FERGIE RISES

'The finest Fergie book of them all. It takes you to the heart of the magnificent absurdity of Aberdeen being kings of Europe'

TOM ENGLISH, *BBC SPORT*

'The glut of books on Alex Ferguson's Manchester United Revolution is exactly why this one is so interesting. A neat idea by an author whose account is superbly written'

THE SCOTSMAN 'BEST SCOTTISH SPORTS READS OF 2014'

'This is a book that takes the evidence from a series of witnesses to burgeoning genius. The testimonies are stunning, insightful, sometimes bitter, mostly awed and regularly funny'

HUGH MacDONALD, *THE HERALD*

'Having interviewed many of those under Fergie's Pittodrie stewardship, he brings much fresh insight into a period covered too briefly in his autobiography'

FOURFOURTWO

'The most fascinating part of Alex Ferguson's career is his eight years taking Aberdeen from no-hopers to beating Real Madrid in a European Final. All the greatest stories have a beginning and this is it'

SHORTLIST

'An excellent new tome'

STEPHEN McGOWAN, *SCOTTISH DAILY MAIL*

'A masterful retelling of how Ferguson was "made" at Aberdeen'

ALAN PATTULLO, *THE SCOTSMAN*

'It is Grant's own passion that permeates and defines *Fergie Rises* and makes it the book that all of us would have loved to have written'

DAVID INNES, *ABERDEEN VOICE*

'Grant has painted a vivid tableau of a bygone age on a giant-sized canvas'

NEIL DRYSDALE, *STV ABERDEEN*

FERGIE RISES

HOW BRITAIN'S GREATEST FOOTBALL MANAGER WAS MADE AT ABERDEEN

MICHAEL GRANT

POLARIS
PUBLISHING

POLARIS PUBLISHING LTD
c/o Aberdein Considine
2nd Floor, Elder House
Multrees Walk
Edinburgh
EH1 3DX

www.polarispublishing.com

First published by Aurum Press in 2014

ISBN: 9781915359179
eBook ISBN: 9781915359186

Interviews have been edited and condensed for clarity.

British Library Cataloguing-in-Publication Data
A catalogue record for this book is available on request from the British Library.

Designed and typeset by Polaris Publishing, Edinburgh
Printed in Great Britain by CPI Group (UK) Ltd, Croydon, CR0 4YY

CONTENTS

For my family, old and new,
and in memory of Donald and Ruby Grant,
with love and thanks

PREFACE

The problem with Sir Alex Ferguson is that his mind games continue indefinitely, and they make unintended victims of the clubs and the supporters who idolise him. Wherever he worked he conjured the illusion that the sun will never set. Then he left, the world turned, and his clubs fell back into shadow. All four of the football clubs he managed in his thirty-nine-year career look back on their period of 'Fergie time' as the very best of days. Decades after he left them, East Stirlingshire, St Mirren and Aberdeen continue to cherish their fading memories and the ageing fans who lived through it yearn for a return to the way things were under Ferguson. Even Manchester United have felt the sting of his departure in 2013. United's global army of supporters may have to resign itself to the truth that the club may never again be so relentlessly successful. So far, Ferguson's unwanted legacy has always been anti-climax and decline for those he left behind.

Nowhere has the chill been more keenly felt than at Aberdeen because nowhere else has his influence raised a team to such unprecedented heights. For seventy-five years that modest club on Scotland's north-east coast had been decent and respected, rising occasionally to make a brief challenge to the Old Firm only to settle back into its accustomed place in Scottish football. Before Ferguson they won one league title and four cups. And then the tornado struck. In his eight and a half years there, Aberdeen won ten trophies.

Between 1978 and 1986 he turned the Dons into one of the most formidable forces the Scottish game has seen and in 1983 one of the greatest to leave these shores and win a European final. For more than 125 years football in Scotland has been a tennis rally, its main honours rebounding back and forth between Rangers and Celtic. Ferguson changed that, leading Aberdeen as the senior partner in a 'New Firm' with Dundee United. The passing of time has only made his impact shine all the more vividly in the record books. Ferguson's Aberdeen remain the only club to challenge and topple the Old Firm over a sustained period.

He lifted Aberdeen, and the 1983 European Cup Winners' Cup final defeat of Real Madrid in Gothenburg elevated him. That was the towering achievement that made his a world-renowned name. When he took his first training session on an Aberdeen public park on 17 July 1978, he began a narrative which would continue beyond Scottish football and find its ultimate fulfilment at Manchester United. Aberdeen was the blueprint. He faced down early disruption and opposition from troublesome players at Aberdeen, as he did at United. There were trophyless early seasons before the floodgates opened for Aberdeen, as there were for United. He imposed an iron will on Pittodrie, as he would at Old Trafford. He built a side around an exceptional leader, Willie Miller, as he did later with Bryan Robson and Roy Keane. He forgave an errant talisman, Steve Archibald, as he did Eric Cantona. He knocked Rangers and Celtic 'off their fucking perch', as he did Liverpool. Crucially, he strived to create an aura around Aberdeen, as he would around United. Aberdeen lost their first two cup finals under Ferguson and then won all of their subsequent six. That was not entirely down to being the better team on the day; part of it was because Ferguson had learned how to prey on opponents' doubts and vulnerabilities.

His post-match Hampden rant about Aberdeen's 'disgrace' of a performance in the 1983 Scottish Cup final, when they beat Rangers, was an iconic incident which captured the energy, hunger, temper and rawness of the young Alex Ferguson. In an official history to celebrate the club's centenary in 2003, he told author Jack Webster: 'There is no doubt that Aberdeen made me as a manager.' That was no hollow platitude, but the truth goes further: his years with Aberdeen made him as a man. Between 1978 and 1986 he lost his father and he lost his mentor, Jock Stein. He also won his first major honours at home and in Europe, saw his sons grow up, and became one of the most provocative, admired and recognisable figures in Scottish life. The transformation was profound: from being not good enough for St Mirren, to being good enough for Manchester United.

From the start, my intention was that *Fergie Rises* would offer a fresh and deeper perspective on Alex Ferguson's time at Aberdeen. I interviewed every member of the Gothenburg team and dozens of others who served under him including his three assistant managers and other club staff. It was hugely rewarding to sit with fine players like Dom Sullivan, Ian Fleming, Jim Leighton, Gordon Strachan, Mark McGhee and Eric Black, all of whom had their problems with Ferguson, either at Aberdeen or subsequently, and all of whom gave their views candidly. Whether favoured or not, these men relayed their personal 'hairdryer' anecdotes like badges of honour. It was soon clear that working with Ferguson was a blast in more ways than one. What came through clearly was what a laugh they all had. Ferguson was controlling, dictatorial, moody and inconsistent, but he was often cracking good fun.

No previous book has been devoted entirely to that eight-and-a-half-year period and none has interviewed players from Rangers, Celtic, Dundee United, Hearts and others to ask how it was to play against those Aberdeen teams. Prominent Old Firm figures, such as Ally McCoist, Charlie Nicholas and Davie Provan gave insights into Ferguson's competitiveness and cunning. They were front-line eyewitnesses to – and sometimes casualties of – those bloody battles at Pittodrie, Ibrox, Parkhead and Hampden. And these guys were winners too, which maybe explains why they spoke approvingly of Aberdeen's nasty streak.

There is testimony from European opponents within these pages, too. 'They were a really difficult team to play. Tough bastards,' said Terry Butcher, a member of the Ipswich team who were Uefa Cup holders until Aberdeen knocked them out. Players in the Bayern Munich and Real Madrid sides laid low by Ferguson's Aberdeen spoke as well. The great Karl-Heinz Rummenigge remembered, thirty years on, how the Dons 'fought like hell, to the last second'. Referees and journalists also shared their tales. There were exceptions, but the overall feeling was warmth and fondness towards the man, if not always his methods. What became clear was just how relentlessly eventful it all was: cup finals, European adventures, broken tea cups, fallings-out, red cards, and always the threat of that 'hairdryer' should anyone step out of line. Never a dull moment.

Occasionally colleagues would ask if Ferguson himself had contributed. Those who have written about him, or about Aberdeen, are aware that for years he has declined requests to be involved with books about himself or his clubs, unless they are official publications or he is providing forewords.

But I had never intended to ask. I had interviewed him in the past and wrote about him at length for a previous book, *The Management: Scotland's Great Football Bosses*. But Ferguson's version of his Pittodrie adventures is already so well-known, thanks to his 1985 account of the Aberdeen years, *A Light in the North*, and his more revealing 1999 autobiography, *Managing My Life*. What more could or would he say now? A time comes when even the sharpest mind has no more nuggets left to mine. What others had to say would be far more revealing.

For those of us who follow Aberdeen, there is a temptation to recoil from the inexorable decline of the last four decades and find sanctuary in the memory of Fergie's revolution. I started to take a serious interest in football around 1975, aged six, when the club had won the sum total of two trophies in the previous nineteen years. Under Ferguson, in those late 1970s and early 1980s, they became a force unrecognisable to previous generations of their fans.

My father was never the type to keep a record of such things but he reckons he missed very few games at Pittodrie between 1948 and 1966, before he moved too far away to attend. He was a regular when they won the league in 1955 but for the most part he watched also-rans in red. The disappointments were endless. In 1953 he travelled to Glasgow and squeezed into Hampden as one of 129,000 who saw them draw with Rangers in the Scottish Cup final. True to form, they lost the replay. A year later he was back when they faced Celtic in front of 130,000. Another defeat. In later years he endured the setbacks from the safety of his armchair.

Around the time I began writing this book, Dad, by then elderly, was hospitalised by an illness. After ten days he seemed comfortable and I was given the all-clear to fly to Luxembourg as one of the football writers covering a

Scotland friendly. There, on the media coach to the stadium, I received a call to say he had deteriorated rapidly over the previous few hours. Then a subsequent call: it might be advisable for the family to gather at the bedside. With their gentle euphemisms the doctors hinted that he was unlikely to get through the night. The family duly gathered but it was impossible for me to get back to him for another nine hours. Numbly, I sat in a little football ground, 800 miles away, quietly trying to compose a match report about a game that did not matter, asking players questions that did not matter, noting answers which did not matter, fearful that at any second the phone would ring with the dreaded conclusion. You think of childhood at a time like that, of shared experiences, of laughter and celebrations. For me, those thoughts were inextricably bound up with Aberdeen under Alex Ferguson.

I made it back to Dad's bedside. He made it through. Over the coming days he improved and after a few weeks he was allowed home. A couple of years later, in March 2014, Aberdeen won the League Cup, their first trophy for nineteen years and only the fourth since Ferguson left. Dad watched it on television. His two wee grandsons were at the final among 43,000 Aberdeen supporters, a bigger following than even the unsurpassable 1980s teams drew. By the time my reports on this new cup glory had been filed for *The Herald* that evening it was too late to call him. I knew he would be away early to his bed but it was lovely to know how pleased he would be. Dad passed away in 2015 and Mam, another Dons fan from Torry in Aberdeen, the following year.

Any mention of 'Fergie' always brought the same reaction from my dad: a laugh, a shake of the head and a remark along the lines of 'What a boy he is'. It was a response that still makes me smile, too, because it affectionately painted Britain's greatest manager as a likeable, irrepressible rogue. Not a legend, not a genius, not the fearsome dictator whose place in history is assured. Just a hugely charismatic leader we all loved having at our club. Fergie could do no wrong in our eyes.

Only once, in the barren years, did Dad show the strain of being a supporter of an underachieving club. It was the afternoon of the 1978 Scottish Cup final, Aberdeen's last game before that 'boy' turned on the lights. I remember being puzzled that Dad's seat was vacant and he was not at home to watch the game on television. A couple of hours later he meandered in after a session at the local. He was rarely a drinker, so why hit the bottle on a miserable day with nothing to celebrate? 'Drowning my sorrows, son,' he said, smiling.

What happened at Hampden that day? Rangers 2, Aberdeen 1.

Now read on.

MICHAEL GRANT
May 2023

ONE

'CUP FINALS ARE TOO BIG FOR SOME PLAYERS'

Glasgow is a city that has always had its no-go areas; neighbourhoods even the streetwise would do well to avoid. In 1978 there was a case for saying Hampden Park was one of them. The famous old home of Scottish football was dirty and dilapidated, so neglected it had been reduced to an eyesore. 'Hampden is dying,' said the Scottish Football Association (SFA) secretary Willie Allan in a mournful plea for external funding. The vast stadium's exterior walls had become a canvas for graffiti about gang rivalries, or bigotry, or the English. Before big matches the area outside the turnstiles was littered with broken glass and muck from police horses. Inside, supporters had to endure an obstacle course of empty whisky and wine bottles, squashed beer cans, discarded ring pulls, carrier bags, food wrappers, cigarette ends and other human debris. Once the crowd was in, streams of urine would slowly snake down the terraces. Those enormous slopes were made out of cinder embankments. They were filthy.

There could be blood, too. The law still allowed fans to bring 'carry-outs' into the ground and segregation between opposing supporters was not strictly enforced. Drunkenness and Scottish football rivalries meant casual violence was inevitable. Heavy beer bottles would be thrown to smash down brutally on rival fans' heads.

On cup final days the sweeping terraces would be filled with block after block of Rangers or Celtic supporters: 30,000, 40,000, maybe 50,000 of them, all noisy, cocksure, an elemental force not just confident of victory but insistent upon it. It felt as though any other team was only there to make up the numbers; to lose without a fuss and clear off home while the trophy was presented to one of its two rightful owners. In Glasgow, and especially at Hampden, day-trippers from Edinburgh, Dundee or Aberdeen were expected to know their place.

That was what awaited Aberdeen in the Scottish Cup final against Rangers on 6 May 1978. Whenever Rangers and Celtic played each other the two sets of fans would divide the ground evenly. When one of them faced any other club their fans would make up three-quarters of the crowd, and maybe more. It took strength of character to turn up in Glasgow knowing that your fans would be outnumbered to that extent. The Old Firm imposed their will on teams. Few who came to Hampden could cope.

Aberdeen were one of the perennial also-rans, outsiders who struggled to withstand Glasgow's psychological onslaught. They had no real pedigree as winners and their only year as league champions had been nearly a quarter-of-a-century earlier. A few sporadic cup successes meant that by the 1970s their history was respectable but Rangers and Celtic usually had the beating of them when it mattered. When Aberdeen routed Rangers 5–1 in the 1976–77 League Cup semi-final it was such a shock that even their own players struggled to comprehend what they had done. They stopped off at the studios of Scottish Television to watch the game again before getting back on the bus for the long drive home. They went on to beat Celtic in the final, too.

That triumph was sufficiently fresh in the memory to make the 1978 Scottish Cup final more interesting than usual. Their recent form had turned Aberdeen into the best team in Scotland. They began a 23-game unbeaten run in December 1977 and chased Rangers all the way to the last day of the league campaign. Between the start of the season and the cup final they had beaten Rangers and Celtic six times. Their impressive young manager, Billy McNeill, was tall and handsome. He was only thirty-eight, had been the iconic captain of Celtic's Lisbon Lions, and came fresh from a decade of lording it over Rangers. The match was a major event. Denis Law turned down an FA Cup final ticket so he could be in Glasgow to support Aberdeen, his home-town club. As one of the BBC's commentary team he even got paid for being there. It felt like the whole north-east migrated to join him. British Rail scheduled five special trains direct from Aberdeen to Hampden and many more fans made the journey in a huge fleet of buses. The *Daily Record*'s front page headline read: FEVER PITCH – HAMPDEN RED ALERT AS BILLY'S ARMY ROLLS INTO TOWN. But this was an army rolling into Glasgow unprepared for the battle. As the Aberdeen support poured off the trains and buses, negotiated the broken glass and the shit from the police horses, and climbed the steps into Hampden, it suddenly hit them. Their first sight of the massed Rangers support, occupying vast swathes of the great open bowl was overwhelming. Suddenly Aberdeen's 20,000 seemed puny. Under the baking May sunshine they listened to the pipe bands and watched an Alsatian dog display team and a balloon competition on the pitch. And as kick-off approached, they grew nervous.

Still, even if they were outnumbered on the terraces and in the stands, surely their representatives on the pitch would be up for the fight? After all, Aberdeen had three men about to go to the World Cup finals in Argentina as part of Ally MacLeod's Scotland squad: big, solid Bobby Clark in goal, tenacious Stuart Kennedy at right-back, the wee barrel of a goalscorer, 'King' Joey Harper, up front. And then there was the captain, the unflappable rock of their defence, Willie Miller. Those four were not the type to buckle. But something was not right. Aberdeen had not been in a Scottish Cup final for eight years and that seemed to prey on some of the players' minds – and on the manager's. On the eve of the game McNeill gave off strange signals to the newspapers. 'There's always tension for everyone involved,' he told the writers. 'But even being in the final is a marvellous thing for the city of Aberdeen.' Some supporters felt uneasy. McNeill was a born winner but with that throwaway line he sounded content – perhaps resigned – simply to be taking part. No Old Firm manager would sound so passive.

There was more. 'It's a big day in their lives,' said McNeill of his players. 'Of course they will be nervous, but I'm sure they will get over that and settle down.' Jock Wallace, Rangers' grizzled, battle-hardened manager, took it all in. Their great wee winger, Davie Cooper, appeared in the papers on the morning of the game to give an entirely different message. He was photographed playing pool in his training gear as if he did not have a care in the world. There was no talk from Rangers about it being a big day in their lives, no mention of any of them being nervous. Cup finals were what Rangers did: 1978 was their ninth of the 1970s.

Aberdeen fell to pieces at Hampden. They were jittery and hesitant, repeatedly giving the ball away and making the wrong decisions. For Rangers, the final became a stroll in their own backyard. Aberdeen no longer looked like a rising force, just another team of pretenders who could not handle the pressure. Rangers' little midfield terrier Alex MacDonald ghosted between static defenders to force a header through Clark's hands after thirty-five minutes. A thunderous, rumbling roar rose up from the Rangers end. Midway through the second half, striker Derek Johnstone planted another header past the goalie. 2–0. Hampden throbbed again to Rangers' support in full voice. Aberdeen pulled a goal back five minutes from time. But even that seemed pathetic. Left-back Steve Ritchie swung his leg at a low cross and scuffed the connection. The ball scooped high into the air and came down to hit the Rangers crossbar and post before going in as goalkeeper Peter McCloy swung on the bar with his back to the ball. The ball did not even touch the net. Aberdeen's performance was so bad even their goal was embarrassing.

They had five minutes to find an equaliser but were too beaten and broken to try. STV's archives have only five minutes of highlights from the game, but even that brief footage says it all. It shows Ritchie brushing off a couple of team-mates as they run up to celebrate; he is shaking his head, muttering gloomily to himself. For a team with momentum five minutes is long enough to score a second goal against suddenly nervous opponents. Aberdeen had no fight for that. No one in red even raced to grab the ball out of Rangers' goal to force a quick restart. They were waiting to lose, waiting to get it all over with. Soon enough they were put out of their misery: Rangers 2, Aberdeen 1.

As the Rangers fans let rip, the Aberdeen end melted away, cursing another let-down. The familiar conclusions swirled around: same old Aberdeen, bottle merchants. Where were the leaders to stand up to Rangers and Celtic? Aberdeen had been men all season but under the pressure of Hampden they turned into mice. Later Joe Harper made another comparison. 'We simply froze and performed like a bunch of rabbits caught in the headlights. We were an embarrassment to all and sundry at Hampden.' More than forty years later the Aberdeen players who lined up that day still shake their heads at the memory. John McMaster, the elegant midfielder, knew they let people down. 'It just caught up with us: the atmosphere, being anxious to do well in front of our families,' he said. 'The next thing it was, "What the fuck am I doing? I'm having a nightmare here." All I did was frustrate myself. I chased Alex MacDonald all over Hampden. I didn't play at all. A boy I'd grown up with said to me later, "John, you're a legend, you've played in a Scottish Cup final." I just thought, "How can you be a legend when you get beat?"'

Stuart Kennedy could not believe what he was seeing. 'Cup finals are too big for some players. We'd beaten that Rangers team four times, beaten them 3–0 at Ibrox, but when you tell some people it's a cup final I just don't know what happens to them mentally. It's like there's more pressure on them. It didn't bother me. I strolled through that game.' McNeill had spoken softly to the players at half-time, assuming they would improve after an 'awful' first half. What they actually needed was a collective boot up the backside, and, too late, he realised it. The newspapers dismissed Aberdeen. 'As one side was so far ahead of the other the 1978 Scottish Cup final will not be remembered as one of the classics,' said the *Glasgow Herald*. 'The Aberdeen heads went down and the shoulders slumped as Rangers turned it on as if taking part in an exhibition.'

By the time the team bus pulled away from Hampden and began the long retreat from Glasgow, the streets were thronged with jubilant Rangers fans, knocking back bottles and cans and pausing to jeer and flick V-signs at the losers from the north-east. Miller scowled out of the window. The captain was quietly seething. He was a hard, born-and-bred Glaswegian who had grown into Aberdeen's leader and icon. He knew the day had been a surrender from start to finish. 'I swore that I would never allow a team that I was captaining to freeze on a big occasion,' he said. But Miller could not change the entire club's mentality on his own. Aberdeen needed someone to worm inside their heads, someone to tell them they were as good as the Old Firm. Better, even. They needed someone unafraid to get right into Rangers' and Celtic's faces. None of that came naturally to the earthy, reserved folk of the north-east.

Back home an open-top bus parade had been organised for the day after the cup final, win or lose. The players wondered if anyone would have the appetite for it but it was a sunny holiday weekend and 10,000 made the effort to line the streets of Aberdeen's city centre, and another 10,000 greeted them inside Pittodrie. They came to acknowledge the fine football their team had played in the five months before Hampden. Such was the dominance of the Old Firm that, as midfielder Gordon Strachan put it: 'Even to appear in a Scottish Cup final was apparently cause for celebration.' A HEROES' WELCOME FOR GALLANT LOSERS, said the *Glasgow Herald*. It was not meant to sound like a backhanded compliment, but the fact remained that Aberdeen were losers. As they disembarked from the bus and walked out at Pittodrie the players looked glum. Their movements were slow and their shoulders drooped. Some held out their empty hands to the supporters in a gesture of apology.

McNeill tried to lift the mood with talk of what Aberdeen were building. Finishing second in the league and cup was only the beginning, he said. Next season they would bring home a trophy, he promised. The north-east had heard it all before. No one really believed anything would change: Rangers and Celtic would share the trophies again the following season, and again the season after that. Who was going to stop them?

A piece of lesser football news made one of the newspapers on the morning of the cup final. FERGIE STAYS ON, reported the *Daily Record*. 'St Mirren manager Alex Ferguson is to stay at Love Street. Ferguson turned down an offer from the United States after meeting with the St Mirren board last night.' It was an apparently insignificant story tucked away on one of the inside pages. Up in Aberdeen, one man read it and made a mental note.

TWO

A DISCREET CALL TO THE JOLLY RODGER

Scotland fans had one thing on their minds going into the summer of 1978. After another long season there was little appetite for the ins, outs and intrigues of club management. There were now bigger fish to fry: Scotland were going to the World Cup finals in Argentina. Their effervescent Pied Piper of a manager, Ally MacLeod, whipped the public into a state of collective hysteria. He was asked what he was going to do after the tournament? His answer: 'Retain it.'

There was no ridicule of 'Ally' and his bombastic declarations. The country hung on his every word. When he decided it would be a good idea for supporters to come to Hampden and give the squad a send-off to the airport, more than 30,000 turned up to wave them away. MacLeod had mobilised a big football crowd, in a big football stadium, just to look at players standing on an open-top bus. Scottish comedian Andy Cameron captured the growing sense of expectation when he submerged himself in tartan and appeared on *Top of the Pops* to plough heroically through his World Cup novelty song 'Ally's Tartan Army'. Feverish excitement propelled the record to 360,000 sales and number six in the UK charts. Scotland had qualified for World Cups before, in 1954, 1958 and 1974, but they had never travelled with this sort of swaggering confidence. Fans were talking about Córdoba, Mendoza and the Pampas as if these places were to be invaded by a friendly but conquering army.

The newspapers' 'number one' football writers had already been despatched to Argentina when the tectonic plates moved back in Glasgow. Suddenly, the World Cup was knocked from the top of the football agenda. In the newsrooms and journalists' watering holes the conversations revolved around two clubs, two men and two dramatic vacancies. It is a major story in Scotland when one of the Old Firm clubs changes their manager. For both of them to do so in the same week amounted to unprecedented turbulence. The sports desks of the Scottish national newspapers – all based in Glasgow, other than *The Scotsman* in Edinburgh – were in ferment. Now the real stories were at home. First the back pages were dominated by the bombshell about Jock Wallace walking out on the Rangers job, without explanation, just days after that cup final defeat of Aberdeen secured the domestic treble. Wallace's reasons remained vague and the sense of affront in the blue half of Glasgow hardly lessened when he took over modest Leicester City a few days later. Who would land the Rangers job? 'St Mirren's Alex Ferguson, the live-wire who has taken the Paisley club to success, became the favourite,' wrote Hugh Taylor in Glasgow's *Evening Times*. Taylor was wrong. Within hours of his paper hitting the streets Rangers had appointed from within. Their long-serving and distinguished captain, John Greig, was given the reins. Ferguson was never an option.

Jock Stein's exit from Celtic after thirteen years as manager was less surprising or confusing, but more momentous given the slew of trophies he had brought the club, including the

1967 European Cup and nine consecutive Scottish titles. 'Now comes the news which will rock the game in Scotland, down south, and indeed in any country where the game is played,' declared the *Evening Times*. If this amounted to a footballing earthquake for Glasgow a secondary tremor was soon to hit Aberdeen. Twelve months earlier the SFA had raided the manager's office at Pittodrie, prised MacLeod out of Aberdeen and given him their top job. When the news about Stein broke, it was immediately obvious that Celtic would attempt the same with Billy McNeill. He was as 'Celtic' as anyone could get: the cornerstone of the Stein era, the first British captain to lift the European Cup, a colossal Parkhead figure. He was also emerging as a young manager with terrific prospects. It was Stein himself who first approached McNeill at an awards lunch in Glasgow and quietly offered him the position as his replacement.

McNeill had been with Aberdeen for less than a year. No one had to tell him he had a squad of outstanding potential or that he might be on the brink of something special despite that cup final let-down. His players liked and respected him, the north-east had embraced him and McNeill and his wife enjoyed the city's comfortable, relaxed way of life. The obvious and sensible thing to do was thank Celtic for their interest but reluctantly let them know the timing was not right. He felt grateful to Aberdeen, too, for giving him a platform in management by taking him away from Clyde and giving him a job with real profile. And yet, and yet . . . The thought nagged away at him that the chance to manage Celtic might never come his way again. Against his better judgment he listened to heart rather than head and tendered his resignation.

In Paisley, Alex Ferguson had turned down that offer from the United States but the story about him 'staying on' at

St Mirren remained accurate for only twenty-four days. On 30 May the club's exasperated board decided they had had enough of a manager they had come to see as confrontational and controlling, and unanimously decided to sack him for breach of contract. Ferguson was summoned to Love Street and a typed, numbered list of thirteen offences was read to him before he was dismissed. A curt statement was issued: 'Because of a serious rift which had occurred between the board and the manager, and because of breaches of contract on his part, it would be in the interests of both parties that the manager's contract be terminated.' The club's supporters could not believe what they were hearing. Many thought Ferguson the best thing to happen to St Mirren in the nineteen years since their last major trophy in 1959. To most of Paisley the decision to sack him seemed as insane then as it has to the rest of football ever since. In essence, the issue was an irreparable personality clash with the chairman, Willie Todd. Ferguson visited his solicitors and insisted he would take St Mirren to an industrial tribunal for unfair dismissal. That decision would become a saga that drained his energy for months, distracting him as he tried to come to terms with his next job, the biggest of his managerial career to date.

The managers of Partick Thistle and Dumbarton, Bertie Auld and Davie Wilson, and the Southampton assistant Jim Clunie, were all linked with the Aberdeen vacancy when Billy McNeill departed. But not for long. It was quickly clear that Ferguson was the man Aberdeen wanted. They were impressed that under his tenures at East Stirlingshire and St Mirren the attendances had leapt significantly, and also that he had built squads without troubling either board for money. In fact, the exciting young team at Love Street was assembled for no transfer outlay and had quickly won promotion to the Premier Division. Yes, the charismatic manager was clearly a handful for both sets of directors, but Ferguson's results spoke for themselves. The more background checks done by Aberdeen chairman Dick Donald and vice-chairman Chris Anderson, the more convinced they were that Ferguson's talent and potential outweighed any questions over impulsiveness or control issues. Anderson had been the interested reader of that snippet in the *Record* about Ferguson turning down the American offer on the day of the cup final. Donald and Anderson were confident in their judgment, having been so successful with MacLeod in 1975 and McNeill in 1977 that both managers were quickly poached for 'bigger' jobs.

Alex Ferguson and unemployment were never likely to suit one another. On leaving St Mirren he was out of work for a matter of hours. Given how quickly he would demonise 'the Glasgow press' for their hostility to Aberdeen it was ironic that the club first made contact with him through the quintessential Glasgow football writer, Jim 'The Jolly' Rodger. Rodger was in his mid-fifties and had been a prominent journalist for thirty years. He was a short, stout, bald, bespectacled man who enjoyed enormous influence and contacts. He was on first-name terms with Prime Ministers Harold Wilson and Margaret Thatcher and in football circles he routinely acted as a go-between in transfers and managerial appointments, effectively an agent in an age before agents. Ferguson had been similarly sounded out by Aberdeen about taking over when MacLeod left in the summer of 1977 but then he had turned them down; 'Insanity,' he admitted in a subsequent autobiography.

St Mirren have always disputed the timing of Rodger's first contact with Ferguson. Their chairman, Todd, later said that Ferguson had let it be known around St Mirren that he was moving to Aberdeen 'four days before he eventually left'. If true, it would mean Ferguson had done so while McNeill was still deliberating over his move from Aberdeen to Celtic. Todd considered that a clear breach of contract because Aberdeen had made no formal approach to speak to him about the job. He claimed he sacked Ferguson because he could not tolerate a manager who was trying to work his ticket out of the club. It was always Todd's view that Ferguson had been 'tapped up' by Aberdeen days, even weeks, before he actually went. But Aberdeen could not have known they were about to lose McNeill. They would have been unaware that Stein was about to leave Celtic. In fact, McNeill later admitted he had been embarrassed that the story broke on 26 May before he had spoken to the Aberdeen board. Whenever the call was made by Rodger, though, Ferguson told him he would jump at the Aberdeen job and the journalist relayed that news to Donald. Ferguson and Donald then spoke by telephone and the following day the young manager travelled north for negotiations. These were concluded so swiftly that a press conference was called for later the same evening.

'I'm thrilled at joining Aberdeen because I want to win things,' Ferguson told the reporters who rushed to Pittodrie. 'You only need to look at the stadium and you can see it is ready for success.' He looked relaxed and comfortable, answering all the questions before posing for pictures alone and with his new chairman. FERGIE HUSTLES NORTH TO BOSS THE DONS, said the headline on the front page of the *Glasgow Herald* the following morning. Journalist Ian Paul wrote that Aberdeen's board 'can be commended for the speed at which they moved' in capturing 'one of Scotland's most exciting managerial prospects'. It was the end of a dizzying spell of activity. Wallace resigned on 23 May, Greig was appointed on 24 May, the Stein story broke on 26 May, McNeill resigned on 29 May, St Mirren's board decided to sack Ferguson on 30 May, Celtic confirmed that Stein would become a director and appointed McNeill to replace him on 31 May, and Aberdeen appointed Ferguson on 1 June.

At last Scotland could take a breath and focus its attention solely on the World Cup. Soon the collapse of that particular dream felt apocalyptic: Scotland lost to Peru, drew with Iran and watched Archie Gemmill score a mesmerising goal in a futile win over the Netherlands. The country turned viciously on MacLeod. Andy Cameron joked that there was a garage somewhere storing tens of thousands of copies of his record. He reckoned 'Ally's Tartan Army' did not sell another copy from the day Scotland went out.

THREE

RESCUING ALEX FERGUSON

Glaswegians have always laughed loudest at jokes about Aberdeen. Scotland's population is concentrated in the central belt, especially around greater Glasgow, whose citizens tend to view the smaller north-eastern city as an inferior outpost. Many would struggle to place it on a map. Others think of Aberdeen as remote, rural, cold and dour. They imagine an all-pervading odour of fish. They call the locals 'sheepshaggers' and make wisecracks about a perceived meanness: 'Copper wire was invented by two Aberdonians fighting over a penny'; 'The first people in Scotland to get double glazing were Aberdonians so that the bairns couldn't hear the ice cream vans'; 'An Aberdonian found a pair of crutches so he went home and broke his son's leg'.

So when Ferguson moved to the north-east of Scotland he stepped into a different culture and way of life. He was old enough to know Aberdeen as a popular holiday resort during Glasgow Fair, the July fortnight when Glaswegians traditionally took their summer break. Until the 1970s many had flocked to its guesthouses and its long, sandy beach. Then the sudden availability of cheap air travel to the

Mediterranean broadened horizons and the traffic between the two cities dwindled. Not that Aberdeen had really enjoyed a picture postcard reputation. For decades its income had been based on agriculture, fishing, textiles and quarrying the famous granite – hence the nickname, 'The Granite City'. The imposing stone made Aberdeen look steadfast and regal, but grey and unwelcoming, too. It also ensured stolidity. For decades the city's population was static and its economy stagnant. During the 1960s it was little more than a regional backwater with no obvious prospect for growth, while 150 miles to the south Glasgow clung to its proud self-image as the second city of the British Empire and one of the world's great hubs of heavy engineering.

But by the time Ferguson arrived at Pittodrie the economic and social landscapes were shifting. In 1969, American drilling rigs struck oil in the North Sea 135 miles east of Aberdeen and by 1975 the first 'black gold' arrived in the city. Then everything changed. The offshore industry needed headquarters and Aberdeen was the only contender. The economic transformation was rapid. Industrial estates were built and money and workers flooded in. Thousands of jobs were created for locals. From a population of around 200,000, by 1978 more than 30,000 were employed in the oil industry. The entire focus of Scotland's economy shifted from the old, declining heavy industries of the central belt to the newly vibrant north-east coast. The boom paid for new housing, offices and schools as Aberdeen gained a reputation for prosperity and affluence. At a time when many parts of Scotland faced decline and hardship, the city was cocooned. The contrast with Glasgow was stark. The great hub of engineering felt blighted. Its tenement slums had been replaced by high-rise flats and soulless suburban housing estates, 'the schemes'. The collapse of manufacturing industries like steelmaking, shipbuilding and the engine factories led to mass unemployment, deprivation and urban decay. If Glaswegians thought of the north-east as a backwater, then Aberdonians looked down their noses at uncouth 'weegies' and the widening economic gap only fuelled the conviction.

Aberdeen supporters never resorted to waving bundles of cash at Rangers or Celtic fans, as fans of London clubs would do during matches against Liverpool, Everton or Newcastle United. But their taunts were no less vicious: 'In your Glasgow slums,' they chanted, 'you rake in the bucket for something to eat/you find a dead rat and you think it's a treat/in your Glasgow slums.' Ferguson never commented on these songs publicly but their mockery of his home city, of its growing poverty and deprivation, must have sat uneasily with a man whose working-class upbringing and socialist beliefs were matters of fierce pride.

Alexander Chapman Ferguson was born in his grandparents' council house in the Drumoyne area of Glasgow on 31 December 1941. His father, also Alex, was a shipwright in the Govan shipyards and brought up Ferguson and his brother, Martin, in the shadow of the Clydeside cranes. The family lived comfortably but had no car, television or telephone during young Alex's childhood.

He was a popular boy, a rough diamond, bright and competitive. Fellow Glaswegians recognised him as 'gallus' – in other words mischievous, opinionated and unabashed. He was also 'handy' – able to look after himself – and could be hot-headed when slighted. He lived life on the front foot. In 1958, aged sixteen, he left school to begin a five-year apprenticeship as a toolmaker in Hillington, four miles from the shipyards. Being street-smart with a readiness to stand up for himself quickly established him as a natural leader and a barrack-room lawyer in the workplace. He was soon active in the trade union movement, becoming a shop steward and taking a prominent role in two apprentices' strikes. He was a product of his time and place. The Fergusons were Labour voters, born and bred.

By the time he was a qualified toolmaker his parallel career as a footballer was already underway. He had played throughout his childhood and earned a reputation as a strong and prolific goalscorer as he rose from playing in the street, through Boys' Brigade and amateur teams, before entering the senior game with Queen's Park in 1958. Ferguson could terrorise defenders and goalkeepers. He was awkward, brave, physical and robust, often inviting retaliation from grizzled Scottish centre-halves. His elbows seemed as important to his style of play as his feet and he would barge his way into scoring positions. Nor did he keep his opinions to himself: he shared them with opponents and officials and was not shy of berating his own defenders or goalkeeper when they conceded goals.

Spells with Queen's Park, St Johnstone and Dunfermline saw his promise steadily grow and when he signed for Rangers in 1967 the fee of £65,000 was a record for a transfer between Scottish clubs. It was the realisation of a personal dream: Rangers were the team Ferguson had supported since boyhood. Yet his twenty-nine months at Ibrox turned out to be the most demoralising of his career. The manager who signed him, Scot Symon, was soon dismissed and Ferguson was bounced between the first team and the reserves, drifting in and out of favour. He felt he was made a scapegoat when Rangers lost the 1969 Scottish Cup final 4–0 to Celtic. He was instructed to mark Billy McNeill but as a striker he lacked defensive instincts and left McNeill unattended at the first goal. The game became unfairly synonymous with Ferguson's inability to cope with McNeill. He also believed his wife's religion had counted against him. He was twenty-four when he married Cathy Holding in 1966. Cathy was a

Catholic, Alex a Protestant, and sectarianism at Rangers was an open secret. His spell at the club ended sourly in 1969. Almost a decade and a half later, when Rangers held out a hand to take him back, the episode would rebound on them.

Ferguson's playing career wound down at Falkirk and Ayr United. Though never called up for Scotland, he was a prominent figure of his day, scoring 222 goals in 432 appearances. Regulars at Pittodrie were familiar with him and not only because he scored eight goals in twenty appearances against them. During a Scottish Cup tie in February 1973, he was embroiled in a scrap with Aberdeen defender Willie Young and was sent off before half-time.

By that point he had been a qualified SFA coach for six years. Those who held such qualifications were always welcome at the SFA's refresher courses but few bothered to return. Ferguson was one of the exceptions. There was no question that he would try to make a career for himself in coaching. His manager in 1973–74, his final season at Ayr, was Ally MacLeod. When MacLeod was flying out to the 1974 World Cup finals in West Germany he bumped into a friend, Bob Shaw, a director at East Stirlingshire. Shaw had admired Ferguson's competitiveness and forceful personality from afar and wondered if he might be available for his club's vacant managerial position. More than twenty men had applied for the job but after meeting chairman Willie Murihead at a Falkirk hotel, and sailing through his interview, it was Ferguson who was appointed to the part-time role in June 1974. His wage was £40 a week.

'The Shire' are one of those little clubs routinely mocked for bumping along in Scottish football's basement. Firs Park was demolished in 2012 but in 1974 it was a tiny ground tucked away in an otherwise drab part of Falkirk; its little stand was barrel-roofed and painted in black and white to match the club's home colours. Ferguson's 117 days as manager remain a badge of honour in their history. Summer departures meant he inherited a squad of only twelve players and a budget to rebuild it of just £2,000. The team was made up of part-time journeymen with recent memories of watching or reading about Ferguson at Rangers. When their new, 32-year-old boss spoke, they listened. From the outset he demanded the discipline and attention to detail that would remain constants throughout his four decades as a manager. Players were told to turn up in collar and tie. He restructured training sessions and started to give them thorough briefings on the opposition. He even told them the local paper, the *Falkirk Herald*, was biased towards the town's larger club, Falkirk. This was nonsense but he repeated it so forcefully the team began to believe him. 'The Shire' had finished sixteenth in Division Two the previous season but under Ferguson they climbed as high as third, with seven wins and only three defeats in his first dozen league games. Attractive, attacking football also reflected through the turnstiles and average attendances rose from around 400 to 1,200.

It was quickly apparent that Ferguson's idea of management involved much wider control of club affairs than any of his predecessors had enjoyed, or expected. When he was challenged by the board for unauthorised spending – he had given £40 to a junior team to come and play a friendly – he startled the directors by threatening to resign. The issue was smoothed over but the club had been served notice: they had a young revolutionary determined to shake 'The Shire' by its roots. As Willie Muirhead would later put it, Ferguson was the best thing that ever happened to East Stirlingshire.

Ferguson's impact did not go unnoticed and in October 1974 St Mirren inquired if he would take over when Willie Cunningham resigned. It was effectively a step down because at the time 'The Shire' were two places above St Mirren in fourth spot in Division Two. The offer left Ferguson uncertain. Both clubs were part-time and he felt a sense of loyalty to the players he had worked so hard to improve. Only when he made a call to Stein, the Celtic manager and Godfather of Scottish coaching, did those doubts clear. Stein told him to sit in the highest point of the stand at Firs Park and then do the same at St Mirren's Love Street. The advice was cryptic but shrewd. St Mirren's ground was far bigger (in the 1970s it had a capacity of almost 50,000, nearly all of it terracing) and Ferguson needed only a brief look to compare the scale of the two clubs' potential. St Mirren had always been one of the substantial names of the Scottish game. They had won the Scottish Cup in 1926 and 1959 and had finished in the top six as challengers to Rangers and Celtic three times since the end of the Second World War. St Mirren had no business languishing in Division Two, down with East Stirlingshire and the other minnows.

After just seventeen games with 'The Shire' he took the job and began a crusade to rebuild and reposition St Mirren as a force. His immersion in the task was absolute, to the frequent detriment of time with Cathy and their sons; Mark, who had just turned six, and twins Darren and Jason, who were two. Further time was devoted to running 'Fergie's', a pub in Glasgow within walking distance of Ibrox Stadium where he was often found serving behind the bar. His working day at Love Street could last for twelve hours or more and again he tried to exert himself over every aspect of the operation, even secretarial duties and maintenance. With East Stirlingshire Ferguson had shown ambition but at St Mirren he had a vision. Paisley, an industrialised town in the shadow of Glasgow, had suffered an economic downturn. The area was depressed and unemployment was climbing. Ferguson wanted to give the dispirited locals a football team of which they could be proud and he bubbled with energy and ideas. A weekly club newspaper was introduced, as was a column by Ferguson in the Paisley *Daily Express*. He drove through the streets with a loudhailer trying to drum up interest ahead of home games. It was an imaginative, almost comic, ploy which made him look like a political candidate ahead of polling day.

After early inconsistency the results came. Due to league reconstruction the top six in the 1974–75 season would be rewarded with promotion. St Mirren just made it, finishing sixth. Instead of being in the second of two divisions they were now in the second of three. Ferguson's confidence grew and he became increasingly decisive. At the end of his first season he released eighteen players. In 1975–76 St Mirren finished sixth again but this was a team coming together. In 1976–77 they clicked. Ferguson led them back to the top flight for the first time since 1971. Between September and March they remained undefeated for twenty-eight consecutive league games and won the title by four points. They scored ninety-one league goals in thirty-nine matches. The most electrifying performance came in the Scottish Cup when they routed Dundee United 4–1 on 29 January 1977. The following month more than 15,000 fans followed them to Motherwell in the next round, where they lost an ugly game 2–1.

The team was young, brash, exciting and dangerous. Ferguson inherited an elegant midfielder, Tony Fitzpatrick, and made him captain at the age of eighteen. Alongside him the tall, languid, curly-haired Billy Stark was good for more than ten goals a season from midfield. Frank McGarvey was a penalty-box livewire and prodigious goalscorer. The team crackled with other young talents, most notably midfielder Lex Richardson and centre-half Bobby Reid. But in signing left-back Iain Munro from Rangers and centre-half Jackie Copland from Dundee United, Ferguson showed he also understood the value of tempering youth with experience. And it did not matter how old anyone was: he dominated them all, even issuing warnings not to dare coming back into the dressing room if they had not won. The players feared him but responded. Fitzpatrick remembers being wrong-footed when Ferguson tore through the team after a comprehensive victory. 'I was silly enough to say, "What the fuck are you looking for? We won 5–0! Are you not happy?" He came over and gave me a Fergie special. He told me in no uncertain terms that he was the manager and it was his standards that counted.' Another time, Ferguson outlined his vision to Fitzpatrick: '"We're going to build a club that's going to overtake Celtic and Rangers." That was his ambition.'

The press latched on to this rising force and coined a nickname: 'Fergie's Furies'. Paisley gave him the response he wanted. Crowds soared from an average of 2,267 the season before he joined to 11,793 in the Premier Division in 1977–78. It said as much about the character of the manager as it did about his team's attacking style. Yet he was still rough around the edges. His reputation for hotheadedness led to conflict with the SFA. After bursting into the referee's room following that Scottish Cup tie at Motherwell and making 'ungentlemanly remarks' he was fined £25 and made to sign an assurance that he would not communicate with officials on match days for the following two years. This was not an isolated incident: his time at Love Street brought confrontations with referees, linesmen, opponents, his own players and the club's directors and chairman.

Coming up against better opposition in the Premier Division put the brakes on the Furies' rise. Their first season back in the top flight, at the end of which he would be sacked, proved a constant struggle. St Mirren finished one place above the relegation positions and lost seventeen times in thirty-six games. Nor was there any respite in either of the cup competitions: Celtic beat them in the League Cup and Kilmarnock put them out of the Scottish Cup, at Love Street. Simply surviving in the top ten was an admirable feat for St Mirren's young manager but it had been a difficult season. Some of the brightness around his young team had dimmed.

Supporters had been unaware of the growing tension between Ferguson, chairman Todd and the rest of the five-man board. The directors were conservative and mindful of their budget. They also felt their ambitious manager had become overbearing and uncontrollable, so they took the unanimous decision to sack him. 'Ferguson, who could claim to be just about the most successful and popular manager the Paisley club has had, was summoned by the Love Street board to be told that his contract had been terminated,' wrote the *Glasgow Herald* on 1 June 1978. If the news came as a shock the paper was nonetheless confident about what was about to happen next. The headline on the report read: SACKED FERGUSON TO JOIN DONS.

It was another step up the ladder. East Stirlingshire were dwarfed by St Mirren, who were, in turn, much smaller than Aberdeen. But at the time of Ferguson's arrival the Dons had won only two major honours in the 1970s compared to Rangers' ten and Celtic's twelve. It was always thus. From the founding of the club in 1903 it had taken Aberdeen forty-four years to win their first major trophy. By 1978 their roll of honour stood at one league championship in 1955, Scottish Cup triumphs in 1947 and 1970, and League Cup wins in 1955 and 1976. Five trophies in seventy-five years. To offset this there was some additional pride in being the only Scottish club, other than Rangers and Celtic, never to have been relegated.

The 1970 cup final had been won under manager Eddie Turnbull against Stein's mighty Celtic. That could – and maybe should – have been followed by one or two league titles. In 1971 Aberdeen went toe-to-toe with Celtic but folded near the end of the season and blew a winning position with two games left. In 1972 they were up against Celtic again when the directors suddenly accepted a £125,000 bid from Manchester United for their outstanding defender and captain, Martin Buchan. The money made sense, the timing did not. Aberdeen were only three points off the top of the league and were in the quarter-finals of the Scottish Cup; after Buchan was sold in February they were immediately knocked out of the cup and finished ten points behind the champions. Turnbull was irascible and confrontational, a disciplinarian and a brilliant coach who provided the kick-start Aberdeen needed after their drab and mediocre 1960s. He sharpened the training, modernised the way the club was run, and shared Ferguson's fearlessness about taking on the Old Firm. Several first-team players were close to tears when Turnbull announced he was resigning to take charge of Hibernian in 1971. Jimmy Bonthrone, a reserved, gentle man, stepped up from assistant manager. He was methodical and well-liked but he lacked both ruthlessness and Turnbull's inspirational touch. Decline set in during his four seasons in charge. When he resigned in October, 1975, Aberdeen were immersed in a relegation battle they would only survive on goal difference by winning on the final day of the season.

By the mid-1970s Aberdeen had become a docile and ordinary club badly in need of a leader. Three men recognised that and decided to take action. Aberdeen's board was unique in Scottish football in that it consisted solely of former players: Dick Donald, Chris Anderson and Charlie Forbes. Donald and Anderson were Pittodrie's twin pillars. Donald, sixty-seven in 1978, was part of a wealthy local family whose business empire had made millions from the entertainment industry, specifically dance halls, cinemas and theatres. At sixteen he began running one of his father's cinemas and also followed in his footsteps, literally, by becoming a qualified ballroom dancing instructor. Long after his seventieth birthday he would amuse himself by doing impromptu little dances in the corridors of Pittodrie. Donald was an Aberdeen man through and through with old values and old money. On most days of the week he would turn up at the ground dressed in a pin-stripe suit, collar and tie, overcoat and soft hat. Jokes about Aberdonians and their supposed meanness might have been cracked with him in mind. When he entered a room at Pittodrie he would ask why all the lights were switched on. He refused to agree to high transfer fees, excessive wages or bonuses and never allowed the club to go into debt. If an attractive offer came in for a star player, Donald was likely to sell him. Such frugality exasperated many supporters but delivered stability and credibility. Club myth had it that Donald could stand at the mouth of the Pittodrie tunnel a couple of minutes before kick-off, look around all four sides of the ground and correctly estimate the size of the attendance to within one hundred.

If Donald was Aberdeen's ice then Anderson, fourteen years younger, was its fire. He had played for the club just after the war and joined Donald on the board in 1967, quickly becoming a challenging, visionary influence. Anderson played a key role in the improvements that saw Pittodrie become the first all-seated, all-covered football stadium in Britain. He was a driving force in league reconstruction and predicted, many years before it became reality, that football would be shaped and financed by broadcasting rights and pay-per-view television. He also held a senior administration position at one of Britain's leading polytechnics, Robert Gordon's Institute of Technology in Aberdeen. There he was exposed to young, dynamic people from the expanding oil industry and he was determined to bring the same sort of energy and ambition to the city's football club. Anderson realised that Aberdeen had to wake up. The whole north-east of Scotland was being propelled by the 1970s oil boom and there was a danger the Dons would be left behind. Flirting with relegation under Bonthrone had been a brutal shock to the system. 'It made us think about what kind of club we should be,' Anderson said. 'Which in turn caused us to look very carefully – certainly more methodically than any other club at the time – at what kind of team we should have and what kind of manager should be in charge.' From November 1975, they appointed three managers in thirty-two months: first Ally MacLeod, then Billy McNeill, then Ferguson.

MacLeod burst on to the scene as a scatty, effervescent showman; an idealist with an infectious personality. Within six months he had staved off the threat of relegation and a year on he won the League Cup. Celtic had been such overwhelming favourites that when the celebrating Aberdeen players arrived for their post-match meal at a Perth hotel they found a 'runners-up menu' had been left out for them. Embarrassed staff rushed to replace it with the winners' version. MacLeod was eccentric and prone to practical jokes. He made the players train on nearby Aberdeen beach even when the tide was in and the freezing North Sea lapping at their ankles. On one pre-season trip to the fee-paying school Gordonstoun he offered a prize to the first player to run, naked, to the nearest pub. When the squad raced off he gathered up their clothes and made away with them.

His coaching was average, but outstanding man-management carried him through, at least for a while. Good signings helped: the robust full-back Stuart Kennedy, cultured midfielder Dom Sullivan, the return of legendary goalscorer Joe Harper for a second spell, and a lanky teenage redhead named Alex McLeish. As far as midfielder John McMaster was concerned MacLeod was a breath of fresh air: 'His training was sometimes out of this world, really good, and then other times it would feel like nothing more than five-a-sides with the same teams for ten months. Eccentric. He wasn't good on technical stuff but he was a fun guy. He lit the place up in Aberdeen, people believed in him. But Ally had eighteen months to two years in a job and then everyone sussed him out.' In his only full season MacLeod galvanised the north-east and added 4,000 to the average home crowd. The SFA had seen enough and decided in May 1977 that Pittodrie's Pied Piper was the man to take Scotland through to the World Cup in Argentina.

MacLeod had been Ferguson's manager at Ayr United and it was he who telephoned his former player to suggest he leave the newly crowned First Division champions at Love Street and take over Aberdeen. Ferguson declined, believing he could realise his ambitions with St Mirren. That decision delayed his arrival by a year. When Aberdeen opted instead for McNeill it looked a good fit. Anderson's headhunting had bagged the club an ambitious young manager with an excellent playing record; as early as 1974 Anderson had been quoted praising the professionalism and technical ability McNeill displayed at Celtic. McNeill was everything that MacLeod was not: meticulous, strong on preparation, outstanding on tactics, measured and deserving of respect by dint of his achievements rather than the strength of his personality. The supporters loved him from the start. Before his first home game, against Rangers, he walked on to the pitch wearing a red shirt to thunderous approval. Like MacLeod, he served only one full season but continued the club's momentum, pushing them as Rangers' closest challengers. And in Steve Archibald and Gordon Strachan he made two outstanding signings who would prove invaluable to his successor.

MacLeod, McNeill and Ferguson amounted to a hat-trick of imaginative appointments. Anderson liked to point out that some thought Aberdeen 'daft and crazy' for following McNeill with Ferguson but the 36-year-old Glaswegian's track record and energy made him the small board's unanimous choice. Not that losing their two previous managers had caught Aberdeen unaware. 'Old Dick got compensation for Ally going to Scotland and then for Big Billy going to Celtic,' said Doug Rougvie, the defender who had played under both. 'He was rubbing his hands, going "ya beauty!" The auld yin knew the right side of a bawbee. Aberdeen were always in the black under him. Dick was amazing.' The club secretary at the time, Ian Taggart, began working for Donald in 1976 and takes with a pinch of salt the board's assertion that the three appointments were part of a phased progression. 'These guys were available at the time. Our board were Aberdonians and not as brash or forthcoming as Glaswegians. The chairman admitted later that he wouldn't have hired Fergie if he'd still been in a job. They wouldn't have poached him from anyone else. Fortunately for us he got the heave at St Mirren.'

Ferguson's greatest gift in the summer of 1978 was not talent but timing: his availability and the Aberdeen vacancy aligned. Some in the north-east had reservations about him. There were those around the city who saw him as typical of the kind of outspoken Glaswegian they instinctively disliked. Many remembered the game against Falkirk five years earlier when he had been sent off. Others worried that he still had much to prove. Under McNeill, Aberdeen climbed to second in the league and reached the Scottish Cup final; they had finished twenty-three points and six places higher than Ferguson's St Mirren. And Ferguson had just been fired somewhat messily and was taking industrial action against a club who had flirted with relegation. The Aberdeen support reacted to news of his appointment quietly. 'Some people wondered if the bad publicity surrounding his departure would put the directors off,' said Gordon Strachan.

Ferguson was certainly nowhere near as polished as McNeill. What did he have that appealed to Aberdeen? 'We believed it was vital to have a manager who had refined coaching and technical abilities,' said Anderson, years later. 'That man, the one with all the warts about him at the time, was Alex Ferguson. And he came here very humble, which might surprise people, but only those who really don't know him. We had rescued him from a rough time.'

FOUR

'BE ARROGANT, GET AT THEIR BLOODY THROATS'

Alex Ferguson took his first Aberdeen training session on Monday morning, 17 July 1978. After only four years as a manager he could claim to be in charge of the most promising group of players in the country. The 31-man squad he inherited contained four current Scotland internationals and six more who would go on to be capped in the years to come. The raw ingredients were already there.

Leading the pack were Willie Miller and the three men newly returned from the trauma of the World Cup in Argentina: Joe Harper, Stuart Kennedy and Bobby Clark. Harper was short, squat and heavy. It was hard to look at his weight and shape and believe he could trouble seasoned defences, but throughout the 1970s he was an instinctive and brilliant penalty-box finisher. He had scored twenty-seven goals for Aberdeen in the previous season and had been scoring prolifically since making his debut nine years earlier. In the 1971–72 campaign he managed forty-two, earning a European Bronze Boot from Uefa as the third-highest scorer across the continent. Defenders found Harper unstoppable. Everton took him south in 1972 and then he had a spell at Hibs before Ally MacLeod brought him home in 1976. 'King Joey' already boasted the highest number of goals in Aberdeen's 75-year history.

At right-back, Kennedy was quick and hard as nails. He possessed unshakeable self-confidence. As far as he was concerned no winger would get the better of him and he affected surprise that they even had the cheek to try. Ferguson first met him when they were both at Falkirk, where Kennedy had a part-time deal. His day job was as an engineer in the Grangemouth docks. One night he was jogging to training when Ferguson's car pulled up alongside and he offered him a lift. Kennedy politely declined. 'He later asked me why I hadn't taken a lift and I told him I preferred to jog. He said, "But it's raining." I said, "That disnae bother me, I work in a shipyard." I ticked every box for Alex Ferguson.'

Clark was the oldest player in the squad. At thirty-two he was only four years younger than Ferguson. His clean-cut features reflected a wholesome and committed professional. He had been Aberdeen's goalkeeper since 1965 and had amassed more than five hundred appearances. He had played seventeen times for Scotland and, like Harper, was synonymous with the Aberdeen teams of the 1970s.

And then there was Miller, who would have gone to the World Cup too had Ally MacLeod not chosen Manchester United's Gordon McQueen instead. No one was likely to describe Miller as clean-cut or wholesome. He would not have seemed out of place in a line-up of the great Italian defenders of the day. His dark hair, thick moustache and swarthy complexion gave him an almost Mediterranean look. For a sweeper he was neither tall nor quick and off the field he was a quiet, aloof figure. But Miller was the unmovable pillar of the Aberdeen team. His anticipation and reading of opposition attacks were magnificent, the timing and strength of his tackling outstanding. He was the quintessential leader.

When Aberdeen had been tested in Glasgow he had been utterly unmoved by the noise and hostility from the Old Firm fans. Above all, he was ferociously driven and competitive. Miller played like a winner long before he lifted his first trophy as captain, the League Cup under MacLeod.

But there was strength beyond the four internationals. Since the start of 1978 Harper had been partnered in attack by Steve Archibald, the 21-year-old Billy McNeill had signed from Clyde. Archibald was nimble, brave, quick and intelligent. His first and second Aberdeen goals had come in a 3–0 victory over Rangers at Ibrox in January and it was clear he would be a growing presence in the team. Behind Archibald, Dom Sullivan and John McMaster were gifted, stylish midfielders. Miller could rely on Willie Garner in central defence, though 19-year-old Alex McLeish was already showing promise in the reserves. Impish winger Gordon Strachan and mountainous defender Doug Rougvie both had plenty to offer. The reserve goalkeeper was 20-year-old Jim Leighton and the coaches were impressed with a 16-year-old midfielder, one of the ground staff boys, called Neil Simpson.

The task of updating Ferguson on the club's young talent, and of shrewdly educating the incoming manager in just about every other aspect of daily life at Pittodrie, fell to Teddy Scott. The adhesive that held the team together, Scott had served every Aberdeen manager since the 1950s and was instantly Ferguson's unquestioning lieutenant. A small man with a heavily-lined face and a wave of thick hair, he had joined the coaching staff as assistant trainer back in 1958 and took on a variety of background roles including trainer, physiotherapist, reserve and youth coach and kit manager. He played for the Dons just once, in 1954, but the contribution he made to the club over his life was immeasurable. He lived and breathed Aberdeen. If Pittodrie was open, he would be in it. If it was closed, he might still be in it. Whenever he missed his last bus home to the village of Ellon, sixteen miles away, he would return to the ground and sleep on the snooker table. To those who did not know him Scott could seem gruff, but he was quiet, wise, popular and respected.

On that first morning of training, with an assistant manager still to be appointed, it was Scott who acted as Ferguson's second-in-command. Ferguson had hoped to take St Mirren's physiotherapist-trainer to fill the role but Ricky McFarlane was unwilling to uproot his family and move north. An approach for Walter Smith, the assistant manager at Dundee United, was also unsuccessful. At the time, Ferguson said the 30-year-old wanted to continue playing. Later he admitted that United's powerful and headstrong manager, Jim McLean, had refused Smith permission to leave.

Scottish football is small and everyone knows one another. Ferguson had encountered Smith at SFA courses and they had been on opposing sides on the pitch and in dugouts as players and coaches. His respect for Smith was rooted in familiarity but his next choice was based on reputation. As a thoughtful midfielder dripping with class for Hibernian and Celtic, Pat Stanton had been one of the most admired figures in the game. Now he was thirty-three and out of work after telling the new Celtic manager, McNeill, that his knee had little chance of making a full recovery from a recent operation. Stanton did not know Ferguson so it came as a surprise when he received a telephone call asking whether he wanted to become the Dons' assistant manager. Off the field he was unassuming to the extent that he was nicknamed 'The Quiet Man'. But he was a shrewd appointment. 'Pat was quiet and self-contained while Alex was vocal and passionate,' said Willie Miller. 'But they formed a complementary managerial team. Both were real football people.'

In fact, Stanton was the only 'signing' Ferguson made before the start of his first campaign. Under McNeill the established players had come within touching distance of Aberdeen's first league title in nearly a quarter of a century and the transformation of the club since the threat of relegation two years earlier was apparent everywhere. The finances were stable, Pittodrie was terrific and in eleven league and cup meetings with the Old Firm in the previous season Aberdeen had won five. Still, one trophy in eight years was a poor return and that worried Ferguson. There were no problems with the club's ambition or even the quality of the team; of the thirty-one players he inherited, nine would subsequently win a European final. What nagged at Ferguson was the mental strength of the club on and off the pitch. He wondered whether they had it in them to take the fight to Glasgow.

Ferguson had always been deeply proud of his Glaswegian roots. Govan shaped him and if he had his way it would shape everyone else, too. The Aberdeen players and coaching staff soon noticed that he instinctively warmed to any schoolboy trainees who came to the club from Glasgow or its suburbs. 'He loved the s-forms [schoolboy signings] from Glasgow,' said George Adams, one of the youth coaches at Aberdeen. 'Nobody, but nobody, was as good as the s-forms from Glasgow. He'd say to the lads from Aberdeen, "Aye, you'll nae beat the Glasgow boys. You're no' as hard as them, you're no' as worldly wise, they're better. Gimme a boy from Glasgow and one from Aberdeen with the same ability and there's only one I'd sign." He was open about that. Didn't hide it. He felt they had a hunger about them that he wanted. But he was also saying it to get a reaction. "You'll never be as good as them . . ."'

The opening results were encouraging. Aberdeen's first match under Ferguson was a 5–0 friendly win at Elgin City on 31 July. Five days later there was another friendly, this one against

Tottenham Hotspur at Pittodrie, the new man's home debut. Gracing the front of the match programme were Spurs' signings Ossie Ardiles and Ricky Villa, who had just won the World Cup with Argentina and were the talk of British football. Difficulties with the transfer paperwork delayed their debuts and neither played, but a 19,000 crowd saw Aberdeen win 3–1 against a team which included Glenn Hoddle and Steve Perryman. The domestic season also saw a good start with a 4–1 win in the rain at Hearts on 12 August – Bobby Clark was injured so young Jim Leighton made his debut in goal – before a home win over Morton and a draw at Dundee United.

Aberdeen's third home game under Ferguson was a mundane League Cup tie against Meadowbank Thistle on 2 September. They had won the away leg 5–0 and the only mild interest lay in whether the aggregate score would reach double figures. It didn't, stopping at 9–0. Just 6,580 supporters paid to get into Pittodrie that Saturday afternoon but those who shelled out an additional 15p for the match programme were treated to something far more interesting than anything they saw on the pitch. Instead of filling his manager opinion column with the bland platitudes familiar to official club publications, Ferguson seized the opportunity to make a powerful declaration of intent:

> The one thing that has annoyed me all my life is this acceptance that Rangers and Celtic must win, that everything is geared around them, that nobody but nobody is expected to beat them. I look at everything round about me and success is staring me in the face. The one thing that is lying hidden inside people's heads is this total belief. We have it in the Beach End [where Aberdeen's noisiest supporters congregated] and that's where we must build and develop from, right through

> the corridors of Pittodrie and into the dressing rooms. I keep getting a picture in my mind when I try to realise ambition and belief in players and the picture is of the Liverpool Kop. When you hear them sing 'You'll Never Walk Alone' even opponents believe the Reds are going to win.

After only three months in the job there it was, the first beat of a drum that he would bang for the next eight years. Belief, belief, belief. When he spoke privately to the players he worded the message more bluntly. How should they tackle the Old Firm? 'Be arrogant, get at their bloody throats.'

FIVE

THE CULL OF THE 'WESTHILL WILLIE-BITERS'

The away dressing room at Ibrox Stadium is one of football's grandest depositories for visiting teams. With its high ceiling, wood panelling and brass fittings, the sunlight flooding in through a row of high windows, it creates a sense of scale and substance which can be intimidating. At his first Aberdeen game against Rangers, Ferguson was too consumed by the task at hand to notice any of that. He had eyes and ears only for the mood of his own players. And he did not like it. Early-season results suggested they had moved on from that dreadful Scottish Cup final performance four months earlier, when they had frozen during what turned out to be McNeill's last game as manager. In fact Aberdeen under Ferguson had made a far more solid start to the campaign than treble-winning Rangers had under their new boss, John Greig. After four games the Dons were already five points ahead and Ferguson saw that visit to Ibrox on 16 September 1978 as an opportunity to lay down a marker by beating them. It was an attitude which crystallised the stark difference between what he regarded as a good result in Glasgow and what his players did.

Rangers played well in the windy conditions and went ahead from a disputed penalty just before half-time. They had further chances and were closing in on their first league win of the season when substitute Gordon Strachan dug out a cross in the ninetieth minute which midfielder Dom Sullivan met with a headed equaliser. The game finished 1–1. Ferguson stood on the touchline and watched how his players reacted. Before kick-off he had heard them talking about slowing down the play, time-wasting, frustrating Rangers and settling for a draw. Now they bounced happily back into the dressing room only to be surprised by Ferguson muttering and moaning. 'The atmosphere in the dressing room was reasonably upbeat, which made the manager even angrier,' said Miller, the captain. Ferguson later took Miller aside and told him he was 'sick' at the team being so happy just because they had drawn with Rangers. There was probably an element of exaggeration in that. The result preserved Aberdeen's lead over the champions and was a decent outcome on a day when they had not performed well. Ferguson even told reporters after the match: 'I'm very pleased. To come to Ibrox in these type of conditions is a good result all right.' But he was convinced that his players' reaction symbolised the attitude that was holding the club back. He was determined to obliterate the inferiority complex Aberdeen had about Rangers and Celtic. Things were going to be different under him: his teams would go to Ibrox and Parkhead and be quick, strong, combative, aggressive, controlling and relentless. Above all they would go to attack.

Ferguson had already demonstrated that his style was to go for it. The previous season his St Mirren, despite being new to the top flight, had lost only two out of eight league games against the Old Firm and beat Celtic twice at Parkhead. He had to instil the same confidence in Aberdeen. Strangely the admiration he felt for the squad he had built at Love Street in itself proved to be an obstacle. It was as if the talented set of youngsters he had left behind at St Mirren were still with him, playing in front of his mind's eye every time he looked at Aberdeen. He began to make unflattering comparisons. During training and in team-talks he kept dropping the names of St Mirren players, intimating he was more impressed with the squad in Paisley than the one he had inherited at Pittodrie. Strachan kept hearing that Tony Fitzpatrick would have been a bigger influence on the play. Joe Harper was not working as hard up front as Frank McGarvey did. If only Miller could defend like Jackie Copland. It was Copland this, Copland that, Copland the other. Miller let it go at first but gradually he began to simmer. Copland was a decent defender at St Mirren and Miller knew, liked and respected him. But Miller had played under three Aberdeen managers, captained the team to a cup victory and represented Scotland. He was in a different class. There was not much he had to learn from a guy who was nudging thirty and who had still been in the lower leagues two years earlier. Miller recalled the prevailing, sarcastic response: 'Tell the St Mirren boys to take their medals up and let us see them.'

Eventually the captain took the new manager to task. Calm and assured, Miller told Ferguson he could rely on his full support and commitment but he resented the constant comparisons with Copland. 'He referred to St Mirren a lot,' said Miller. 'That's what got my nose up a little bit. I had my own way of doing things. I liked to organise at set-pieces. So when Fergie kept referring to how St Mirren did things I didn't take it that well. Eventually I pointed it out to him. "Let me organise this. I'm not really that interested in how Jackie Copland did things." It wasn't eyeball-to-eyeball, not on that occasion. It was more of a "Look, gaffer, I've had enough of Jackie Copland and St Mirren". The thing with Fergie is that he's a good judge of character. I wasn't trying to undermine his authority in any way and he knew that. He was pretty rash when he came in to Aberdeen. He was only thirty-six. He wasn't schooled in man-management. He wasn't the type of manager he became later. He was abrasive. He spoke his mind.'

It was not simply a matter of wounded pride. The comparisons rankled on the basis of plentiful recent evidence. Over the previous two seasons Aberdeen had played Ferguson's former team six times and the results were 3–2, 4–0, 4–0, 3–1, 2–1 and 4–2. Aberdeen had won the lot. 'He really wasn't liked when he first came in,' said Willie Garner, Miller's central defensive partner in Ferguson's first season. 'He wasn't that much older than a few of the players and I think he was doing a lot of things for effect. It was the whole "deal with the monster"-type thing, and he was the monster.' John McMaster recalled the mood: 'The boys were getting pissed off with it. He was like a bull in a china shop. Face-to-face stuff, pouncing on things, not thinking. Stuart Kennedy used to go in and say, "Boss, you're going to lose that dressing room if you continue to talk about St Mirren players."'

Ferguson liked Kennedy's style and the feeling was mutual. Kennedy was a senior and popular figure among the players and an invaluable advocate for the new manager. As resentment slowly grew, Kennedy's role became key. After a few weeks he intervened: 'Eventually the St Mirren thing was pointed out to him . . . although it had to be eased into the conversation! We were strong, proud players as well. He still had affection for that St Mirren team and players but he realised it wasn't the way forward.' Perhaps Ferguson had been attempting to rile Aberdeen into becoming a new set of 'Furies', but he was perceptive enough to see when he had made a wrong call. The point made by both Kennedy and Miller hit home. There would be no more reminiscing about Jackie Copland.

The task of remaking Aberdeen in his own ferocious image remained. The crucial early battle of wills was fought between him and Miller and the outcome would shape the team for years to come. Both were Glaswegians. Miller, the younger by fourteen years, came from Bridgeton, Rangers territory like Ferguson's beloved Govan, and he shared the manager's hard upbringing and deep-rooted hunger and ambition. They were as competitive as each other, though they had different ways of showing it. Ferguson was expressive, Miller reserved. The early friction between them was down to just one factor: they had yet to appreciate how the other worked.

At first they circled each other. Because Miller lacked pace he relied on his magnificent reading of the game and so tended to defend from a deep position. Ferguson felt that invited pressure from opponents and wanted Miller to push up and hold a higher line. Miller ignored him, not out of disrespect but because he felt Ferguson did not know enough about him or the art of defending to suggest such a fundamental change of tactic. Miller also had a sluggish attitude to training – he was one of those players who only came alive in matches – and the combination did nothing to endear him to Ferguson. A confrontation was inevitable.

'Willie kept getting booked for mouthing to the referee,' said Garner. 'There was this game when he'd been booked and then gave out another couple of dull ones fifteen to twenty minutes into the second half. All of a sudden our physio's out with the subs' boards, banging them together, clack-clack-clack. I look across and he's holding up number six. Willie's coming off. I'm laughing to myself, thinking, "This'll be fun." Willie didn't even look across. I says to him, "You're going off." So he looks across, stares at it and just waves his hand at the touchline, dismissing it. A few seconds later, clack-clack-clack with the boards. Same again, Willie looks across and just waves it away again. He just keeps playing. So Fergie tells the physio to come back into the dugout. At the end of the game, what an argument that one was! Fergie versus Willie. "You tried to undermine my authority!" They were nose-to-nose.'

Miller asserted himself more than once. Several minutes into one of Ferguson's longer dressing-room post-mortems he got up, protesting he was cold, walked to the shower room and said he could listen from there, if necessary. In a match at Partick Thistle he was unhappy about Aberdeen playing five at the back and at half-time told Ferguson it had to change. Other players were startled by the open challenge to the manager. Ferguson told him to be quiet, Miller continued to rant. The tension was palpable. Ferguson was furious but, revealingly, the confrontation petered out. He would take it from Miller – and no one else – because he knew the captain was as committed to improving the team as he was. He had no interest in usurping the manager's control. Indeed, it was soon clear to Ferguson that Miller had exactly the qualities he wanted in his team's leader. If anything it was Ferguson who compromised as Miller's relentlessly impressive performances rendered their initial clashes irrelevant. In time he would hail Miller as 'the best penalty-box defender in Europe'. In the meantime the captain was about to prove himself as indispensable to his manager off the pitch as he was on it.

Though Aberdeen's early results under Ferguson were satisfying, including progress past Marek Dimitrov of Bulgaria in the European Cup Winners' Cup, they disguised the ongoing friction with the players. The disaffection was heightened by a geographical divide. The Ferguson family had yet to move north and the manager was often absent when the team bus made the long journey home after away games, returning instead to Glasgow to see Cathy and the boys. Not travelling with the team encouraged dissent. On the journey back from Aberdeen's first league defeat of the season, against Hibs at Easter Road on 23 September, the players discussed the tactics Ferguson had employed. There were complaints. His approach had been uncharacteristically conservative and he had Joe Harper up front on his own in a 4–5–1 formation. Hibs had won 2–1 and could have scored more.

When the players arrived for training the following Monday they were told to get changed and then sit in the centre circle at Pittodrie, where the manager would address them. Ferguson emerged from the mouth of the tunnel and strode purposefully on to the pitch. None of them knew what was coming and most assumed they were in for some shouting and bawling. Instead he declared an amnesty: they could raise their complaints to his face. Whatever they had to say, they could say it there and then without fear of repercussion.

Harper was the first to pipe up: 'I don't think the tactics worked, boss,' he said. Harper was a dominant character among a small clique of first-team players who lived within a few streets of each other in the pleasant little suburb of Westhill. Harper, Dom Sullivan and Ian Fleming often shared lifts to training and they harboured early reservations about Ferguson. All of them had thought the world of either Turnbull, MacLeod or McNeill, and in Harper's case all three. They did not think so much of their successor. After Harper another player had his say, then another. Ferguson could take only so much before his temper boiled over and he spat out a response: 'Fucking Westhill willie-biters.' The unusual line stuck. 'We were nicknamed "the Westhill willie-biters",' said Sullivan, laughing about it more than thirty years later. 'We were apparently openly conspiring against him and we all lived in Westhill! That's what he called us. It wasn't true. Not at all. It just came off his tongue one time and it stuck with the boys. It became banter to the rest of them in the dressing room.'

Apart from provoking that memorable phrase the summit in Pittodrie's centre circle seemed to pass without any strong reaction on Ferguson's part. In fact, it was the calm before the storm. After the training session Harper was summoned to the manager's office. 'Bloody sit down,' Ferguson barked. He then castigated Harper for questioning his tactics in front of the team. As he wagged a finger in Harper's face the player's anger rose up. He snapped and grabbed Ferguson's finger, momentarily bending it backwards. 'Don't you ever point a finger at me like that again,' he snarled. 'I was brought up to show good manners. I would never do that to anyone. If you don't want my opinion, don't ask for it.' Then he stormed out of the office. Though Ferguson took the incident no further, his mind was made up about Harper. Their relationship would never fully recover.

As a city, Aberdeen is a goldfish bowl. Inevitably, people heard rumours that things were not going well behind the scenes and gossip circulated about mutinous players and their antipathy towards the new manager. It did not help that they lost four games in a row including a 3–0 collapse in the first leg against Fortuna Düsseldorf in Germany on 18 October. After that match Ferguson allowed the players to drown their sorrows but was irritated when his generosity was abused and some of them embarked on a heavy session which ended in a nightclub. His anger intensified when they played poorly and lost at home to Hearts three days later. On the day of the second leg against the Germans local reporter Andy Melvin wrote a comment piece for the *Evening Express*: 'During the past fortnight rumours have swept through Aberdeen like a fire through a forest. Stories of mass transfer requests and even physical confrontation between Alex Ferguson and a player have been born, cultivated and allowed to mushroom by those characters who always claim to be "in the know" . . . Three Premier League defeats and Pittodrie is looked upon as a cauldron of hate. Three wins and I suppose all is well again. Alex Ferguson and his players are deeply worried about the situation and that is not doing their Premier League and Cup Winners' Cup preparations any good at all.'

Stories about tensions between Harper and Ferguson reached supporters. The striker was a hero to those fans in the cavernous, noisy Beach End who Ferguson himself had yet to impress. By the time he left the club Harper was Aberdeen's leading goalscorer of all time. But Ferguson saw problems beyond the goals. Harper was no natural athlete and had little enthusiasm for fitness training. He would duck and dive to get out of long runs, or look for cheeky shortcuts. Ferguson also thought him disruptive. Though Harper went on to contribute thirty-three goals that season, he was too much of an individual and refused to follow the manager's instructions. Ferguson was intent on building a team who defended from the front, with strikers constantly moving and closing down opponents. That was not Harper's style. Stuart Kennedy, who enjoyed Harper's company, was clear-sighted about Ferguson's dilemma: 'A lot of managers might have buckled down to wee Joe. He might have dominated them because he's a dominating wee guy. He was the top scorer and all top scorers have an ego. He was "The King". The fans loved him. But Fergie looked at the team. Maybe at Pittodrie you weren't being asked to run so much but he looked at playing in Europe, playing away games. Joe would score goals, that was a guarantee, but he wasn't going to run out to the flanks and shut down a full-back.'

Years later, in his 1999 autobiography, *Managing My Life*, Ferguson described Harper as a long-term problem for him at Aberdeen: an artful dodger; a player with weight problems who lacked discipline. He even claimed to have lapped him on a training run. Harper responded in his own book, *King*

Joey, in 2008, concluding that Ferguson hated and despised him. 'I cannot help wondering if Fergie considered my hero status as some sort of threat to his authority.' He denied being unsupportive but accused Ferguson of showing him little respect and pursuing a vendetta. 'I do not wish to speak to Sir Alex Ferguson ever again,' he wrote. True to his word, in 2014 Harper declined to be interviewed for this book because it would involve discussing Ferguson. Ferguson, meanwhile, has never publicly responded to Harper's autobiography.

Harper's Westhill pal Sullivan was a skilful and smooth midfielder who had made a major contribution to the club's 1976 League Cup win. Unlike Harper he was one of the fittest players at Pittodrie. Among the Aberdeen squad he had a unique history with Ferguson. They had once played against each other when Ferguson was coming to the end of his career at Falkirk and Sullivan was a young lad starting at Clyde. During that match Ferguson had smashed in two of Sullivan's teeth. 'There was a corner kick five minutes in,' Sullivan remembers. 'I was back covering, picking up Fergie. Thirty seconds later I was picking up my teeth. He swung an arm and broke two teeth. I got off the ground, the ball's at the other end of the park, I've got blood everywhere and didn't know where I was. That was Fergie: win at all costs.'

Their reunion at Pittodrie got off to a bad start. Sullivan's version of events is that Billy McNeill made an offer to take him to Celtic soon after moving there as manager. Ferguson interpreted it as collusion and a lack of commitment on the player's part and Sullivan found himself dropped to the reserves. He insists he knew nothing about Celtic's bid and did not deserve to be marginalised. 'I went to Fergie and asked about it. He said, "You're no' for sale." I said, "But I'm not playing in the first team, you're no' giving me a chance." But I was dismissed. I kept coming in and out, being put back into the reserves. Playing well, but in and out. He was fucking me about, to tell you the truth. He admitted it in later years. Eventually I decided, "Ach, I'm not putting up with this," and I asked to see the chairman, Dick Donald. I said to him, "Mr Chairman, I'm really unhappy, I don't know where I'm going, I don't know what I'm doing, I don't seem to be getting a game and I'm training with the reserves." He said, "I'm sorry to hear that, Dom, hold on a minute." He phoned down for Fergie. Fergie came up. Dick says, "Alex, Dom isn't happy. What's the situation?" Fergie says, "Well, he's in my squad, he's not for sale." So Dick goes, "If he's in your squad surely he should be in here training?" Fergie didn't like it. Dick Donald was very straight. So Fergie says he needs a certain number of players for set drills and so on. Dick says, "I don't see how another one would upset that."

'I was dismissed from the room. About ten, fifteen minutes later I got summoned to Fergie's office, just a wee cubby hole. He was sitting behind the table and I just stood. "What is it, boss?" He says, "Don't ever go to my fucking chairman." I said, "Excuse me, he's my chairman as well, and you don't need to swear at me, you can express yourself and I can perfectly understand what you're saying." "Get out of my fucking office!" He cleared the table. I always say I was the first to get the hairdryer [treatment]. That was his way. And he sorted out many bigger superstars than me.'

The third of the so-called Westhill willie-biters, Ian Fleming, was a small, gutsy, street-fighter of a striker who had been brought to the club by Ally MacLeod and had subsequently proved himself invaluable to McNeill. Fleming suspected that Ferguson had a problem with him because of on-field issues from the past, in particular challenges he had made on two St Mirren players, Bobby Reid and Iain Munro. On both occasions Ferguson's dugout exploded in angry protest at Fleming. Now

Ferguson was his boss. Fleming said: 'I was quite hard. If I thought defenders were going out to nail me my attitude was that I would get in there first. I remember those St Mirren games. Their dugout were out shouting at me, "Fleming, ya dirty . . . Yer an animal." I turned and said, "Sit on yer arses, I never touched him." So me and Fergie had history. I just got it in my head that he didn't want me. He did say, "I want you here as a pool player." But I'd always been a first-team player with Kilmarnock and then with Aberdeen. I kept going in to see him. I'd tell him it wasn't working. Stevie Archibald and I used to sit outside his office at dinner time, both waiting to see him. He'd say, "You two again?" Did I give him a chance? Maybe I didn't. I should have sat tight and fought my case. He thought there were cliques. He thought the likes of me and wee Joe were troublemakers. Maybe I was wrong and was too sharp in wanting away. But I loved the club. I still do.'

The Westhill lads may have grumbled about Ferguson's methods but they never short-changed Aberdeen on the pitch, nor moaned to the press. Nor did they attempt to enlist others to provoke a mutiny. There would have been no point. Three of the most powerful figures in the dressing room – Willie Miller, Stuart Kennedy and Bobby Clark – were supportive of the changes Ferguson was imposing and the more they got to know him the deeper their loyalty grew. Miller was aware of the mutterings against Ferguson and resisted them: 'I was never part of that group. I was the captain and felt I had a responsibility to support the manager. Even if it was a bad manager I would have felt that responsibility. But he wasn't a bad manager, he just rubbed people up the wrong way. He wanted to win titles and he kept drilling that into us. I assessed it and I thought if someone's that determined to be successful then he would do for me. Alex assessed it pretty quickly; he didn't really need me to tell him. He knew who was for him and who was against him. One of his great attributes is judging characters and knowing who he can trust, who is 100 per cent with him and who is not. But he found it tough going in the first year.'

Clark was the team's elder statesman and a highly respected professional. He recalls those early tensions with frustration: 'Some of the older boys had been Billy McNeill's boys. I remember grabbing some of the guys and saying, "Billy's not coming back, so why are you doing this? First of all give him a chance." I said, "Let's get this thing going again because you're just taking money out of your own pockets here, you're self-destructing, you're winning the league for Celtic." And then Alex grew and people began to realise that he was very, very good.'

Ferguson needed people he could trust. Chairman Dick Donald and vice-chairman Chris Anderson were influential allies, so was trainer and reserve-team manager Teddy Scott, while the loyalty of his assistant, Pat Stanton, was beyond question. One player made the mistake of going to Stanton with a gripe about Ferguson. 'It was a football issue, but it was about Alex,' said Stanton. 'I stopped him and said, "Listen, before you go any further, Alex Ferguson brought me here to help him and I'll no' help him by talking behind his back. So if you continue this conversation, and say what you're about to say, I'll tell the manager because that's what I'm here for. I'm on the manager's side. I owe it to him to cover his back."' Stanton was respected by the players, and they confided in him, but his commitment was to Ferguson. When the pair of them discussed the squad in that first season they reached similar conclusions. Anyone they had reservations about would have to go. Stanton said: 'I remember sitting talking to him one day, just running through the players. One thing about Alex Ferguson is that he saves himself a lot of time. He clears things up quickly and he can spot a phoney. I just said to him, "Some of these players here, they're not going to do it for you so what's the point of them being here?" I felt there was a wee bit of resentment towards him. I said to him, "Just get rid of them or they'll get rid of you."'

Ian Taggart, club secretary during Ferguson's time, observed the fate of dissenters at close quarters: 'The directors were aware of it and they talked about it. I don't think they talked to Fergie about it. But the senior players nipped it in the bud and that was the end of it. Too many of the players could see that he had it. He weeded out the other players. They all disappeared.' Defender Doug Rougvie put it more bluntly: 'The Westhill willie-biters? He got them out. They all got bombed. He slaughtered them.'

Fleming was first to go. He made more than 100 appearances for Aberdeen but he did not last five months under Ferguson before he was sold to Jack Charlton's Sheffield Wednesday in February 1979. 'I regret leaving so early,' he says now. 'I would have liked to have played for him because I would have suited him. But the damage was done. That's the regret of my football life, but how could I know they were going to win so many trophies? In football there are people you get on with and people you don't. He's maybe the greatest manager there has ever been. But the best manager for me was Billy McNeill. I'll always say that.'

Sullivan was next. Eight months later Celtic came in for him again. He received a phone call from Ferguson: McNeill wanted to see him and this time there would be no objections. 'Come in at 7 o'clock, get your boots, be out of the place at half-seven.' Sullivan was a fine footballer and the move to the club he had supported since childhood would result in him winning two league championships. Eventually he would make peace with Ferguson as well. 'We met years later at the opening of a pub in Glasgow. I sat with Fergie, "How you doing, boss?" I sat with him for two hours. And he says, "I was probably too hasty with you." I said, "Boss, I was never against you and I never wanted to leave."'

Surprisingly, the Westhill ringleader, Harper, survived far longer than the others. After the clash in Ferguson's office he vowed to keep his head down and lasted another two-and-a-half seasons at Pittodrie. However, serious knee injuries kept him off the pitch for long spells and his solitary appearance in the 1980–81 campaign, in a home defeat to Kilmarnock in the final match of the season, marked the end of his Aberdeen career. He had lost the battle with Ferguson but he preserved his regal status as far as the fans were concerned. He left Pittodrie with tears in his eyes after Ferguson broke the news that he would not be getting a new contract. The mutual mud-slinging of their later autobiographies showed that the bitterness between the pair was irreparable. But supporters have refrained from picking sides, then and now. Harper remains 'King Joey'.

There was one other powerful character in the Aberdeen dressing room who travelled in from Westhill. He was as headstrong, stubborn and potentially troublesome as any of the other three, but Steve Archibald was no 'willie-biter'. Nor was he rushed out by Ferguson. Archibald was his own man; a serial complainer who was rarely without a grumble, often to do with his wages. But he had no inclination to resist or undermine the new boss. Unlike the others he was young, his best years in the game still ahead of him. Ferguson saw this and in an early display of his capacity for pragmatism, giving leeway to those who were valuable to him, he shrugged off the player's moaning. In turn, Archibald blossomed. When he left for Tottenham, at the end of Ferguson's second season, it was on his own terms, having completed an £800,000 move the Dons could not refuse. It pained Ferguson to lose him.

Whether the dressing room was united in support or not, Ferguson's ultimate vindication lay in results. Aberdeen's first clash with Celtic on 7 October would be another test of the team's nerve. They delivered a stirring 4–1 win at Pittodrie and Ferguson purred: 'In all my years associated with football, both as a player and as a manager, I have never seen an Old Firm team demolished so successfully or beaten so easily as Celtic were here.' Gradually the worries about his handling of the job began to ease. The season continued with a European exit at the hands of Fortuna Düsseldorf but only after a performance of character and quality in the second leg on 1 November. 'German clubs always fear playing in Scotland, and this is why,' Fortuna manager Dieter Tippenhauer said after losing 2–0 at Pittodrie but going through 3–2 on aggregate. 'Aberdeen were strong, aggressive and never gave up. The Aberdeen team is young. I will be looking at their fortunes with interest in the future. Their day will come in European football.'

That result was the beginning of a ten-game unbeaten run which continued until the penultimate day of 1978, when Morton won at Pittodrie. Five of those matches may have been drawn, but at the turn of the year Aberdeen were sitting third in the Premier Division. Beating Meadowbank Thistle, Hamilton, Ayr United and finally Hibs in a semi-final won by Stuart Kennedy's extra-time goal, the Dons had moved through to the League Cup final where they would face Rangers in March. By now a Ferguson team was emerging. Clark was the regular in goal, behind full-backs Kennedy and Chic McLelland. Miller and Rougvie provided a physically formidable central defence – the latter stepping in for the injured Willie Garner – and Strachan was emerging as a wee, red-haired box of tricks in the middle, offering far more than he had in his debut season under McNeill. Alongside him, completing a midfield quartet, were John McMaster, Drew Jarvie and either Sullivan or winger Ian Scanlon. And up front there were goals in both Archibald and Harper. In fact, between that finger-bending confrontation in the manager's office and the end of the year, Harper scored fifteen goals. The presence of a couple of 'willie-biters' in the side evidently did nothing to disrupt the team's spirit, nor its improvement. The threat of rebellion they had presented to Ferguson had petered out. The results eased him out of trouble. On the field at least.

Even when the football offered solace, the second half of 1978 remained relentlessly stressful for Ferguson. On 2 November, the day after Aberdeen were eliminated from Europe, the *Evening Express*'s front page headline was FERGUSON CHEATED ON EXPENSES. He had carried out his threat to take St Mirren to an industrial tribunal and now the dirty laundry was being hung out in public. The tribunal sat over four days between early November and early December and was an unwelcome distraction when Ferguson was still finding his feet at Pittodrie. There were more long journeys between Aberdeen and Glasgow, more long phone calls, and more meetings with solicitors. For reporters it was a dripping roast of juicy stories. Sacked football managers rarely take their former clubs to court and this revealed why: the questioning was done under oath and inevitably details emerged that neither party wished to make public. Among the reasons St Mirren gave for his dismissal were the drawing of £25-a-week unauthorised expenses and his payment of bonuses to players without the board's permission. (In his defence, Ferguson produced a club letter from 1977 which he said showed he was entitled to all the expenses he had claimed.) The tribunal was also told that Ferguson was unhappy that St Mirren were prepared to pay three players more than he earned himself. There were vivid accounts of arguments with the directors and of Ferguson walking out of a board meeting and threatening to sue. He was accused of engineering his own dismissal in order to earn £50,000 compensation and of receiving a case of champagne for acting as an advisor to a bookmaker friend. He denied all the allegations against him.

St Mirren's lawyer remarked pointedly that it was 'an extremely happy coincidence' that Aberdeen should approach him with a job offer on the very day of his dismissal. St Mirren vice-chairman John Corson claimed that Ferguson had been described as 'impossible to live with' and revealed that most of the board had decided to sack him on 15 May, eleven days before a full meeting could be convened to ratify the decision. There was also evidence presented that he had had poor relationships and rows with office staff at Love Street, and an allegation that he had sworn at his female secretary when they argued about paying tax on a player's expenses. His income was disclosed, too: a basic salary of £15,000 at St Mirren compared with £12,000 at Aberdeen, though at Pittodrie there was the incentive of bonuses of £6,000 for winning the league, £4,000 for finishing second and £2,000 for third place. Aberdeen, incidentally, had also given him an £18,000 interest-free loan to buy a house and provided a £7,500 Rover club car. For a man so guarded about his private life, it was galling to have such personal information disclosed in public. In response, Ferguson's solicitor accused St Mirren chairman Willie Todd of pursuing a vendetta against the manager and of being 'vicious and underhand' in the way he handled the sacking.

Having heard all the evidence the tribunal took a fortnight to deliver its verdict. Although some of the individual charges were dismissed, including the one about advising the bookie, the tribunal ruled in favour of St Mirren and Ferguson lost the case. The dismissal had not been unfair, the tribunal concluded: relations between Ferguson and the board had become irrecoverable and he had charged £25-a-week expenses without permission; the club had been entitled to sack him on those grounds. It was his 'impatient energy and single-mindedness, which so contributed to his success as a team manager, that led to his downfall', said the sixteen-page conclusion. In regard to the incident with the secretary, though, the report's choice of words soon looked comical: 'It shows him as one possessing neither by experience nor talent, any managerial ability at all . . .'

The verdict, delivered four days before Christmas, shattered Ferguson. 'I would not like to go through something like that again. It took me away from my players at Aberdeen for three weeks and that is what is important to me now. I am strong enough to take it,' he said afterwards. Fortunately his relationship with the Aberdeen directors, especially Dick Donald and Chris Anderson, had deepened as they stood by him. Donald dismissed the tribunal's verdict as irrelevant to Aberdeen: it was a matter between Ferguson and St Mirren. Case closed. Such unquestioning loyalty made a lasting impression.

The episode had been an embarrassing career low. Ferguson then suffered a far greater personal trauma.

After four decades in the Clydeside shipyards, Alexander Beaton Ferguson reached pensionable age the year before the eldest of his two sons took over at Aberdeen. Alex senior spent nearly all his days in Govan, Glasgow, living and working in the shadows of the giant cranes. He was a plater's helper, assisting the men who bolted iron plates on to the sides of ships. Later he was an assistant timekeeper in Fairfields. His son would name his house after that shipyard.

Ferguson senior was a Protestant and the product of an area riven by sectarianism. Yet he married a Catholic girl, Elizabeth Hardie, and went against the grain by supporting Celtic rather than Rangers, even becoming chairman of the local supporters' club. That showed his independent mind and he did not care when his boys, Alex and Martin, took the more conventional path and followed Rangers, the club based less than a mile from their tenement home.

He was a quiet, almost reserved man, well known and respected both at work and around the community. He avoided the two curses that so often blighted West of Scotland working-class life, bigotry and heavy drinking. And the long hours and endless overtime he put in at Fairfields meant his family lived in comparative comfort. Their home was clean and tidy and the boys always had clothes and regular meals. There was even an inside toilet, which was more than the neighbours could say. But he was also impatient, punctual and demanding, and possessed a volcanic temper. Discipline under Alex senior was strict and that extended to his sons' growing enthusiasm for football. When he watched them play he would bark instructions from the touchline. It was always 'Ferguson' he shouted, not Alex or Martin. He was a harsh judge, sparing with praise and quick to find fault. But he understood the game and his criticism was always constructive. The boys were told to keep their feet on the ground, never to get carried away. 'He never allowed me to be satisfied,' said Ferguson of his father. 'Without him I would never have made it into football.'

Alex had been forced to take on less physically demanding work in the yards after surgery for bowel cancer in 1961. His health remained an ongoing concern for the family thereafter. In the second half of 1978, aged sixty-six and when his son was 150 miles away in Aberdeen, he fell into poor health and was diagnosed with lung cancer. Shortly before Christmas he was admitted to the Southern General Hospital in Glasgow. Already shuttling back and forth for his industrial tribunal hearings, Ferguson now crammed hospital visits into his relentless schedule. He saw his dad as often as possible, accepting that their time together was becoming increasingly precious.

On 24 February 1979, Aberdeen played St Mirren, taking Ferguson back to Love Street for the first time since the tribunal's verdict. An hour into the game they were ahead thanks to goals from Archibald and Scanlon. The points looked certain. But it was a fractious afternoon; at half-time Ferguson breached the conditions of an undertaking he had given the SFA by entering the referee's room to remonstrate. Soon after St Mirren pulled a goal back, Scanlon and later Miller were sent off. Ferguson was livid and again directed his frustration at the referee. With seven minutes left St Mirren equalised for the point they needed to go top of the league. Jackie Copland, of all people, scored. At the final whistle Ferguson was pulled into a side room by his friend, Fred Douglas, the stadium electrician at Love Street. Douglas told him that the club had received a call while the game was going on: his dad had passed away. In fact the time of death was recorded at 4.23pm, coinciding with the spell of trouble when Aberdeen lost two men and a goal. Donald and Anderson did what they could to comfort Ferguson but it was insufficient. 'I was completely broken up,' he said. 'I was beyond consoling.'

The funeral was four days later. Ferguson got through it without any public display of grief. That evening Aberdeen had a home game against Partick Thistle. His work ethic kicked in and he decided he would take charge of the team as usual, because that was what his father would have wanted. On the long drive back to the north-east he pulled into a lay-by and cried.

SIX

'DOUG ROUGVIE IS INNOCENT'

Ferguson was not the type of man to stand still or retreat into his shell while grieving. Over the following weeks there was no dimming of his relentless energy, no indication that his focus had wavered. His mourning was a private affair. His dad passed away just thirty-five days before a date the whole family saw as hugely significant. After 304 days in charge at Aberdeen the Scottish League Cup final against Rangers on 31 March 1979, was the first national occasion of his managerial career. It felt fresh and exciting, yet his mood was clouded by some old baggage. 'If the cup is to travel north then Aberdeen must beat the Hampden freeze,' wrote Jim Reynolds in that morning's *Glasgow Herald*. 'That is not an amateur weather forecast but a question of doubt about Pittodrie temperaments at the national stadium. They have players of undoubted class . . . they have shown in lesser matches that they can beat Rangers . . . but they have still to prove they can do it when it really matters.'

Reynolds was right. Under Ferguson Aberdeen had drawn with Rangers at Ibrox in September and at Pittodrie in November. They had beaten Celtic at home in the league and away in a Scottish Cup replay. They had reached Hampden having lost only one out of seven games against the Old Firm. Days earlier they had set a league record by beating Motherwell 8–0. But Reynolds' article struck at an uncomfortable truth: the team had yet to prove to Scotland, to Glasgow, and to one Glaswegian in particular, that they could do it when it mattered. Memories remained vivid of that Scottish Cup final collapse under McNeill ten months earlier. Aberdeen versus Rangers would become the sourest, ugliest fixture of Ferguson's time in Scotland and what happened in his first cup final contributed enormously to a rapid deterioration in relations.

In the first minute Rangers striker Derek Johnstone cut down Archibald in a tackle Ferguson called 'disgraceful'. Archibald played the rest of the game as a subdued figure. Fifty-eight minutes in Aberdeen took the lead when Duncan Davidson's header was fumbled over the line by Rangers' lanky goalkeeper Peter McCloy. For nineteen minutes they had one hand on the cup. Then Johnstone accidentally collided with Clark during a Rangers attack, dislocating a vertebra in the goalkeeper's neck. The pain was instant and Clark's entire arm went numb. He was down on one knee and clutching his arm when Rangers began the move from which they equalised. 'If I'd stayed down we might have won,' Clark said, bemoaning his decision not to seek instant treatment. 'From then on I really struggled. I had no idea what was wrong with my arm.' Alex MacDonald struck a long-range shot which took a deflection off McMaster and spun away from Clark. Suddenly it was 1–1 with thirteen minutes to go. Ferguson came on to the pitch to console Clark and check whether he could continue. Archibald volunteered to take over in goal but Clark refused to go off and continued with his left arm heavily bandaged.

What happened next has been the subject of dispute and controversy ever since. There is no surviving television footage of the off-the-ball incident between Doug Rougvie and Johnstone which turned the game. Today in the plush, modern offices of STV in Glasgow there is only a small grey box containing a *Scotsport* storage tape with brief highlights of the match. Most of the footage was destroyed years ago, as was customary for many games from that era, before there was an appetite for re-watching classic matches. The surviving tape from 1979 offers no clues. One moment McCloy is shown kicking the ball from his hand and when the camera pans across to the middle of the pitch Johnstone is already lying face down on the ground with no-one near him. Referee Ian Foote had no doubt about what happened between the two big men. Rougvie had already been booked for a bad foul on winger Davie Cooper. The film shows Foote walking towards Rougvie and pointing to his own elbow before flashing the red card. Rougvie drops to his knees and puts his forehead on the turf, distraught.

Aberdeen were incandescent. Harper had been at the 1978 World Cup with Johnstone and the pair were friendly, but he can be seen rushing to the scene in obvious anger to try and haul Johnstone up off the ground. When Harper himself is yanked away by Sandy Jardine he turns to see Rougvie already trudging off. 'Derek will swear blind that I karate-chopped him,' said Rougvie, who has steadfastly maintained his innocence. 'But he backed into me and dived. He just wanted to change the game and he did. We knocked fuck out of each other on the park for a lot of games before and after that.'

Ferguson had anticipated Rougvie versus Johnstone being a big part of the match. McMaster recalled: 'Before the game Fergie says to Dougie, "Big man, see the first couple of times, whack big Johnstone, naebody's been sent off in the final."

So he whacks him and gets sent off! But he didn't even do anything wrong. Big Johnstone just went down.' Aberdeen battled desperately but could not hold on against a Rangers team sensing the kill. In the fourth minute of injury time Tommy McLean whipped over a corner and Colin Jackson soared to connect with a header which beat Clark again. Rangers had their winning goal.

Ferguson was seething. His first instinct was to direct his wrath at Rougvie but the uncomplicated big defender protested his innocence so vehemently, to the point he was reduced to tears, that it was clear he was genuine. As he prepared to face the media Ferguson turned to assistant Pat Stanton: 'Don't let Rougvie out of your sight because if he goes out there and sees Johnstone, God help him.' The *Evening Times* carried a picture of Ferguson glaring at Foote as Rougvie went up the tunnel. Its football reporter, Hugh Taylor, wrote: 'Was Rougvie unlucky? Did Derek Johnstone fall – or was he pushed? Arguments will go on. My own view was that it was too harsh a punishment.'

Aberdeen kept a lid on their opinions at the post-match press conference but soon their anger flared into public view. I WAS VICTIM OF A BLATANT CON TRICK screamed the headline in the *Evening Express* two days later. Rougvie was quoted at length: 'I'm absolutely disgusted with what happened at Hampden. Derek Johnstone backed into me and then dropped to the ground. I was left standing there looking astonished. I was being "conned" and there was nothing I could do about it. I can honestly say that I never touched Johnstone. I wouldn't feel so badly now if I had. But I'm absolutely disgusted that a fellow professional, a former player of the year, could behave like that. The injustice of it all has shattered me. I love football but it has suddenly gone sour for me.'

The nature of Aberdeen's relationship with the local media was such that both Ferguson and Clark wrote columns for the city's Saturday evening sports paper, the popular *Green Final*. Even after several days when their immediate bitterness might have faded, both men put their names to remarkably strong pieces. Clark's was headlined 'I'd rather be a loser than a cheat'. He wrote: 'Throughout the week, in calm, objective inquisitions, he [Rougvie] still pleaded complete innocence of violent conduct towards Derek Johnstone. The big 13-stone Rangers skipper, who remained motionless for about two minutes, made a remarkable recovery. Anyone who dropped as if pole-axed by a sledgehammer would not, I feel, be up and running about minutes later. If it was a case of acting it makes one wonder if winning at the price of cheating a fellow professional is worth it. I hope that Aberdeen never stoop to this sort of practice. But, having said that, we can't allow ourselves again to be naive enough to think that the world is full of honest people. After last Saturday I begin to wonder if there was any truth in the joke which says, "Football is a rat race, and it looks as if the rats are winning."' For his part, Johnstone has always maintained that he was an innocent victim and that the referee was right to protect him.

In his own article Ferguson chose his words carefully to ensure he would not be disciplined by the SFA. The manager's piece – headlined 'when you lose respect, you lose greatness' – lambasted Johnstone without referring to him by name. 'Every now and then a player emerges who looks set to become one of football's greats. We have a young man who has all the opportunities to make himself a football great. He is made captain of his side at a very young age. He is treated like a hero by the fans. Then suddenly something happens which knocks him off his pedestal. And we all realise that the player isn't really the man we thought he was. We see him as a child who has just had his rattle taken away and who cries until he gets it back and gets his own way. Well after last Saturday I have lost all the respect I had for one player whom I felt was really going somewhere. I needn't explain myself further.'

The letters page showed Aberdeen supporters had been whipped into an unprecedented level of anger by Foote and Johnstone. This would carry through games against Rangers for years to come. Each letter had its own little headline: 'Foote left without a leg to stand on'. 'Despicable act against a fellow pro'. 'Biggest farce of the season'. 'Action needed to stop faking'. 'Rangers should get Oscars'. 'System loaded in favour of Old Firm'. 'Bring in an English referee'. 'I saw it – nothing happened'. 'I nearly kicked in my radio'. Only one made a different point: 'Excuses – for the second year running'. But for once that was not the general view. Aberdeen were seen as victims, not losers. Ferguson was as satisfied as he could ever be in defeat and praised the team for competing hard even when the cause looked lost. 'The most important thing for us at the club to realise is that it's all over,' he said. 'There's nothing we can do about it now. We must rise above the disappointment and become greater. It is my ambition to build a side who can beat Rangers and Celtic consistently even when faced with adverse circumstances like last Saturday. We now know we can match Rangers. I am quite confident of beating them the next time we meet in a cup final.'

When Rougvie and Johnstone next faced each other at Pittodrie there was derision towards the Rangers man. A supporter stood in the Beach End with a home-made T-shirt declaring: 'Doug Rougvie Is Innocent'. Rougvie came on as a substitute and got two enormous cheers: one for scoring in a 3–1 win, the other for booting Johnstone into the air. The pair eventually made peace, the process helped by a brief period as team-mates at Chelsea. 'Derek is a nice bloke,' said Rougvie. 'I was fuming at the time, though. I still hear boys saying, "That fucking Johnstone . . ." but I say to them, "Ach, me and Derek get on different class, we're good mates."'

Ferguson's first season had amounted to an incredibly turbulent and uncomfortable trial: the 'willie-biters', the industrial tribunal, the upheaval of moving his family north, the death of his father and the stuttering form of his team. They knocked Celtic out of the Scottish Cup at Parkhead in March but finished eight points behind them in the Premier Division. Reaching the League Cup final was the modest highlight. Aberdeen lost to Hibs in the Scottish Cup semi-final and eventually finished fourth in the league, two places and thirteen points lower than they had been a year earlier under McNeill. 'My first season at Pittodrie was terrible for me, it couldn't end soon enough,' Ferguson admitted in a television documentary years later. 'But then I decided to stop worrying about my predecessors, their past records and all the rest of it, and be myself.'

In the summer of 1979 he allowed himself a proper holiday and plenty of thinking time. He now credits this as the turning point: 'What made Alex Ferguson and brought me success at Aberdeen was getting a summer break. Going away to rethink. Not once did I doubt my own ability.' He was also overcoming his initial doubts about his players. Clark, Kennedy, Miller, Strachan, Archibald, even Harper: they were strong. For all the friction with Harper, the striker still delivered thirty-three goals. Archibald weighed in with twenty and in the closing weeks of the season Ferguson added Mark McGhee from Newcastle United, his first signing for Aberdeen after ten months in the job. He had given debuts to an intense, focused young goalkeeper, Jim Leighton, and to the combative midfielder Neil Simpson. And he had turned the effervescent young central defender Alex McLeish into a regular.

One game stood out for Ferguson in the closing weeks of that season. When Aberdeen drew 1–1 with Celtic in the

Scottish Cup quarter-final at Pittodrie no one fancied their chances in the midweek replay. Parkhead was at its brooding, intimidating worst, with play interrupted in the second half as beer cans rained down from the home supporters on to the pitch. The game was an ugly battle. 'Some of the tackling by players of both sides had those of us in the press box ducking,' wrote Ian Paul in the *Glasgow Herald*. The report was headlined: IT'S MAYHEM AS CELTS GO OUT OF THE CUP. Aberdeen were 2–0 up in thirteen minutes and survived an onslaught which yielded only one second-half goal for Celtic. Ferguson saw it as the night his team proved their steel. 'For many of the players that certainly was the most important game of their lives because it proved they could beat the Old Firm and they could beat them in an atmosphere which was at the very least intimidating. It was the measure of them. It made them as men.'

The victory came two-and-a-half weeks before the ugly League Cup final. Those two games gave Ferguson what he wanted: belief in the players he had, and the realisation he could take them to another level. A Glasgow referee inexplicably showing a red card in the cup final? Glasgow fans throwing missiles at his players? Ferguson hoarded injustices as ammunition. 'It gave him something to work with,' said Miller. 'It helped him build up this "west coast bias, they're all against us" mentality. He had us believing that not only did you have to deal with the fans and the referees in Glasgow, but that everyone including the press was against us. He built that up and he gave us a helluva resolve. He knew exactly what he was doing.' Ferguson had another seven-and-a-half years at Aberdeen. Neither Rangers nor Celtic beat him again at Hampden.

SEVEN

1980: THE CHAMPIONS

Pittodrie has never been one of those grounds which thrums with noise and electricity. Aberdeen's old home can fall into lulls of funereal silence during games, partly because it is so exposed and open to the elements. With the North Sea only 300 yards away supporters are often too cold to sing. When bracing winds whip through even the seagulls overhead can make more noise than the chittering fans. Ferguson once observed that he could tell when Aberdeen fans were unhappy: 'You hear them rustle their sweetie papers.' He was joking but the natural reserve of the Pittodrie support niggled at him. The backing of a large, passionate, vociferous crowd was a constant accompaniment for Rangers and Celtic and Ferguson believed it lifted their players and gave the Old Firm a major advantage over his own team. At the start of the 1979–80 season he decided to do something about it. Again his platform was the club programme. Those fans who read his column at home games would soon feel they were being nagged into noisy obedience.

Whenever Rangers or Celtic came to town, he urged, the home supporters should compete for decibel levels just as the team had to do in battles on the pitch. When Rangers visited on 15 September 1979, he wrote: 'Get behind the team from the start and compete vocally with the Rangers support and we'll do our best.' When Celtic came a week later: 'Our support once again, as they did last Saturday, must drown out the Celtic support.' When Rangers returned in the League Cup: 'Our players will be going out there tonight to die for us so I hope you, the supporters, will remember that. Sometimes you get carried away and criticise one or two players when they are not doing too well but please try and get behind the whole team.' When Celtic returned: 'Tonight will also be a test for our support. Let's hear you!'

Ferguson was openly envious of Rangers and Celtic for the huge followings they enjoyed. He liked the warmth and decency of people in the north-east and the affection and pride they felt for their club. But he was a Glaswegian and when it came to football that meant unbridled fanaticism. He wanted volume and passion that could intimidate visiting teams. Only the dark, yawning Beach End, home to the more boisterous fans, delivered what he required. The rest of the home stands were often a source of frustration. He developed a tactic of being demanding with them before major games and praising them afterwards. 'I still feel that you are too quiet and don't get behind the side enough,' he said. 'People say that it is impossible to change the personality of the support but I certainly do not believe that. Our support always matches the Rangers and Celtic crowds when they are visiting so there is no reason why this cannot be the case every week.' Eventually he became blunter: 'Get rid of your inhibitions this afternoon and let yourselves go.' He had taken it upon himself to manage not only his players but the fans too.

In his first season Aberdeen had finished eight points behind the champions, McNeill's Celtic. But it was obvious that they were capable of more without the need for radical surgery. Only Dougie Bell, the 19-year-old midfielder he had known at St Mirren, was added to the squad. In the boardroom Dick Donald and Chris Anderson had been impressed by how Ferguson handled a traumatic first campaign. It was clear that the players were responding to him, but he wanted more. On the first day of pre-season training in 1979 he told them 'the honeymoon's over' and declared that things would now be done his way. There would be changes to the shape of the team including Gordon Strachan moving from central midfield to the right and Alex McLeish beefing up the midfield. Ferguson felt that one of the reasons the team had defended too deep in his first season was they did not have natural tacklers in central midfield. It had been too easy for opponents to get through to Miller and his back four. From now on they would be aggressive, far quicker to pressurise opponents on the ball, and afraid of nothing. There would be no playing for a draw; the intention was to go for a win in every game, including European ties and all trips to face the Old Firm in Glasgow. 'It definitely did the trick with the players,' he said later. 'I could see a whole change in attitude.'

Even so, Aberdeen's second European campaign under Ferguson ended in the first round when they went out of the Uefa Cup to Eintracht Frankfurt, who drew 1–1 at Pittodrie before a 1–0 win in Germany. There was no shame in being eliminated by Eintracht, who went on to win the tournament, but of greater concern was continued inconsistency in the Premier Division. By December they had beaten Rangers home and away but lost twice to Morton and won just seven of fifteen league games.

Aberdeen made it back to the League Cup final, which was brought forward to December. The feeling around Scottish football was that they had done the hard part simply by reaching Hampden. They had faced both Rangers and Celtic over two legs and won all four games with an aggregate score of 9–3. Indeed, the quarter-final against Celtic at Pittodrie saw a demonstration of virtuoso finishing by Archibald and evidence of how unpredictable and pragmatic Ferguson could be when wayward characters were useful to him. Archibald scored a hat-trick and defied Ferguson's instructions by taking the match ball home as a souvenir. He was a strong character and a law unto himself, but he rubbed along with Ferguson even though the potential for conflict was never far from the surface. When Ferguson found out about the missing ball he called Archibald into his office and ordered him to return it. The following day he was sitting in the coaches' room with Pat Stanton and Teddy Scott, drinking tea and chatting, when the door burst open. Archibald shouted: 'There's your fucking ball,' and booted it hard into the small room. The three of them ducked and spilled tea over the floor as it ricocheted around. Others would have been crucified but no action was taken against Archibald. 'That was Steve,' said Ferguson.

Intelligent, strong-willed, capricious and ambitious: the blond, tousle-haired Archibald shared many of the manager's own characteristics. He turned up to moan about one thing or another so often that Ferguson said there was 'an Archibald chair' in his office. 'Stevie liked to have his say and Fergie liked that about him,' said Stanton. 'He'd probably have done it himself when he was a player because he was volatile too. He recognised something of himself in Stevie. He didn't want his players to be wee choirboys. Even when he was angry with Stevie he appreciated where he was coming from. They had respect for each other.' Archibald also happened to be a dashing, reliable goalscorer with great instincts and reactions. He gave Aberdeen real menace.

The League Cup momentum continued with a semi-final win over Morton to book a place in the final against Dundee United. For the first time since 1962 neither Rangers nor Celtic had reached the final. No one realised it at the time but it marked the first chapter in a new story for Scottish football; the beginning of an eight-year period in which a new order, the 'New Firm', took hold. The phrase came into common usage in the Scottish newspapers' football pages as Aberdeen and United rose as twin challengers and developed an unusual rivalry.

United's manager was Jim McLean, a small, balding man whose public persona had two modes: miserable or furious. McLean was incredibly highly-strung and intense, a tracksuited martinet who commanded total authority over every aspect of Dundee United. His reputation for tactical and coaching brilliance was matched only by that for being uncompromisingly demanding. He was from Ashgill in South Lanarkshire, twenty miles from Ferguson's Govan, and had been a journeyman player before becoming a coach at Dundee. That was the older, more successful and better-supported club in the city but in 1971 he moved to the smaller Dundee United to become manager. McLean put an emphasis on finding and developing talented young players and then dominating and shaping their characters just as Ferguson did. United grew through the 1970s, reaching the 1974 Scottish Cup final and posting steadily improving results in the league. They had been third, behind Celtic and Rangers, in 1978-79.

Ferguson and McLean were great pals. They had roomed together on an SFA coaching course way back in 1966 and remained close. Both grew up in Rangers strongholds but they were now fanatically committed to overturning the Old Firm. They entered into what amounted to an informal alliance: if their clubs could take points off Celtic and Rangers, or knock them out of the cup competitions, those tournaments would be opened up for Aberdeen and United. As managers they publicly teased each other, each claiming to have the upper hand in an affectionate sparring that Ferguson never repeated with any other manager likely to challenge his team for honours. United defender Maurice Malpas eventually got to know them both: 'In some ways they were out of the same mould: had to win at all costs, crabbit shites, football daft. They spoke so often they knew what each other was doing. And they helped each other. They were desperate to skelp each other, but in terms of "them against us" with the Old Firm, the two of them were in cahoots.'

Regular five-a-side games were organised between the clubs' management teams. Ferguson and McLean recorded the scores and obsessed about winning the next one. Ferguson also liked McLean's assistant, Walter Smith, the man he had initially wanted to appoint as his own number two at Pittodrie. Aberdeen had a larger support and eclipsed United's achievements but Ferguson found McLean's teams the most frustrating and difficult to compete against. Over the years United inflicted some painful setbacks on the Dons. The 1979–80 League Cup final would be the first of them.

The lowest crowd recorded for the tournament's final, only 27,173, turned out on the vast Hampden slopes to see the first game, which Aberdeen controlled in a lively but goalless draw. 'We played United off the park at Hampden,' Ferguson said later. 'I knew then in my heart that we had thrown the cup away. But I had to hide my feelings. I had to try to motivate myself and my team, decide on tactics and team formation for the replay.' The second game was held at neutral Dens Park in Dundee – only a few hundred yards from United's own stadium – and was one of the bleakest experiences of Ferguson's Aberdeen career. His players never got to grips with the swirling wind, heavy rain and slippery pitch. The night got off to an appropriately embarrassing start when Miller inexplicably led his team into the wrong half of the pitch for the warm-up, provoking loud jeers from the United support. Things never improved.

Willie Pettigrew scored twice to give United a commanding 2–0 lead. The Aberdeen support was in a foul mood. Tayside Police had estimated that there would be 18,000 Aberdeen fans to United's 8,000, but Dens Park was so packed that the turnstiles were closed with 2,000 Aberdeen supporters locked out. In the second half hundreds spilled on to trackside because of crushing and fighting, and play was suspended for two minutes. Paul Sturrock, United's thin, quick, elusive striker, had been troubling the Aberdeen defence and no sooner had the game restarted than he embellished his performance with a goal. It was a 3–0 rout and the mood became uglier still. When the United players went on a post-match lap of honour with the club's first trophy they were forced to retreat to the centre circle after being pelted with cans. Bobby Clark criticised the louts in his *Green Final* column the following weekend: 'Surely Aberdeen with its clean reputation for beautiful parks, gardens, good schools, hospitals and other amenities wants to preserve its good name right down the line to its football team? Let's not be sheep and follow the example of the Old Firm.'

The root cause of the anger was not United. Aberdeen had now lost three cup finals in a row. When the team bus arrived back at Pittodrie, well after midnight, Ferguson and his players saw fresh graffiti scrawled across the metal grille on the stadium's front door: 'You've let us down again Dons'. Ferguson felt wretched. 'I remember coming back up the road from Dens Park that night and really feeling worse than I have felt in my life. I lay awake in bed all night expecting the phone to ring for some reason. In the morning I just felt like packing everything in because the season had promised so much and we had been beaten by United and lost our first chance of a trophy. I'm quite sure if I continue to manage for another twenty years I'll still wake up in the middle of the night and relive that awful experience.' Pat Stanton was taken aside for a quiet word by Dick Donald. 'He's really down,' said the chairman. 'You'll have to pick him up from this.'

'The "bridesmaid" tag is not good enough for the Pittodrie faithful,' said the *Evening Express* on 13 December, 1979. 'Aberdeen have blown hot and cold for most of the season.' It urged Ferguson to sign a new striker. The manager's next column for the paper was headlined: 'SHATTERED – BUT OUR DAY WILL COME.' He did not spare himself. Yes, he had picked the wrong team for the conditions. Yes, McLean had got the better of him. Yes, United played so poorly in the first game that it was obvious they would make changes for the replay. He acknowledged that including the replay his personal record in cup finals as player and manager now stood at five without a win. But he rallied. He turned up at Pittodrie early on the morning after the defeat and personally met every player and congratulated them on the excellent effort they had shown over the whole cup campaign. Supporters did not share his enthusiasm. In the next game only 5,000, the lowest home crowd of the season, bothered to show up against St Mirren. Ferguson gave 16-year-old John Hewitt his debut. Hewitt would eventually carve his name into Ferguson's career but for now the manager simply needed someone to lift spirits with the promise of something new.

Aberdeen were fourth in the table and six points behind leaders Celtic with a game in hand. They were not even halfway into the 36-game campaign. Celtic had already won at Pittodrie in September but the home-and-away League Cup wins proved there was nothing between the teams. 'He sat us down,' John McMaster recalled. 'He says, "I see winners in this room and I see losers." That was clever. Everyone's sitting there looking at themselves going, "Who're the winners and who're the losers?" He was more or less saying, "I'm getting rid of a few."'

Another defeat by Morton dropped them to sixth place in January, but then they began to gather points steadily. Rangers were beaten at Pittodrie before a 0–0 draw with Celtic left them ten points behind the leaders but with three games in hand. When Kilmarnock came and won in late February, Aberdeen's challenge seemed doomed. Ferguson looked at the balance of his team and knew it was close to being a really strong unit. The defence was solid, with Miller growing in stature all the time. Crucially Ferguson had solidified the centre of midfield by moving McLeish forward from defence. McMaster and Drew Jarvie were fine players but neither were natural tacklers. When McLeish was moved back to his preferred position in March, becoming Miller's regular defensive partner for the first time, young Andy Watson replaced him to maintain the steel in the middle of the park. The midfield provided an extra layer of protection for the back four and when they won possession they would funnel the ball to the team's creative men, little Strachan and bearded winger Ian Scanlon, or the forwards. Moving Strachan out of the engine room to a wider position allowed him to blossom. He had great technique, could dribble, and was a finisher. His size and red hair made him a focal point in the team. Fans began urging the side to 'get it to wee Gordon'. It was a side with a good, natural shape, with energy, pace and strength.

Up front, Mark McGhee had become the preferred partner for Archibald. Harper had suffered a serious knee injury and been out since November, effectively ending his Aberdeen career. The changes galvanised the team and four wins and two draws hauled them up to second. Celtic still looked in control and spent a Scottish transfer record of £250,000 to add striker Frank McGarvey from Liverpool. The signing was a blow to Ferguson because he had been trying to bring the player to Aberdeen. Celtic had already taken three points out of four at Pittodrie and Aberdeen still had to meet them twice in Glasgow. Surprisingly the defending champions then began to wobble without being under any initial pressure. They struggled to score goals and won only once in seven league games between January and March, drawing the other six. 'They're getting worried,' Ferguson told Miller privately.

Celtic steadied themselves with important wins against Hibs and Rangers and still had a seven-point lead on 5 April 1980 when Aberdeen went to Parkhead. Ferguson interpreted the situation in a way no previous Aberdeen manager would have: his team had a game in hand, which could cut the lead to five (it was two points for a win then), and if they won their two remaining clashes with Celtic the gap would be down to just one. 'A few weeks ago Celtic seemed to have it cut and dried,' he said. 'Everything now is in a different perspective.' Ferguson's chutzpah was compelling. He was talking about winning twice in a month at Parkhead when only one team had won there in any competition since the start of the season. Even Real Madrid had lost 2–0. But the one team which had gone there and won? His Aberdeen, in a League Cup tie in November. That was the spring of Ferguson's optimism.

More than 40,000 filled the enormous Parkhead terraces, the vast majority of them Celtic supporters coming to see Aberdeen's challenge killed off. The sun was beating down, fans were in short sleeves, and Ferguson was buoyant. Four days earlier a 4–0 win at Kilmarnock had left him purring. 'You could have set it to music,' he said. At Parkhead they were confident and assured, playing forcefully from the start. Jarvie gave them an early lead, Johnny Doyle soon equalised, but McGhee put Aberdeen 2–1 up in the second half. Bobby Lennox had a penalty to equalise but Clark saved well and Aberdeen held on. 'We had a great record at Parkhead,' said Ferguson. 'I simply knew we were going to win.' They were now five points behind with a game in hand.

Suddenly the newspapers realised they had a title race to cover. They printed lists of Celtic's seven remaining games and Aberdeen's eight. One fixture stood out. 'For those who like their football tough and raw, pencil in the date of Wednesday, 23 April,' wrote the *Glasgow Herald*. 'That is when these two giants are scheduled to meet at Parkhead again. That could really be the decider.' The veteran *Sunday Mail* journalist Allan Herron wrote: 'Aberdeen have the players, the skill and the driving ambition to win the league championship for the second time in their 77-year history. But do they have the nerve?' Trained fatalists, the club's supporters suspected they would mess things up eventually, but they were drawn by the improving results. Home crowds rose from 7,000 to 19,000 in the space of five games. A home draw with Hibs on 16 April prompted an angry Ferguson to tell reporters his team had thrown away the title. But three days later Strachan, McGhee and Archibald delivered a 3–1 win at Kilmarnock and then heard the staggering news that Celtic had crashed 5–1 to a Dundee team who would be relegated within weeks. UNBELIEVABLE, AND I'M NOT CONVINCED IT REALLY HAPPENED said the headline on Ian Paul's match report in the *Glasgow Herald*.

Aberdeen returned to Parkhead for the third time in nineteen days (between league games they had lost 1–0 there to Rangers in the Scottish Cup semi-final). This time they had to win. 'It couldn't be done, that was the media's outlook on it,' said Miller. 'I remember reading the papers. We might be able to get one victory there but we certainly weren't going to get two. I remember Mark McGhee's performances, his strength of physique and character, were so important for us. At the time it was unthinkable but we had a belief we could do it.' Ferguson said: 'This is it, the league decider. If we lose, it's Celtic's title.' It was a hot, sweaty spring night in Glasgow's east end.

The Celtic support turned out in force again. The crowd was the biggest Aberdeen played in front of all season, officially recorded as 48,000, although some thought the true figure might be closer to 60,000. The vast terraces held a swaying, baying, noisy army in green-and-white, preparing to crank up the volume and test the nerve of the pretenders in red. Archibald scored early but Celtic equalised from the penalty spot within two minutes. Aberdeen came again: Strachan had a penalty saved before McGhee nodded them back into the lead just before half-time. It was a rousing match. When McMaster and Scanlon opened Celtic up again in the second half Strachan made it 3–1 and the battle was won. He clenched his fist at the hard-core Celtic support in the intimidating covered enclosure known as 'The Jungle', just as Archibald had after his opening goal. Ferguson approved: 'It was letting Celtic know that we were there to win. We wanted to beat Celtic on their own ground, in front of their own people. We proved we were there not just to make up the numbers but to win the league.' Aberdeen were now top of the table on goal difference with four games left.

'I think we knew then that it was really in our hands,' said Clark. 'That was the first time I felt that the Aberdeen fans got behind us and realised that something special was about to happen.' It had become an Aberdeen-Celtic staring contest – and Celtic had blinked first. They had been eleven points ahead in the first week of January but Aberdeen relentlessly clawed back the difference. When Celtic folded in April, losing four times, they allowed Ferguson's men to pull level and then move clear. No club had broken both halves of the Old Firm since

Kilmarnock won the league in 1965. Otherwise Scotland's list of title winners read like a relentless tennis rally: Rangers-Celtic-Rangers-Celtic-Rangers-Celtic, ad nauseam. But on the morning of 3 May 1980, Aberdeen knew their vastly superior goal difference meant they would effectively end that sequence if they won at Hibs and Celtic dropped a point at St Mirren.

The main route to Hibs' Easter Road ground in Edinburgh is via the city's London Road with its bank of trees along Royal Terrace Gardens. The Aberdeen squad were startled by what they saw as the bus wound its way towards the stadium: thousands of their supporters. 'The amount of red shirts,' said Stanton. 'It was like an army was camped in the trees! Fergie said to the players, "Look! Look! You can't disappoint these people."' They didn't. Poor Hibs were already relegated and now became the hosts of someone else's party. It was a stroll in the Edinburgh sunshine. Archibald scored his twenty-second goal of the season and Watson added another before half-time. Scanlon, McGhee and Scanlon again turned it into a 5–0 rout. Now they simply needed to hear the Celtic result. During the second half Clark kept turning to the dugout, or to fans, desperate to know the score. At full time Ferguson and his players waited on the pitch for around a minute as play continued in Paisley. It had been goalless there all day, despite the brief scare of Celtic being awarded a penalty before a linesman changed the referee's mind. Ferguson was on the point of detonation. Then came the moment of confirmation. He watched the press box and one of the Aberdeen *Evening Express* reporters gestured to him, circling his hands into two zeroes: Celtic had drawn 0–0.

Ferguson erupted, jumping this way and that, not knowing who to go to first. 'I sprinted on that park hugging everybody who got in my road.' He spotted Clark and ran across the Easter Road pitch with his arms outstretched and his suit flapping and threw himself on to his goalkeeper.

'Can you blame the man for going out of his mind?' cheered commentator Archie Macpherson in a memorable commentary for the BBC. 'I remember him galloping down the pitch,' Macpherson recalled. 'There are great images in Scottish football that you retain and that was one of them: that Forrest Gump run by Fergie towards his own support. That's burned on the retina like some of the great goals or Billy McNeill lifting the European Cup. After the game he was incoherent. The league was what he wanted.'

Of the players, Clark was visibly the most emotional, holding his head in his hands and unable to stem the tears. His team-mates and the supporters assumed he had been overwhelmed by the moment after so many years of expectation and failure. But that was only part of it. He had also struggled through personal tragedy. In March, in the space of a fortnight, his father-in-law and then his father had died suddenly.

Hibs invited Ferguson to make use of the stadium's public address system and he took a microphone and offered his thanks to the Aberdeen support. 'If any of you want a drink later, come round to my house,' he joked. At 3am two fans rang his doorbell. Laughing, he took them in, poured a couple of glasses and showed them a video of the game.

Even on the day of his greatest managerial feat so far Ferguson showed his uncompromising streak. When Aberdeen were 2–0 up and coasting at half-time he let rip at referee Brian McGinlay in front of a scrum of onlookers in the tunnel. McGinlay's crime? Giving a throw-in to Hibs which Ferguson saw as Aberdeen's. While the celebrations continued on the pitch and in the stands Dick Donald broke away to visit the referee's room and quietly apologise to McGinlay. No sooner had he left than Ferguson himself entered with a bottle of champagne under each arm, placing them on a table. He was all smiles, and then came to the point: 'So, can half-time be forgotten about?' McGinlay can still remember his response: 'I said, "No, Alex, it can't. I've already spoken to your chairman and it will have to be reported to the SFA because you did it in front of too many people, too many saw it." So off he went, mutter, mutter under his breath. He got to the door and paused. Then he turned around, came back, grabbed the two bottles of champagne and disappeared with one under each arm. The two linesmen were ready to give me a doing, they were gasping for a drink! If I'd told him he wasn't being reported the whole crate of champagne would have come in . . .' The SFA later handed Ferguson a £250 fine and a year-long touchline ban.

The Aberdeen players were blissfully unaware of this comical little episode. Outside their celebrations continued. For the older heads like Clark, Miller, Rougvie and Kennedy the significance of what they had done was immediate. 'Winning the title was the big breakthrough for us,' said Kennedy. 'I felt I had arrived.' At just twenty-one, Alex McLeish was one of the calmest amid the euphoria. 'I didn't see winning the league the way the older boys did, the tears and all that,' he said. 'I'm thinking, "What are they crying about, this is natural evolution." I'd been used to winning at boys' club level. Since I'd come to Aberdeen they'd won a League Cup and reached cup finals.' When the Aberdeen party eventually left the ground for a joyous bus journey home, Strachan, born and raised in Edinburgh, stayed in the capital with his wife and young son. 'There were lots of Hibs fans there,' he said. 'People came crowding around to congratulate me and to say how glad they were that a club like Aberdeen had at long last cut in on the Rangers-Celtic monopoly. They were sick of it.'

The season was not quite over – they had one final match to play, at Partick Thistle four days later – but the title race certainly was. Aberdeen's superior goal difference meant Celtic could snatch the league from them only if Ferguson's men lost to Partick by ten clear goals. It finished a low-key 1–1 draw. Aberdeen formally entered the record books as champions by one point. Ferguson had delivered something incredible after just two seasons. 'Winning the league gave us total confirmation that what he was doing was right,' said Miller. 'Whatever it is that changes you from being a loser in cup finals to being a winner, being league champions gave us that.'

The celebrations lasted for days. One night Ferguson was asleep in bed when his telephone rang at 2am. He answered to hear a chorus of singing and good-natured abuse. The players were having a party at Miller's house. Ferguson joked that they were all fined and suspended for irresponsible behaviour, which only provoked further derision. He hung up and put his head back on the pillow. 'I lay back and reflected how satisfied I was that my relationship with the players was close enough for them to have reacted like that.' The players feared Ferguson but generally they liked him, working within his boundaries and often enjoying the theatre of how unpredictable and volcanic he could be. It was never, ever boring. Behind his back they came up with nicknames. Sometimes he was 'The Dark Lord' but more often it was a shortening of his frequent description as 'Furious Fergie' at the start of newspaper reports. To them, he was usually just 'Furious'.

He struck a masterful balance between ruling with a fist of iron while also appearing generally fair, interested and often good-humoured. After the Westhill willie-biters had been weeded out there was no real dressing-room dissent at Aberdeen, certainly nothing so premeditated. There was plenty of laughter around Pittodrie. Players would gossip about Ferguson when he was not there, like pupils discussing a stern headmaster. They talked about the little nervous cough he would develop as matches drew nearer, which often acted as an early warning that he was about to enter a room. 'You could laugh with Fergie,' Strachan recalled. 'He'd get on the team bus and have fun with you, or he'd have a quiz, or he'd play his shitey music. Somebody chucked his tape out of the window one day. To this day he thinks it was me, but it wasnae me. I would have wanted to but I wasn't brave enough.' In one match programme there was a news snippet about the groundsman's dog chasing Ferguson and club secretary Taggart until they escaped by jumping over the perimeter wall into the Beach End. It could only have been printed with the manager's approval.

The full extent of Ferguson's red revolution was yet to be seen, but Aberdeen's championship victory represented a major unsettling of the established order. And it seemed to mirror deeper shifts in Scottish life, with the newly affluent north-east providing a stark contrast with Glasgow's industrial decline. That once-proud city was struggling and with hardship came division. At the end of the 1980 Celtic-Rangers Scottish Cup final the two sets of supporters leapt the Hampden fences and hundreds went at each other like savages. Live television coverage showed the fans charging each other, running battles on the pitch, punches, kicks, bottles and cans being thrown and frightened children cowering from the trouble. It was all played out to a soundtrack of sectarian chanting. Condemnation poured down on the two clubs from all over Britain. 'The Old Firm's meetings next season will begin as they ended on Saturday, with violence and shame,' said the *Glasgow Herald*.

The following day, when Aberdeen were presented with the Premier League trophy, the riot was a major talking point. Supporters revelled in the Old Firm's disgrace and how ugly and backward all of that seemed compared to the Dons' joyous ascent. Aberdeen had played Rangers and Celtic thirteen times over the season, winning nine and losing only twice. Now their supporters' newfound sense of authority was enhanced by the images of rioting Glaswegians. The sun shone and 24,000 packed into Pittodrie in noisy appreciation, a jubilant cauldron of red-and-white shirts, scarves, banners and flags. The Old Firm felt like Scottish football's dark past, Aberdeen its progressive future. Ferguson stood in the centre circle and soaked it all in. This was the Pittodrie he had wanted all along.

EIGHT

LIVERPOOL

A mob of angry Aberdeen supporters awaited Alex Ferguson when he arrived for work at Pittodrie on Saturday, 11 October, 1980. It was shortly after 10am and about thirty of them were crowding around the players' entrance. 'Disgruntled fans hurled abuse at the Dons boss, who had to force his way into the stadium,' reported the *Press & Journal.* The mob's problem was not Ferguson, it was Liverpool.

Aberdeen's reward for winning the league was entry to the European Cup for the first time in the club's history. After a narrow win over Austria Vienna they were handed the most ominous draw of all. Aberdeen versus Liverpool instantly captured the imagination on both sides of the border. 'This is what the public want,' said the Liverpool full-back Phil Neal. In Scotland the hysteria was feverish. It was the biggest clash between the best teams in Scotland and England since Celtic versus Leeds in 1970. The novelty of someone other than Rangers or Celtic winning the league had made the rest of Britain sit up and take notice of this new, vibrant Aberdeen team and its brash young manager. Liverpool were European aristocracy, English champions in four of the previous five seasons and European Cup winners in 1977 and 1978. To drizzle further spice over the tie the Liverpool machine was propelled by Scotsmen: Kenny Dalglish, Graeme Souness and Alan Hansen. The demand for tickets for the first leg at Pittodrie was phenomenal. The ground's record attendance had been set at 45,061 in 1954 but the capacity was now just 24,000. The club calculated that around 60,000 wanted to see Liverpool. Within minutes of the draw being made the Pittodrie phone lines were jammed. Both of them.

When tickets were put on sale the first supporter began queuing at 3.15pm the previous day. Fans brought sleeping bags, deck chairs, radios and heaters to see them through the night. The numbers grew until at one point the queue snaked more than a mile away from the stadium. Police estimated that at least 15,000 were in the line. When faced by a level of demand they had never encountered before the club's management made the mistake of allowing supporters to buy up to four tickets each on the basis of first come, first served. The entire allocation was wiped out in forty-five minutes and those more than a few hundred yards away when the gates opened – regardless of whether they went to every home game or not – got nothing. Some milled around to protest, angrily voicing their frustration at Ferguson when he arrived. The ticket distribution had nothing to do with him, he just happened to be in the wrong place at the wrong time. He could do nothing but sympathise.

A bigger headache was how his team were going to cope with a unit as strong as Liverpool as he sought to introduce Aberdeen to football fans south of the border. He knew the English inclination to disparage Scottish football and he would be damned if they saw anything to snigger about when they watched Aberdeen. Miller spoke for the players. 'We all get reports up here of how the English players rate our football,' he said. 'They call it the "funny half-hour" when snippets of our games are shown on television. That gets under my skin. The crazy moments in our games always seem to be shown on the box. But everybody here knows the standard of our game is rising.'

Neither club was happy about being drawn against strong opposition so early in the tournament. 'Thanks very much, Uefa,' said Dalglish. Bob Paisley's powerful team was packed with seasoned England internationals – Neal, Ray Clemence, Phil Thompson, Terry McDermott, Ray Kennedy and David Johnson – but they were wary of their opponents. Paisley had the Dons watched in all four games between the draw and the first leg. 'The moment we knew it was Aberdeen the mood around the dressing room changed,' said Dalglish. 'Scarcely had the draw been made than all sorts of noises flooded out of Scotland about what Aberdeen would do to Liverpool and about us Anglos being sent homeward to think again. We had to win. Graeme, Al and I kept telling each other that if we didn't get a result we were going to be crucified, completely slaughtered, every time we went back to Scotland. They would rub it in forever.'

Ferguson wanted to improve Aberdeen's European record, which he had described as 'abysmal'. They had first competed in the European Cup Winners' Cup in 1967 and in nine previous campaigns on the continent had been scuttled out at the first or second hurdle. The bookmakers did not expect that to change: Liverpool were 1–4 to go through and Aberdeen 7–2. The tie represented the biggest examination of Ferguson's managerial career so far. What he said about the games publicly contrasted sharply with the reality. 'Liverpool will present perhaps the most formidable task Aberdeen will undertake for many years,' he said. 'Yet in no way are we worried about the game.' Years later he candidly told an entirely different story: 'The fixture dominated and interrupted everything. It was nothing less than a nightmare. It got to us, it got to everyone.'

Pat Stanton had stepped down as Ferguson's assistant in May. He wanted to go back to live in Edinburgh and the pair parted as firm friends. His replacement was Archie Knox, an uncompromising disciplinarian in the manager's own image. Knox had been a midfield journeyman with Forfar, St Mirren and Dundee United before becoming player-manager at Forfar, just fifty miles south of Aberdeen. He was only thirty-three when he arrived at Pittodrie as a formidable, barking assistant manager. Ferguson liked his style and also admired the quality and variety of his training drills. The pair travelled to watch Liverpool beat Middlesbrough on 7 October and met Bill Shankly in the Anfield directors' box. Shankly had already been quoted in the newspapers describing Aberdeen as a credit to the Scottish game. He said their performances in the previous round had reminded him of Inter Milan in the 1960s and the current European Cup holders, Nottingham Forest. When he bumped into Ferguson and Knox he gave them a genuine, warm welcome and then smiled. 'So you're down to have a look at our great team? Aye, they all try that.' Ferguson recalled 'stuttering my thanks' and that he and Knox had 'behaved like groupies' in the presence of managerial royalty.

Bob Paisley's own intelligence-gathering on Aberdeen had him questioning 'whether they have enough up front' without Archibald, who had departed for Tottenham Hotspur in the summer. The Liverpool manager went out of his way to praise Strachan, identifying him as a major talent and a threat to his team. The phrase Liverpool had for this was giving 'a little bit of toffee', in other words lavishing public praise on an opponent with the intention of placing the spotlight on him and affecting his game. Strachan was quiet over both legs.

Liverpool intended to fly home straight after the first leg but encountered trouble. The local council's refusal to allow an extension to Aberdeen airport's opening hours prompted Liverpool's general secretary, Peter Robinson, to remark: 'We have had more difficulty on this than we have when going behind the Iron Curtain.' On the night, there would be no mistaking Pittodrie for some Soviet outpost. With the floodlights on and the stands packed to capacity – including the away allocation of just 500 from Liverpool – the scene was set for a quintessential Battle of Britain. Outside, touts sold tickets for ten times the face value. Inside, the atmosphere was hostile. 'The Beach End ferociously booed everything that Liverpool did,' reported the *Press & Journal*. 'Horrendous, real vitriol spitting from the terraces,' Dalglish recalled later. Liverpool's three Scots attracted the worst of it, but to no apparent ill effect. In fact, they opened up Aberdeen after only five minutes. Dalglish played a ball square to Johnson and he played an instant through ball for McDermott to float a sumptuous chip over Jim Leighton. It was the only goal of the night. Liverpool had done a job on Ferguson's team and everyone knew it.

McMaster remembered: 'The Liverpool boys came up the tunnel at half-time, cocky. Dalglish, Souness, all of them. They're going, "Game done." "Half-time in the first leg!" "Game done." "What a result." "That's it finished." They're clicking their fingers in the air. They were doing it for show. We were raging but they hammered us 1–0.' McMaster himself barely got his shorts dirty: he suffered serious knee ligament damage in a tackle by Ray Kennedy at the very start of the game that put him out for the rest of the season. Despite the beating Aberdeen had taken, Ferguson's admiration for Paisley's team remained undimmed. 'The Liverpool players had a bit of grit and nastiness about them

– good qualities when you need them – and they were well armed in the psychological war department.' He spoke like a young manager who had taken copious mental notes.

Two days before the second leg Peter Robinson was back in the newspapers complaining again, this time that Uefa had still not revealed where that season's final would be held. This was no attempt to play mind games with Aberdeen – there was no longer any need for that – but an indication of Liverpool's certainty. The second leg at Anfield was about damage limitation for the visitors. Liverpool had not lost in their last seventy-five home games, a record that stretched back thirty-three months. 'These players have the opportunity to become immortal in Scottish football,' said Ferguson as he put a brave face on their task. 'What greater incentive could they have than that?' Neither Kennedy nor McMaster was available. Andy Dornan, a 19-year-old full-back, made only his second competitive appearance while Neale Cooper and John Hewitt, sixteen and seventeen respectively, went on as a substitutes. 'I remember warming up,' said Cooper. 'The Scousers were shouting at me, "Make the most of this, son, this is the closest you'll get to big-time football."'

The Dons had one chance to level. McGhee dispossessed Thompson and rode two challenges before facing the Liverpool and England goalkeeper, Clemence. He shot straight at him. 'I always think I should have done better,' said McGhee. 'I shot too early. I shit myself a bit.' Then the roof caved in. Miller saw a ball fly off his head past Leighton for an own goal after thirty-seven minutes, then a Dalglish back-heel put Phil Neal through and he curled the ball inside the far post to make it 3–0 on aggregate before half-time. As Aberdeen prepared to go back out after the interval one shout stood out among all the noisy encouragements. 'C'mon lads, three quick goals and we're right back in it,' said Drew Jarvie. He had opened his mouth without thinking. Several players froze and turned to him. Three goals in forty-five minutes? Liverpool had conceded eight at Anfield in the whole of the previous league season.

The second half was a bombardment. Johnson had a goal ruled offside. Leighton saved from Ray Kennedy, then from McDermott. When Avi Cohen hit the crossbar Sammy Lee retrieved the ball for Dalglish to bury a header. A five-man move put Hansen through to make it 4–0 on the night and 5–0 over the two legs. Ferguson watched the devastation from the stand with Knox in the dugout. 'I was acting as his runner that night,' said Willie Garner, who had lost his place at centre-half to Alex McLeish. 'Midway through the second half he says to me, "Go down and tell Archie to take Rougvie off." I says, "Who's going on for him?" He says, "Anybody . . . fucking anybody."' It was the heaviest defeat Ferguson ever suffered with Aberdeen.

Souness was the Liverpool captain, a majestic combination of midfield steel and silk who had been playing for Scotland since 1974. Nobody messed with Souness. In an Anfield dressing room full of hard cases he was the driving force and undisputed leader. He had been determined to assert Liverpool's authority over the upstarts from Scotland. McGhee said: 'Souness wanted to put us right in our place and to be fair he did. I don't remember any two other games where I felt as much a spectator. There was a strength and confidence about Liverpool that was different from anything we'd faced before. Remember on *Spitting Image* they used to make some characters small, like David Steel? I always felt it was like we were really small at Anfield and Souness was huge. He was swatting people away. I remember him hitting a diagonal from one touchline to the other. I'd never seen a ball hit like it. Magnificent to watch.'

Ferguson had received his hardest lesson since coming into management six years earlier. Liverpool's combination of ability, character and aggression, the noise generated by their passionate support, the psychology of their players as they hammered home Aberdeen's inferiority, all of it registered with him. He envied it. The Anfield night had been a painful exposure to proven masters. 'Football is a learning process. Above all, our players had to appreciate that there is no forgiveness in such games for teams who surrender possession cheaply. Those kind of memories burn deeply and they hurt. It's the kind of night you don't wish to suffer again. To avoid it there is only one answer: be prepared to battle with all the traditional passion and aggression for which Aberdeen and Scottish football are renowned.'

The second leg had been sponsored by the snack manufacturers KP. At full time the Aberdeen players returned to the dressing room and found a bag of crisps and nuts hanging on each peg. McGhee remembered: 'We come off the bus at our Liverpool hotel with our faces tripping us, our ridiculous Aberdeen tracksuits and our KP nuts. And then in walks Souness. Over his shoulder he's got the raincoat with the fur collar. I think he was with his missus and her sister. They were in for a meal with his pals.' Souness was not there to gloat – the hotel was a regular haunt – but his arrival did little to lift Ferguson's mood. He had a face like thunder. The players were told they would get something to eat and then they were going straight to their beds: 'If I catch anybody laughing you'll get fined a week's wages.' McGhee can still recall the scene: 'In the background was Souness's mob popping champagne corks. We can hear the laughter. Fergie's swivelling round every few seconds, trying to catch us out. We're trying not to laugh.' Dougie Bell said: 'I made faces at [striker] Stevie Cowan and he started laughing. Fergie caught him. "Do you think it's fucking funny, son?" He never played again for months!' Cowan added: 'As we were leaving he said, "Cowan, I'll see you in the morning." In the morning he didn't say anything . . . but for three months he never even looked my way. Nothing. And when I got back in favour, all of a sudden it was, "Cup tie! You're back in! You're the man!" And it came from nowhere.'

Aberdeen flew home the following morning. Ferguson was not finished with them yet. Rougvie recalled: 'He's going, "You're a bloody disgrace, every cunt in Scotland is laughing at you." He had us running laps of the pitch on the Thursday afternoon. All because we've lost 4–0 at Anfield! We're thinking, "He's a fucking maniac, he's aff his heid!"'

Two days later Aberdeen went to Parkhead and beat Celtic.

Ferguson soon showed that one of his managerial strengths was an ability to absorb even the most harrowing setback, learn from it and rebuild. Anfield became Aberdeen's ground zero in European competition. He felt the team's inexperience had been obvious and players had taken the wrong options in possession. When to pass and when to run with the ball? His own managerial record in Europe extended to ten games – only three of them wins – but the Liverpool tie had shown that the levels of concentration, technique and decision-making were far higher than Aberdeen were used to in Scotland. He noted how often a game against foreign opposition might seem to be going to plan and then in a matter of minutes 'the roof falls in'.

Miller admitted: 'Liverpool was too early for us. We didn't feel we were going to get hammered the way we did at Anfield. It showed that we had done okay in Scotland but there was a gap to be bridged if we were going to compete in Europe.' Liverpool came to be seen as a great lesson for Aberdeen; a clear punctuation mark in their European record, after which the improvement was startling. Though he spoke about inexperience and players making wrong decisions, what had really troubled

Ferguson was their attitude going into both legs. McGhee said: 'He recognised that we were all in awe of Liverpool. We never thought we could beat them. We didn't consider ourselves in the same league and so we had no chance before the games even started. He hated the idea of feeling inferior. He sensed that was a huge failing. He was very, very angry about it.' It was like an aftershock of 1978 and the lack of belief Ferguson had seen initially in his players when they faced the Old Firm. Those days were long gone domestically but Liverpool proved that Aberdeen still had much to learn in Europe.

There would be no opportunity for another crack at the English champions, or anyone else for that matter, in the following season's European Cup. Aberdeen's defence of the Scottish title crumbled through inconsistency. They were unbeaten in the league until December, compiling a 30-game run without loss that included the end of the previous campaign. They even finished with more points and a better goal difference than they had as champions. But stomach problems finished Strachan's season in December and with Aberdeen winning only seven out of eighteen games in the second half of the season Celtic cantered to the league title by seven points. The League Cup campaign featured the curiosity of a Belgian goalkeeper, Marc De Clerck, scoring on his Aberdeen debut in a rout of Berwick Rangers. But, distracted by their impending visit to Anfield, Aberdeen were knocked out by lower league Dundee. Then, Morton's maverick Andy Ritchie scored a stunning goal to bundle them out of the Scottish Cup.

The element of surprise they had enjoyed in the previous season had gone. Teams now raised their game against Aberdeen and every fixture was vigorously competitive. 'Since becoming champions we have found that we are the side everyone is gunning for,' said Stuart Kennedy. 'They pull out that little bit extra against us. We don't mind.' But it made the team vulnerable to dropping points, a problem compounded by a lack of goals. Celtic scored twenty-three more than Aberdeen in league games alone. When Archibald left for Tottenham soon after the title was won it was the first departure of a player Ferguson would have wanted to keep, and the lack of an adequate replacement showed. McGhee was powerful and a growing influence who scored seventeen goals but the only other player to reach double figures was Walker McCall, a squad player who Ferguson had brought back for his second spell at the club. Harper returned only on the final day of the season after a knee injury that had kept him out for eighteen months.

Ferguson felt his team lacked 'personality' players. 'It was brought home to me again when Joe Harper made his comeback in the reserves and nearly 3,000 fans turned up to see the game. He is a character who adds that special something to an afternoon in the same way that Bobby Clark, John McMaster and Gordon Strachan can.' The words were generous but Harper had no future. At thirty-three, that game would be his last. The manager wanted to bring more invention, unpredictability and, above all, goals to his team. If there was any doubt about the board's readiness to match his ambition, a declaration of intent from Chris Anderson dispelled it. 'I want Aberdeen to be the best team in Scotland and able to compete on level terms with the best in Europe,' said the vice-chairman. 'We must consolidate and win the title not just again, but again and again and again.'

NINE

CRIME AND PUNISHMENT UNDER THE BEACH END

At the time of his retirement in 2013 the public perception of Sir Alex Ferguson was of a managerial grandee, a greying and bespectacled figure who was still at the coalface in his seventies. That was not the Ferguson Aberdeen knew. He was only thirty-six when he arrived and just thirty-eight when he won the league and took on Liverpool. A young, physical, robust, athletic man, Ferguson went on runs, joined in during training sessions and threw himself into five-a-sides. Nothing worked up a sweat more than the gladiatorial battle of 'tips'.

The Pittodrie gym was a cramped, windowless box under the Beach End with a solid pillar in the middle and six painted goals around the four walls. The dust and gloom ensured that it would not have passed modern health and safety inspections. Players would come out of it coughing. Tips was a crazily fast and intense game of first-touch attacking and defending, which could start at 20-a-side before being whittled down as players lost a 'life' by conceding a goal. Eventually it got down to one-v-one, though sometimes it started as a personal duel between two in the first place.

Ferguson played tips against Archie Knox every Friday afternoon. The youth players would line the walls to watch, sometimes voluntarily, sometimes conscripted. The shrewder ones knew how to make a quiet exit if it looked like Ferguson was going to lose. 'As soon as you saw Alex getting beat you'd get out because he'd be looking for bodies,' said Tommy McIntyre, who was a 17-year-old witness to the combat. Most unfortunate of all was the poor soul who was chosen to act as referee. Ferguson or Knox would challenge every decision. One day McIntyre was told he was in charge. 'Fergie and Archie were knocking lumps out of each other; the sweat was lashing off them. So the final goal wins and I had to make a decision. The pressure! Fergie was looking into my eyes saying, "Well, what *are* you gonna do?", and Archie was looking at me saying, "Yeah, what are you gonna do?" So I goes, "I have to say it was a goal for you, Archie . . ."' That was probably McIntyre's biggest mistake, as he quickly recognised. 'Fergie storms out. He shouts, "Right, get your boots, you're outside." He took me to the track around the pitch and he ran me and ran me and ran me. Round and round the pitch. He walked away and said, "Just keep running." So I kept running and running and running. It seemed like forever. Eventually I stopped and asked someone, "Is the manager around?", and he said, "Oh, he's away home, he's away a while ago."'

Other young 'refs' would be accused of being corrupt and ordered to wash the manager's car. Ferguson and Knox were so competitive the scores of these weekly tips games were carried in Aberdeen's match programme. Tips bred an atmosphere of brutal rivalry which sometimes bubbled over from fun to brief animosity between players. 'It could be ten people trying to kill each other,' said Stevie Cowan. 'One time me and Simmy [Neil Simpson] fell out and were rolling around. I went home but Fergie sent for me, told me I had to come back to Pittodrie.

I was expecting an absolute mauling from him. He said, "You need to rein in your aggression . . ."'

When Ferguson took on anyone in the Pittodrie snooker room the game would end only when he was winning. If he lost the first frame he would demand it be the best of three. The floor was tiled and the wooden cues had no rubber plug at the end. When his opponent was about to take a shot Ferguson would loudly bang his cue on the ground, hoping to put him off. 'I can't be 100 per cent certain,' said Pat Stanton, 'but I reckon when the other player was putting his score up on the board Alex would move the white. Especially if he'd had enough of the guy.' Ferguson and Knox would borrow trainer Teddy Scott's tartan bunnet and compete at throwing it on to a peg on the dressing-room wall.

Everyone on the staff took an interest in whether the manager or the assistant had won the weekly tips. From the administration workers, ground staff and management to the coaches and players, the club employed about fifty people. It felt like a family operation. A few pensioners came in for daily voluntary work, proudly keeping Pittodrie spick and span. Ferguson made it his business to be familiar with everyone. He knew names, wives' and husbands' names, children's names, where people had been on holiday, whether someone's relative was ill. Hand-written cards from Ferguson turned up on their birthdays and at Christmas. Everyone was made to feel important. Ferguson believed that if everyone felt involved and appreciated they would give that little bit more. He would tease and torment them: 'These boots aren't clean, look at the state of them!' 'What kind of soup's this today? It's rotten.' These little digs were delivered with a huge smile.

The Pittodrie canteen was the social focal point of the club. Before training every morning one of the ground staff boys would go around the players and management asking if they were staying for lunch. He would write their names down and collect 50p each for a two-course meal and glass of orange squash. There was no pasta in those days: the menu included soup, sausages, mince and tatties. After lunch Ferguson, Knox, Scott and maybe one or two of the senior players would sit around telling stories over a cup of tea. No one had a treasury of anecdotes to match Scott's. Ferguson once jokingly threatened to sack him for packing the wrong socks. Gordon Strachan quipped: 'And where will you get the six people to replace him?' Scott represented decency, tireless service and loyalty. He was streetwise, too. Willie Garner, who played for Ferguson, left to manage Alloa and then returned as assistant manager in December 1983 – when Knox left to become a manager in his own right at Dundee – remembered Scott asking him to help pace out 100 yards on the training pitch before the players arrived for running exercises. Garner got to the required spot only for Scott to shout, 'Keep going to 110 yards, the buggers always stop at ninety.' The players reckoned Scott had his various training drills written into the lining of his bunnet. He would deny it and point to his head: 'It's all in here. Army training!' He was kind and helpful to the players and they adored him. Not that he was a man for extravagance. 'Trying to get a pair of boots off Teddy was incredible,' said McIntyre. 'You would get wind that there were new boots in, Copa World Cups or whatever, and you wanted a pair. You'd ask Teddy and he'd say, "Let's see the pair you have." The toe would be hanging out of them but he'd say, "Ach, you've got a couple of games left in them." He looked after the pennies as well.'

Deep in the heart of the stadium was 'Teddy's room', a den which was part football museum, part bric-a-brac shop. Scott gathered all the souvenirs and gifts Aberdeen accumulated and stored them in his Aladdin's cave. Strips, pennants, caps, medals, salvers, gloves, boots, balls, scarves, books, flags, scrapbooks, cuttings, autographed man-of-the-match champagne bottles and assorted memorabilia from all over the world. There were hidden gems everywhere, even a cricket bat signed by Ian Botham and Allan Lamb. Mischievously he added to the mystique by restricting access. 'He wouldn't let you into his room where the boots were,' said Garner. 'He'd make you stand outside like a schoolboy while he handed you what you needed.' One day Ferguson turned to Stanton: 'You know, I've never been in Teddy's storeroom. What's in it?'

Scott took to Ferguson straight away, feeding off his energy, ambition and integrity. He had worked under eight Aberdeen managers and as early as 1980 had declared that Ferguson was the best of them. Ferguson quickly saw that Scott was an invaluable lieutenant and the pair became exceptionally close. Scott would not dream of imposing his views but he could cleverly get his point across. Sitting beside Ferguson on the bench during a game he might say such and such a player didn't look himself today. Ferguson would say nothing in reply, but he might fidget for a minute or two and then make a substitution to take the guy off.

Now and again Pittodrie's inner circle would be visited by a small, charming elderly man in a suit and a soft hat. Bobby Calder had a unique football career. He was a leading referee who had taken charge of the 1947 Scottish Cup final when Aberdeen won their first major trophy. After briefly managing Dunfermline he was appointed Aberdeen's chief scout in 1949. It was a job he held for thirty-two years. Rangers and Hibs, among others, tried to lure him away but he remained loyal. Aberdeen famously failed to spot a young Denis Law, the city's greatest football talent, who went straight from school to Huddersfield Town. 'If we were to lose a Denis Law again the man responsible would be sacked,' said Ferguson. But Law was an Aberdonian who had been right under their noses, whereas Calder lived and worked in the central belt. Ironically they would have been more likely to spot and sign Law if he had emerged from around Glasgow. When manager Eddie Turnbull performed a ruthless cull of the club's scouting network in the 1960s, Calder was considered invaluable and kept on.

He worked in Glasgow along with his deputy Jimmy Carswell. Calder could not drive and Carswell acted as his wheels. They were quite a double act. Both had an excellent eye for talent and Calder was especially blessed with an easy manner which convinced parents to release their boys into the care of a club 150 miles away. He would turn up at the front door with chocolates or flowers for the boy's mum, cigarettes or cigars for his dad, even loose change for any brothers or sisters who might be around. He would tell boys of fourteen or fifteeen: 'Son, you're signing for Aberdeen and signing for Scotland at the same time.' His instincts and network of contacts allowed him to repeatedly beat other clubs, notably Rangers and Celtic, to outstanding young players.

There was a sense of mischief, too. When he turned up at a match he relished the ripple that went round as the other scouts suddenly became anxious about his potential target. He persuaded a teenaged Charlie Cooke to move north from Fife by first signing one of his best pals and making sure Cooke found out about it. When he learned Rangers wanted young goalkeeper Clark he nipped in and beat them to it. When he discovered the winger Arthur Graham was going to sign for Celtic on the Sunday, Calder watched Graham play for his junior team on the Saturday, got on his team bus after the game, went home with him, and persuaded him to join Aberdeen instead. Celtic were furious. He beat the Glasgow clubs to the punch on outstanding talents like Tommy Craig, Jimmy Smith and Willie Young.

Of the squad Ferguson inherited in 1978, Willie Miller, John McMaster, Alex McLeish and Jim Leighton had all arrived via the Calder-Carswell conveyor belt. Calder also wanted Aberdeen to sign an 18-year-old Andy Gray in 1973 but the club told him they already had enough forwards. Gray signed for Jim McLean's Dundee United instead and later became Britain's first £1.5 million player. Calder tried to snare the teenage winger Davie Provan only for his parents to insist it was too early for him to go full-time. Provan went on to a decorated career with Kilmarnock, Celtic and Scotland.

Once Calder and Carswell had delivered a young player he came into Ferguson's orbit. The Aberdeen youth programme and coaching sessions were under the control of Lenny Taylor, deputy headmaster at a local school, helped by Scott and the oldest first-team player, Clark. Ferguson was staggered to learn Taylor and Clark were doing the work voluntarily. Clark said: 'I remember when Fergie came in and he said to Lenny and me, "You two have never been paid for this? You've been doing it for nothing?" And he had us back-paid immediately!' When Calder relinquished the chief scout role to Carswell in 1981, Ferguson became more involved and put an even greater emphasis on identifying, recruiting and developing young players. Aberdeen opened coaching schools in Glasgow and Edinburgh, taking on the Old Firm, Hearts and Hibs in their backyards. Ferguson was determined to land a higher proportion of Scotland's best raw talent and shape them for his first team.

Pittodrie was energised by the hubbub of young players in the corridors, the dressing rooms, the pitch or the red blaes car park-cum-training pitch. There were sixty under-13s, thirty under-14s, twenty under-15s, all training three nights a week. When Clark left the club he was replaced by George Adams, a player Ferguson had signed at East Stirlingshire. 'The standards were fantastic,' said Adams. 'Alex was always there, asking, "Who are the good ones?" He was always helpful and supportive. He was so confident in his own ability, so confident in the structure and organisation. Everything had to be right. He would make sure the boys were looked after, he would guarantee that to the parents. The boys would be put up in digs where landladies would look after them. He would go to their digs unannounced. He looked after the landladies at Christmas or whatever with presents and boxes of chocolates. The landladies were expected to grass, of course, if any of the lads misbehaved. And they did.'

Ferguson was as shrewd when it came to scouting teenagers as he was with managing seasoned internationals in his first team. He would assess not only the boys' talent but their attitude and body shape. He would surreptitiously size up their parents, either on the doorstep of their homes or on the touchline at a youth game, to gauge how the boy himself would fill out. He would ask his scouts: 'Is the dad big? Is he a smoker?' 'I can spot a winner a mile away,' he said. 'When a boy walks into my office I can tell by how he stands, how he holds himself, if he has the competitive instinct. You can't instil it into a player; it's got to be there.'

Aberdeen were doing everything right: one talented young player after another emerged through the system into Ferguson's early teams: Jim Leighton, Neil Simpson, John Hewitt, Ian Angus, Neale Cooper, Bryan Gunn and Eric Black. All of them would go on to win leagues, cups, Scotland caps or even European medals. Within a month of taking the job in 1978 Ferguson had surprised Black's teacher at a remote Highland secondary school by calling him personally. The school was 120 miles from Aberdeen and Ferguson had never seen Black play. But Billy McNeill had invited the 14-year-old to Pittodrie for summer training and Ferguson wanted to reassure the highly-talented schoolboy that the invitation still stood despite the change of manager. 'We changed near to the first team and he would come to the sessions, he would watch the games,' Black recalled. 'Alex Ferguson knew exactly what he required from his players and it was pretty clear what you had to do. If you weren't doing it, you were told. As a striker you had to put defenders under pressure, you had to link, you had to work extremely hard. Press. Constantly make runs.'

Ferguson's ambition did not come without a price. Paying the youth coaches and meeting the bills of running sessions in Glasgow and Edinburgh amounted to additional expenses and Dick Donald was not a man for unnecessary spending. Every penny was a prisoner around Pittodrie. Ferguson decided the players should travel to away games wearing all-red Adidas tracksuits. This fashion statement was relayed in an amusing snippet in the match programme, which had no name beside it but doubtless echoed Donald himself: 'It sounds a sensible move that will do away with the prospect of spoiling or creasing of expensive clothing on lengthy coach trips.' Donald was fastidious about paying all his bills on time. 'It was a tight board, in more ways than one,' said Ian Taggart, the secretary. 'Dick was very careful with money. If you wanted money for something you just went and asked him. Sometimes you got "yes" and sometimes you got "no", but if he turned it down it wasn't because of limits, it was because he didn't think it was a good idea and it didn't stand up on its own merits. His instincts were good."

Even so, Donald often deferred to his vice-chairman, Chris Anderson. Taggart revealed: 'Dick Donald was a very strong character. But he was happy to take a more background role and let Chris Anderson front it up. He didn't feel as eloquent as Chris, so he was happy to let him do that. They worked well together.' It was Anderson who pushed hardest for Pittodrie to be modernised and expanded. Both ends of the stadium were converted from terracing to bench seating by the middle of the 1970s. From Ferguson's position in the Main Stand dugout he could look across the pitch to where the vast south terrace was seated and then covered by a £500,000 roof in 1980. Aberdeen's crush barriers would not stand up to new safety standards, and because grants were available to subsidise seating that was a cheaper option. Complete covering was necessary because supporters could not be expected to sit exposed to the north-east's cold winds and rain. All the same, the result was that Aberdeen could proudly declare that they had the first all-seated, all-covered stadium in British football. Anderson wanted electronic scoreboards and there was talk of a double-decker stand at the Merkland Road end to increase Pittodrie's capacity from 24,000 to 30,000. Planning problems meant neither of those proposals came to fruition. There was one further innovation, though: Aberdeen became the first club in Britain to have executive boxes where corporate guests could eat, drink and watch a match behind glass.

Ferguson had a board of directors who shared his ambition. He was building up the club from a foundation of scouting and youth coaching, with young players continually refreshing an already powerful squad. The city of Aberdeen, and the whole of north-east Scotland, was buying into a growing club. Taggart was entrusted with the job of selling the executive boxes and could barely believe how easy it was. The whole lot were immediately snapped up on three-year leases. He was pushing at an open door: 'In those days everyone seemed to be an Aberdeen supporter.'

TEN

IPSWICH FALL TO THE JOCK BASTARDS

If there was a club in England that should have been twinned with Aberdeen at the beginning of the 1980s the natural candidate was tucked away in the pastoral Suffolk countryside. Just over 540 miles separate Pittodrie and Portman Road but the home of Ipswich Town was in many ways the Scottish club's mirror image. Aberdeen and Ipswich were geographically remote from the bigger clubs they challenged. They were well-run 'family' operations. They were located in one-club cities, with the undivided attention of their local support, and had comparable populations to draw on. And both were enjoying the best years in their history under charismatic managers.

There is a compelling argument for saying that in the autumn of 1981 Ipswich had the best team in England. Terry Butcher, Paul Mariner, Eric Gates and Mick Mills all played for the national team, the latter sometimes as captain. John Wark and Alan Brazil were Scotland internationals. Arnold Mühren and Frans Thijssen were capped by the Netherlands. In the previous season Ipswich had finished second in the league and won the Uefa Cup. They had drawn twice with the Liverpool side who pummelled Aberdeen and they had beaten the eventual league champions, Aston Villa, home and away. Ferguson took a deep breath when Aberdeen were drawn against Bobby Robson's team in the first round of the 1981–82 Uefa Cup. His first European tie since the scarring ordeal of Anfield could not have been any tougher. He was deeply impressed by Ipswich and Robson. He had once contacted Robson and asked if he could spend time with him during a pre-season trip to the Netherlands. The Ipswich players were intrigued to see him on their bus, showing great interest in their formation and tactics. Ferguson watched Robson giving his team a dressing down. 'Robson went right through the lot and I thought, "That's the way to do it,"' Ferguson recalled.

The first leg was at Portman Road on 16 September and few thought Aberdeen would cope. In Ipswich's two games immediately before the tie they beat Manchester United and Liverpool. England remembered Aberdeen folding against Liverpool and expected Ipswich to pile on new misery. They duly went ahead just on half-time. Thijssen elegantly deceived Andy Watson and Doug Rougvie before driving a shot which spun over the line despite Leighton's attempt to save. So far, so predictable. But six minutes into the second half Aberdeen earned a corner. The kick was straight out of the Ferguson training manual: a high cross to the edge of the box, a powerful header into the goalmouth, and a nimble forward pouncing to score. It was a move which brought them goals time and time again. On this occasion Peter Weir crossed, Alex McLeish connected with the header and John Hewitt reacted in the goalmouth to nip in front of the goalkeeper and score a precious away goal. Aberdeen held on comfortably for a 1–1 draw and suddenly Ipswich realised what they were up against.

Ferguson and his players had gone down and taken them on, toe-to-toe, in a gruelling physical battle. Weir and Strachan had been told to play deep and wide to run at Ipswich's full-backs and also help tighten the midfield. That forced the Dutchmen, Thijsen and Mühren, into territory being policed by the rugged Neale Cooper and Watson. Miller swept up behind them. Ferguson had shown himself to be a match for Robson. 'We all thought, "Aberdeen, nah, we can beat them,"' said Terry Butcher. 'But they were a really difficult team to play. Tough bastards. Fucking hell, really strong bastards. We really didn't know much about that Aberdeen team before being drawn against them. We went into the first leg thinking we were going to be okay, but we were taken aback by their power. Jeezo, they were a strong side. An away goal wasn't good, but we still felt confident that we could win.' Alan Brazil felt the same way: 'At the time we had a bloody good side and we honestly felt that we would beat anyone. But we came off the pitch thinking, "Christ, we've got a game on our hands here."'

Ipswich were entitled to interpret the result as a blip. By the time they went to Pittodrie they had won three more league games to go top of the table, unbeaten in seven matches in the old First Division. England striker Mariner was back in the team having missed the first leg through injury and he told reporters: 'Aberdeen will be forced to be more adventurous in their home leg and that will mean more chances for us. They are bound to leave holes at the back if they come out and take us on in an attacking, open game.' What really caused a stir was a remark made by Robson at his press conference on the eve of the second leg. 'Aberdeen did surprise us at Portman Road, but I have a feeling that may be as well as they can play. We, on the other hand, can do a lot better. Although Aberdeen will be tough, it is not an ordeal.' Even if it was not meant to be provocative or condescending, that was how it was interpreted around Pittodrie. Ferguson made sure his players knew about it and they took it as badly as the supporters.

Stuart Kennedy said: 'I don't like to talk badly of Bobby Robson, I loved him, but he gave a bad interview. He said he felt Aberdeen were lucky and that Ipswich had played the better football. We took it as an affront. It was like getting spoken down to. He thought he'd come and play us off the park at Pittodrie . . . oh no, no, no.' In his 1984 autobiography, Strachan wrote that Robson had 'shown some of that arrogance for which his nation has been known'. Ferguson did not share his players' view. He had exploited the notion of English arrogance to fire a reaction from his team, but he understood Robson's comments and sympathised with them. 'What he said was for the benefit of his own team,' Ferguson said later. 'Not for anyone else.'

Aberdeen's confidence was quiet and understated and it derived from a belief they had improved their team over the 1981 close season. Only one signing had been made, but at around £300,000 (plus Ian Scanlon) Aberdeen had set a club and Scottish record transfer fee to bring Peter Weir from St Mirren. Weir was a left-winger with a stooping, unusual run, which could make him look a little awkward. But he was quick and blessed with magnificent technique and balance. Crucially he could dribble and shoot off either foot, which meant full-backs did not know whether he would go past them down the line or cut inside. Against Ipswich, he did both. Weir's gentle, placid personality left him vulnerable to Ferguson's insatiable demands. 'He used to kick my backside, many a time,' he said. Ferguson always felt he lacked confidence and could have developed into a truly world-class talent had he shown more belief. But he also knew this much: when Weir was in the mood he could be unplayable.

Mick Mills was thirty-two when he played at Pittodrie on 30 September 1981. Ipswich's short, moustachioed captain was still playing for England, still the darling of his club. Weir looked at him and saw vulnerability. He sidled up to Hewitt before the return leg and told him: 'If I'm on form I can destroy this guy.' His reasoning was sound: 'Mills was still an England international but he had slowed up a bit. I felt if I could get the right service I could really run at him. On the night it happened: I got two goals, right foot, left foot.'

Pittodrie was packed and electric. Ferguson was facing one of his biggest tests. 'We stirred up a hornets' nest when we drew at Ipswich and they will react to that,' he said pre-match. It was a night when Knox made an intriguing discovery. In the minutes before kick-off he was standing on the trackside when he realised he could hear a man talking from deep inside the stadium. An air vent was carrying the noise from inside, all the way from the away dressing room. Knox said: 'I could heard it quite clearly. It was Bobby Robson talking to his players. That was the first time I heard that. I could stand and listen in to what they were saying in the dressing room. But we didn't do it every week!' That night he heard Robson addressing his Ipswich players, telling them how much better they were than the 'Jock bastards', telling them to go out and show it. He was writing off Aberdeen. Knox and Ferguson knew it was all done for effect, but they used it to wind up their own players and produce a counter-reaction.

The stage was set for a pulsating night. Strachan scored a penalty to put Aberdeen 2–1 up overall, but John Wark levelled the aggregate score with another penalty before half-time, and the away-goal advantage was gone. Watson and Cooper had a grip of Thijssen and Mühren but Ferguson felt his team were sitting back too much and allowing Ipswich to press. That had to change. At half-time he turned to Weir. It was not a left-midfield player he wanted, it was a left-winger. He told Weir to push forward. After fifty-five minutes Weir ran at Mills. Ipswich's captain backtracked and backtracked until Weir cut inside and drilled a low, right-foot shot into the far corner. Pittodrie sensed an English kill. Half an hour later Weir staged an almost perfect reenactment. This time he ran at Mills and went outside on to his left foot, flashing another shot across goalkeeper Paul Cooper into the net. Aberdeen were home and dry and the holders were out. If Strachan had converted a second penalty in stoppage time it would have been a rout.

The stands rose to Weir. During his first dozen games for Aberdeen there had been the inevitable criticism that comes when a player arrives for a record fee. On his thirteenth appearance he delivered the performance of his career. McMaster said: 'I've never seen a display in my life like Peter Weir's against Mick Mills. I reckon Mick Mills was lying in his bed for a week after that with an ice bag on his heid. Peter terrorised him. What a terrific player he was. Very, very underrated.' Mills trooped off the field, dejected. 'Weir diddled Millsy twice,' said Terry Butcher. 'He just turned on the magic. We had worked so hard to win the Uefa Cup; it had been such a journey for us. Bobby Robson wasn't happy that night . . . wow. Not happy at all. I think we might have stayed at the Thistle Hotel in Dyce after the game and we just got absolutely smashed because we'd lost the Uefa Cup at the first hurdle.'

Alan Brazil was left with two abiding memories: Rougvie's brutality and Weir's brilliance. 'Doug Rougvie kicked everything that moved. Launching himself at people. Fuck me, he was taking you out chest-high. Miller and McLeish were hard but fair. Rougvie was the hatchet man. He looked like he'd just escaped from Barlinnie prison. And the doing that Weir gave Mick Mills! Mills needed cartilage operations after that game, he'd been twisted so much. Weir murdered him.'

Bill Shankly had died suddenly three days before the Pittodrie game. There was something of Shanks' unshakeable certainty in the comment Robson made to Ferguson at full time. He entered the home dressing room to congratulate Ferguson and Miller: 'You'll win this cup easily now.' Ferguson was not so sure. Real Madrid, Inter Milan, Hamburg, Valencia, Feyenoord and Arsenal were still in the competition, and so were Dundee United. The other half of the New Firm had beaten Monaco while Aberdeen were dealing with Ipswich. But both Celtic and Rangers had tumbled out. Journalist Ian Paul reflected the nation's mood in the *Glasgow Herald*: 'If a few of us in this less talented corner of the country are currently feigning north-east accents, that is only a tiny tribute to the two teams who have kept Scotland's European interests alive.'

Aberdeen avoided the more powerful clubs in the second round and were paired with Argeș Pitești of Romania. Ferguson's growing stature was reflected in the fact he felt confident enough to contact Brian Clough for information. Clough's Nottingham Forest had beaten Argeș Pitești home and away two years earlier. In the first leg at home Aberdeen duly raced into a 3–0 half-time lead, but did not add to it, prompting a managerial outburst. 'That second half was dreadful,' said Ferguson. 'In fact it was a disgrace. Probably the worst thing I could have done was telling them that they were doing well. I praised them at the interval and then they let things slip . . .' No praise came from him at half-time in the second leg. Instead it would go down in football folklore as the occasion for one of Ferguson's most infamous performances. The Romanians scored two first-half goals to make it 3–2 on aggregate. Aberdeen were in real trouble and Ferguson erupted. Weir and especially Strachan got the brunt of it for sitting too deep. Strachan chirruped back, further infuriating Ferguson. Finally he blew his top and sent a tray of tea cups up in the air before attempting to deliver a forearm smash to a tea urn. The urn was ceramic, heavy and immovable. Ferguson continued ranting and raving while desperately trying to disguise the pain shooting through his arm. The players bit their lips to stop themselves laughing. The histrionics turned out to be more dramatic than the match. Second-half goals from Weir and Strachan defused Aberdeen's problems. In his next programme notes Ferguson airbrushed the tea urn episode entirely. 'A half-time briefing was all that was needed to restore the players' confidence in their work,' he wrote.

Aberdeen had made it beyond the second round of a European competition for the first time. But Uefa's draws had rarely been kind to Ferguson and the pattern continued when they were paired with Hamburg, who were top of the Bundesliga and favourites to win the Uefa Cup.

Ernst Happel's team was home to German internationals Felix Magath, Manny Kaltz, Horst Hrubesch and the peerless Franz Beckenbauer. At thirty-six, 'The Kaiser' had returned to German football after a spell in the United States. Such was his stature at the club that he also did scouting work on Happel's behalf. The weekend before the first leg Beckenbauer was among a delegation from Hamburg who watched Aberdeen play Hibs at Easter Road. Afterwards he spoke effusively about Neale Cooper, who reached his eighteenth birthday three days later. 'He said I was possibly the closest he had seen to a player like himself at that age,' said Cooper, who cherished the anecdote. 'That was quite a compliment. But I always say that it just goes to show, even Franz Beckenbauer can talk some amount of shite . . .'

If Aberdeen had been taught a lesson by Liverpool, Hamburg continued their education. The result was one of the most frustrating they experienced under Ferguson. They took on an outstanding German team and scored three times against them through Black, Watson and Hewitt. A handful of other chances came and were allowed to slip away. A penalty by Strachan was saved. 'I was very impressed by this young Aberdeen side,' said Beckenbauer. 'Their work-rate was tremendous.' Ferguson was also effusive about his team and felt the scoreline could have been five or six–nil. Kaltz went further: 'They could have scored seven.' But they hadn't, and that is where the lesson lay. Aberdeen had twice switched off and handed Hamburg two goals. Leighton and Kennedy had got into terrible trouble and given the ball away, and Hrubesch was left with a tap-in. Three minutes from the end, as an injured Rougvie was carried along the trackside, Aberdeen naïvely left themselves open again and Hrubesch scored another. For all their domination Aberdeen were travelling to Germany with only a 3–2 lead and two away goals conceded. 'The Germans must be going back to the continent truly amazed that they got off so lightly,' wrote the *Glasgow Herald*.

Ferguson was bold in Hamburg, not only throwing in Black and Hewitt as his attack but announcing on the day before the game that the two 18-year-olds would start. He also gave McLeish, twenty-two, a blunt warning via the media. 'If Alex can't handle Hrubesch then he shouldn't be thinking about the [1982] World Cup, because somewhere along the way he is going to be asked to look after Hrubesch or someone like him.' The jibe proved prophetic. Tall, strong and commanding in the air, McLeish had emerged as a defender of outstanding potential alongside Miller, but he could not contain Hrubesch on the night. The German scored the opener with a first-half header, his third goal over the two legs, before Hamburg rattled in two more in the second half. McGhee struck a lovely goal with eleven minutes left and another would have levelled everything, but Hamburg held on to progress to the quarter-finals 5–4 on aggregate. The tie had been scuppered by those two away goals at Pittodrie.

Ferguson singled out Strachan for not doing enough: 'Great players don't accept man-for-man marking. I could have wept watching a man with his ability being marked out of things.' He said Strachan was a good player but had still to become a great one. 'I've made these points to Gordon. Now it's up to him.' The disappointment was obvious but there had been no repeat of the collapse at Anfield and no disgrace. Their opponents had been formidable – eight of Hamburg's second-leg team played in their European Cup final win over Juventus at the end of the following season – and the Dons had looked comfortable in their company.

Aberdeen still had much to prove, though, at home as well as abroad. It was December and they were fourth in the league. Ferguson warned that unless the team's concentration and focus improved there would not be any Hamburgs to worry about the following season. While they were in the Uefa Cup they won only seven of their opening fifteen league games and went out of the League Cup to Dundee United. Post-Hamburg, they lost only two of their remaining twenty-one league games and finished two points behind the champions, Celtic. Strachan and Hewitt stepped up as goalscorers and by the end of the season Aberdeen had scored forty more goals than the previous campaign. Still, Liverpool, Ipswich and Hamburg had been exciting distractions from the fact that Aberdeen had gone nearly two full seasons without a trophy. The sense of progress and momentum was there but there was little silverware to show for it. Ferguson was still asking his team if they wanted to be thought of as 'one-trophy' players. The same question could be put to the manager.

There was still the Scottish Cup, though. The campaign began on 23 January when Hewitt put the ball in Motherwell's net 9.6 seconds after kick-off, setting a record which still stands for the fastest goal scored in the tournament. It turned out to be the winner. Celtic, Kilmarnock and St Mirren were seen off in the following rounds. Aberdeen were in the Scottish Cup final for the first time in four years, and the first time under Ferguson. The team waiting for them were Rangers.

ELEVEN

DECLARING WAR ON THE GLASGOW PRESS

Scotland has always been fertile territory for newspapers. More than 730,000 people bought the *Daily Record* every day at the start of the 1980s, the equivalent of one in every five adults in the country. The *Record* was the leader in a voracious and plentiful daily market. Readers who did not fancy it could instead buy tabloids like the *Sun*, *Daily Mail* or *Daily Express*, or broadsheets such as the *Glasgow Herald* or *The Scotsman*. In Aberdeen there were the *Press and Journal*, selling more than 100,000 copies per day, and the *Evening Express*.

The *Record* marketed itself as a national paper but many saw it as the quintessential Glasgow title, its pages reflecting the interests and agendas of the central belt. The foundation of its huge appeal was Scottish news, entertainment and sport. And the *Record*'s definition of sport was Scottish football, which primarily meant Celtic and Rangers. Those who supported, played for or managed any other club often found the coverage in the Scottish press immensely frustrating. Aberdeen, Dundee United and the rest had their space – and the newspaper men travelled with them on European trips – but the default position was that Old Firm stories tended to lead the back pages. Commercially that made perfect sense because most readers lived in the populous central belt and Celtic and Rangers mattered far more to them. Ferguson knew all of that but refused to accept it nonetheless. He bridled against the cosiness between national newspapers and the Old Firm.

When he played for Rangers he was impressed by the skill and cunning shown by Celtic manager Jock Stein in manipulating press coverage to his club's advantage. When Rangers seemed to have a comfortable lead towards the end of the 1967–68 title race – with Ferguson as their top scorer – Stein used the newspapers to insist they could only throw away the championship. The comment seemed to wobble Rangers. They won only three of their last six matches and Celtic snatched the title by two points. From the infancy of his own managerial career Ferguson tried to use the press to his advantage. He told the East Stirlingshire players that the *Falkirk Herald* favoured Falkirk FC. At St Mirren he would point out to his team that they were not getting the column inches they deserved. He would phone national reporters with stories to increase St Mirren's coverage. From his earliest days Ferguson recognised the role of the media. He used the press to drum up interest in his teams and privately seized on negative coverage – real or imagined – to tell his players the reporters had it in for them. 'You remind yourself of the number of people who don't want you to win,' he said. 'It fires you up, it gets you going, so we use it to our advantage.'

Ferguson had not been at Aberdeen long when he began to tune into a long-standing local complaint about reporters favouring the Glasgow clubs. Soon it became a grievance he exploited to his benefit. He began talking to his players about 'the West of Scotland press' as a group that resented Aberdeen and was inclined to preserve the status quo. All they wanted to write about was triumphs for Rangers and Celtic, he said.

What's more, they disliked having to travel long distances to the cold north-east to report on the upstarts at Pittodrie. His captain, Miller, enthusiastically echoed the message in the dressing room: 'He believed every word that he said. And he was absolutely right. Some might argue that a bias towards the Old Firm does not exist but it is palpable.'

When the Scottish Football Writers' Association voted Strachan their player of the year in 1980, Ferguson gave the decision a cynical welcome: 'It's a mark of Strachan's ability that he has earned the respect of fans throughout the country and the admiration of a Glasgow-orientated press which at times seems to have difficulty recognising ability when it's parcelled in a red shirt.' Ferguson's apparent suspicion of the press verged on the obsessive. Every morning he would insist on having all the main daily titles ready for his forensic inspection. If there was a story or comment which he perceived as negative about himself or Aberdeen the point was noted. Sometimes his response was to ban the journalist responsible from his press conferences. Other times he would simply tear out the page and stick it on the dressing room wall so he could use it to anger and motivate his players. Midfielder Neil Simpson explained: 'It was that siege mentality: the press are against you. Things would go up on the board. "Look at this, look at what they're saying about you guys, about us." You would get angry about it. We totally bought into it.'

The bigger the match, the more likely Ferguson was to draw on some aspect of the newspaper coverage to find a little edge. In the spring of 1979 Aberdeen had drawn 1–1 with Celtic in the Scottish Cup quarter-final at Pittodrie and faced a daunting replay at Parkhead.

Stuart Kennedy said: 'We went down to Glasgow on the Wednesday night. The Glasgow press wrote, "The replay is a waste of petrol money for Aberdeen." We pinned this stuff up in the dressing room. Basically it was not worth our while turning up.' Ferguson milked it for all it was worth. Aberdeen won 2–1.

Rougvie said: 'The press didn't want Aberdeen doing well. Oh aye. They hated us; they hated Fergie with his arrogance and his power, his power to ban people. "You, you cunt, you wrote something I didn't like, you're no' getting in."' When Rougvie made his one and only appearance for Scotland he was one of six Aberdeen men who played in the match against Northern Ireland. 'It was an Aberdeen Select that night. The only thing wrong was we got beat, so the Glasgow press didn't like that. It didn't matter how good we were they didn't want a Scotland team of sheepshaggers, they wanted Rangers and Celtic players in so they could write about them and sell their papers.'

Not all of the players believed what Ferguson was feeding them. Mark McGhee drew his motivation from elsewhere: 'I don't know if it was a conscious decision by Fergie to start doing it, to use it as a ploy, or whether it was just something that developed. But he used to say, "They hate driving all this way up here." I don't know if that was true or not. He gave us the impression that the Glasgow press were all Celtic or Rangers supporters and didn't want Aberdeen to achieve things. I don't think from the players' point of view we particularly cared. We didn't give a toss what the press men thought. It was more a west of Scotland thing: we didn't like the idea of the fans, the people there, being disrespectful to people from the north and thinking less of us. Thinking of us as yokels.'

Ferguson would indoctrinate his players with the same message about the Glasgow press for the entire duration of his Aberdeen career. He never let it go. One of his last signings for the club, Robert Connor, arrived only six months before the end. Connor said: 'If you were to ask me what he went on about the most, that was it. Especially when we were going to Parkhead and Ibrox. "All the press are against you, they want to write about how great Rangers are, or how great Celtic are." He just built and built on that. The likes of Miller and McLeish had heard it a million times and it was ingrained in them. But for people like me coming in it had to be drummed into us, just in case we hadn't realised.'

Hammering home his mantra about the press being biased in favour of the Glasgow clubs had one consequence that even Ferguson might not have imagined: it unsettled some of the Celtic and Rangers players. It was uncomfortable for them to be portrayed as favoured or indulged while another team was supposedly resented. Billy McNeill spoke of the impact it had on his Celtic team: 'Alex's thing about this "bias", and always being in the press about the bias that his team experienced against the Old Firm . . . that unsettled your players, it annoyed them. It maybe disturbed their concentration. Undoubtedly it did at times.'

There is a hierarchy of football reporters on every newspaper. The chief football writers were nearly all based in Glasgow. Ferguson demanded that they abandon the Old Firm more often and come to Aberdeen matches instead. The club tended to be covered by the regional men who lived within travelling distance of Pittodrie. He began berating reporters in front of their colleagues at post-match press conferences, aggressively challenging them about how many times they had been to Pittodrie that season. On one occasion, after Aberdeen had dropped points at Motherwell, he walked into the press room simmering with anger. The first reporter he saw was the Glasgow-based Hugh Keevins. 'You fucking cunts!' he shouted, unprovoked. 'You don't know anything about Aberdeen. We never see you up at Pittodrie.' In fact that season was only a few weeks old and Keevins had already been to Aberdeen four times. When that point was quietly made to Ferguson later he said: 'I know. He just happened to be the first in my line of vision.' He let the football writers know he was keeping a notebook recording how many Aberdeen games each of them attended. Who covered the games was the newspapers' decision, the sports editors' decision, but Ferguson made it his business. Did the fabled notebook actually exist? Or was it, as some maintain, an early example of Ferguson's 'mind games'? It didn't matter. Ruse or not, what counted was the threat.

He would talk about individual reporters to his players, telling them how much this or that hack disliked coming all the way to Aberdeen, that they made the effort only because it was a game against Celtic or Rangers. Simpson said: 'It would be, "Oh aye, they'll all be up today, we're playing Celtic, aye, look, here they are." They were like hated characters, some of these boys! You didn't know any different because it was almost like you were behind the lines. Everyone was in it together.' Ferguson extended this domineering stance to even the Aberdeen press and periodically banned any local reporter who displeased him. He also had several skirmishes with the journalist for Grampian Television, Frank Gilfeather, often because of tension over Ferguson's demand that he be paid for interviews. Ferguson also caused trouble if a player appeared on television without his prior approval. When he wanted to be, he could be wantonly awkward. Grampian once asked Gilfeather to contact all ten Scottish Premier Division clubs and ask if they would submit a team for a televised summer indoor five-a-side tournament to be held in Perth. Nine clubs said they would. Only Ferguson refused.

On the way back from the Argeș Pitești tie in Romania Gilfeather asked Ferguson if he would agree to be filmed for an interview during the flight. The mood on the plane was relaxed and Ferguson, happy with the result, said yes. The piece was broadcast two nights later and the content was innocuous, but when Ferguson next saw Gilfeather he lambasted him in front of other reporters. He said his wife Cathy had watched the interview and thought he looked as though he had had a couple of beers. He had, but Ferguson blamed Gilfeather for talking him into doing the piece. The argument continued in front of an increasingly uncomfortable press pack. Gilfeather, a former Scottish amateur boxing champion, let slip his usual affable and courteous demeanour: 'Eventually, tongue in cheek, I said, "Alex, if you continue this you'll force me to make a comeback."' The situation was defused, but Gilfeather's refusal to kowtow meant the pair were never close.

The mythology of the Glasgow press working to obstruct Aberdeen does not square with the private behaviour of either Ferguson or the club. When Ally MacLeod was identified by Aberdeen as the man they wanted in 1975, Chris Anderson initially contacted Alex Cameron, chief football writer with the *Record*, to act as an intermediary. Jim Rodger had been the similar conduit to bring Ferguson north in 1978. Anderson, in particular, had open channels of communication to the Glasgow sports desks and was shrewd enough to know the press could be used to Aberdeen's advantage. Dick Donald was less trusting and kept his distance, though he was not beyond cowing the local press pack with threats about leaking stories straight to Glasgow if they failed to toe the line. 'We'll get the boys from the south on to this,' he would growl.

Ferguson derided the 'pro-Glasgow' press but he had a keen appreciation of its needs and its market. He knew newspapers had space to fill and it was within his power to give them material. It was harder to get prominence for Aberdeen stories than for Celtic or Rangers ones, because of the respective size of their supports, but a winning team with a dynamic and outspoken manager was a seductive combination. His relationship with journalists was complicated. He would occasionally bully, intimidate and ban them, and yet he enjoyed their company and the feeling was generally mutual. After games at Pittodrie he held court. He would sit with them for his post-match press conference and then a select few would move through to an ante-room for long and relaxed conversations over drinks. Ferguson always insisted on pouring the booze himself. He would tell stories which were funny, rude, revealing, gossipy and indiscreet, while picking the reporters' brains about what other clubs and managers were up to. After a while the mood might temporarily darken as he got something off his chest. Most of those present lapped it up and enjoyed him, though not all. 'There were some people who wanted him to fall on his backside, absolutely,' said football commentator Archie Macpherson. 'Those who were Glasgow-inclined, if I could put it that way, thought of him as just a bombastic loudmouth at times. But I think winning the league changed things.'

On European trips he would make a point of knowing which hotel the press were in so he could pay an evening visit. His readiness to buy a round was much appreciated. And so was his participation in the journalists' cards schools, not least because he was a poor player who could be quickly cleaned out. There were times, on the eve of a European away game, when Ferguson might still be with the press at 1 or 2am. His ability to charm even an unfamiliar group of reporters was evident when Aberdeen were in Hamburg for the European Super Cup late in 1983. Tottenham Hotspur were playing Bayern Munich in the Uefa Cup in the same week. A number of leading English journalists had travelled to Germany for that tie and they decided to make a detour to familiarise themselves with the charismatic young manager of Aberdeen. Ferguson had them eating out of the palm of his hand, letting them run up a large bar bill at his expense. He told them Tottenham would be too strong for the Germans. Bayern narrowly won that first leg, but Tottenham turned the tie around at White Hart Lane. The Fleet Street gang, remembering Ferguson's prediction, were impressed.

Until Ferguson's emergence only Stein displayed such an astute understanding of the role played by the football press in Scotland, and of how to work the journalists. Archie Knox said: 'Fergie was always aware of that, he knew he had to give them something. Something controversial, maybe make something up, plant a seed with them. He was very conscious of all that. He knew they had their job to do and space to fill. But he really did feel there wasn't enough recognition for Aberdeen. How would a paper sell in Glasgow with an Aberdeen headline? He was aware of that and that it meant Rangers and Celtic would get more publicity.'

During his time with Aberdeen, Ferguson attended a management and coaching course at the SFA's complex at Largs. He was asked at what point on a match day did he start thinking about his post-match press conference. To a room full of hardened football men, his answer came as a revelation: 'Twenty minutes or maybe even half-an-hour before the end of the game.' To illustrate the point he gave an example from a match when Aberdeen had lost and Miller had been shown a red card. Tony Higgins, the former Hibs and Partick Thistle striker who later became a prominent figure in the players' union, was in the audience: 'He said that twenty minutes before that game ended he knew they'd get a doing in the press, that the papers would doubt Aberdeen's ability to win the league. So he decided to berate the Glasgow press. "You can't wait for us to get beat, Willie Miller should never have been sent off," all that stuff. So for the next couple of days Fergie got slaughtered. The columnists were saying, "Is this the way you behave, Fergie?" On the Saturday they won again. He stood there and told the room the last thing he wanted was for those players to have doubt in their minds, so he was prepared to take the criticism on to himself. Most of the coaches couldn't believe he was thinking about all of this long before the game was over, thinking about his press conference while he was still sitting in the dugout. None of the other coaches could understand that. He was miles ahead of them.'

TWELVE

THE OLD FIRM: 'WE DIDN'T LIKE ABERDEEN, THEY DIDN'T LIKE US'

In many respects the 1982 Scottish Cup final looked like a replay of 1978. Aberdeen were back at Hampden to face Rangers. Miller, Kennedy and McMaster were in the team, just as they had been four years before. Lining up against them were Sandy Jardine, Colin Jackson, Davie Cooper, Bobby Russell and Tommy McLean, all of whom had been in that winning Rangers side. John Greig, captain in 1978, was now manager. This was a squad of proven winners. And on the terracing their support again vastly outnumbered Aberdeen's. Many knew that Aberdeen had managed only three wins in the previous eighteen Scottish Cup meetings between the clubs. This time Aberdeen were heavily fancied, but that had been the case in 1978 when they froze. 'I don't care how many make the journey from Aberdeen,' said Rangers captain Ally Dawson on the eve of the final. 'Our fans will outnumber and outshout them. That will give us a tremendous lift and maybe even unsettle them a bit.'

The remark was revealing. Few now doubted Aberdeen's ability, only their character. They had beaten Rangers and Celtic twenty-one times since Ferguson took over and nine of those wins had been in Glasgow. But he had yet to take them to Hampden and triumph when it mattered most, in a cup final. In his *Sunday Mail* preview of the final Don Morrison wrote of Aberdeen: 'The in-form team, talented and skilful, they look stronger in practically every respect. Yet there is one question which niggles away at the back of the mind: do they really have the temperament?' Dawson's line about Rangers' support unsettling Aberdeen was understandable. A Rangers crowd in Glasgow is a force of nature, matched in scale, volume and fanaticism only by neighbours Celtic. For decades Rangers had seen club after club crumble and fold when faced with this assault on the senses, Aberdeen among them.

Greig and his team prepared for the final in the seaside resort of Largs, an hour out of Glasgow. The intention was to release them from the pressure of the city and allow them to relax. But it also gave them thinking time. Time for doubt. No matter how hard they tried to convince themselves that Ferguson and this Aberdeen team would buckle, the evidence was in short supply. They worried that something had changed at Pittodrie.

No longer did Aberdeen travel south to Glasgow cowed and with an inferiority complex. That had become clear from something that had started to happen when they visited Celtic. Parkhead could hold close to 70,000 and often did. It was huge, dark and menacing. But no part of the neglected, misshapen stadium was more intimidating than 'The Jungle', the bare concrete terrace with its low roof that ran the length of the pitch. The fans who packed it for the big games were the Celtic hard core. They were noisy, aggressive if they wanted to be, and unforgiving to any team they saw as a threat. Rougvie was Ferguson's first-choice left-back, an enormous, straight-backed, broad-chested Fife giant. Because he was from .Ballingry, was missing his front teeth and would stand with his long arms and legs spread wide when protesting to referees, team-mates nicknamed him 'The Ballingry Bat'. Yet, although he looked fearsome, Rougvie had a gentle, easy-going nature and possessed the serenity common to many big men who have no need to fear physical confrontation. He was provocative in just one respect, one that became a symbol of Ferguson's Aberdeen mentality and swagger. Instead of staying well infield during pre-match warm-ups at Parkhead, Rougvie would remove himself from the other players and start doing his exercises right in front of the baying Jungle. There he would be, running up and down the trackside, stretching his arms out wide, doing side-to-side moves or leaping to head imaginary balls. It was an act of mischief and an unequivocal declaration that, however much they tried to intimidate him, he did not care. No one had ever shown such nerve to a Glasgow crowd. They went wild, screaming at him, hurling abuse, jabbing their fingers. Rougvie looked back with a huge beaming grin.

'I used to run past the Jungle pumping my arm at them,' Rougvie recalled. '"Up ye, ya bastards." Terrible, wasn't it? I just did it to noise them up. It was us saying, "We've come down to beat youse and we're not bothering our arse how we do it." Oh, I got pelters. Absolute dog's abuse! It was brilliant! I'd be going, "Oh, I've never heard that one, I'll take a note of that one." Ach, I'm a big coward really. I'd have run if anyone came on! I knew they wouldn't catch me because I was quick as fuck.' Everyone who saw it knew exactly what it was, including the Celtic players. Davie Provan said: 'It was like a statement. "You're not going to intimidate us."'

Rougvie initially took on the Jungle in the first of the two visits to Parkhead in April 1980. It was his own idea rather than a stunt suggested to him by Ferguson, but it sent out exactly the kind of message the manager wanted. Miller said: 'Let's just say Fergie didn't discourage it.' Rougvie's antics subsequently became a theatrical ritual of Aberdeen's visits to Parkhead. Ferguson encouraged his younger players and new signings to take in the show. Tommy McIntyre remembered: 'He said, "Go and watch The Bat doing his warm-up." It was a right hot sunny day, he takes his top off, and he's ripped. They're howling at him! He was just winding them up. And Fergie wanted them wound up.' Miller said: 'I loved it. I'd say to him, "Big man, on you go; we'll just quietly do our warm-up over here while you take all the flak." He loved it. It seemed to energise him. He enjoyed being that kind of figure.'

Ferguson wanted to reverse the status quo in which visiting teams could seem submissive or meek against the Old Firm. He wanted his teams to be harder than Celtic and Rangers, better than them, mentally stronger than them. And he wanted to make sure the Old Firm knew it. No team had taken such a provocative approach but Ferguson had players with the skill and attitude to carry it off. McLeish said: 'When we played Celtic, if we dumped Frank McGarvey on the ground, we used to rub him on the head and say, "Ach, you're all right, Frank, get up." He hated it!' When he was wary of one of the opposition's key men, like the rugged Celtic captain Roy Aitken, Ferguson would instruct one of his team to confront him from the start. Dougie Bell remembered: 'He'd say, "Roy Aitken? Roy Aitken? The Celtic fans all sing, 'Feed the Bear' about him . . . he's a big shitebag. He's scared of you, Dougie." Whatever Fergie told you, you believed. So the first chance I got I tried to get in about Roy Aitken and wind him up. Roy probably wasn't at all bothered about me, but Fergie had me believing he was running scared.'

The Old Firm did not take it well. Animosity and bad blood developed. After three seasons and a league title Ferguson's

Aberdeen had become hate figures for Rangers and Celtic supporters. Tellingly, this also extended to the dressing room. Davie Provan said: 'The thing about that Aberdeen side was this: even after an Old Firm game there is a mutual respect between the two sets of players. Most of the players shake hands. That didn't always happen against Aberdeen. We didn't like them and they didn't like us.' At the end of one season Aberdeen and Celtic were both booked into the same resort in Majorca, a fact which became evident only when the Celtic players walked into a pub and found several of the Aberdeen team already inside. Provan said: 'You could have cut the atmosphere with a knife. It was bizarre because everybody had been drinking. Normally you'd meet another Scottish team and it would be, "How you doing, how long you over for?" Not this time. It was a very curt "aye" and that was it. That was the feeling between the teams.'

Both halves of the Old Firm were of a similar mind. Aberdeen got right under Rangers' skin, too. 'It wasn't a nice experience playing against Aberdeen,' said defender Davie McKinnon. 'That was part of their strength. They wound people up something awful on the pitch. Rangers players and Aberdeen players just didn't get on whatsoever. There was a huge amount of needle. I think there was respect from both teams for the abilities of the players, but when you played against them there wasn't a respect for the way they went about their business because they were in your face quite a lot. That's a strength, I suppose. You don't need to be liked to be a winner. And they had that winning mentality.'

The 1981–82 league season finished a week before the cup final with a dress rehearsal. Rangers were smashed 4–0 at Pittodrie. If Celtic had suffered an unlikely home defeat to St Mirren, Aberdeen might have snatched the league title on goal difference. Instead they came second, ten points above third-placed Rangers. It was a strong finish to the season and Ferguson said: 'The present successful spell reflects the all-round efficiency of this club from the top to the bottom, from match-day stewards to the highly competent office staff who look after the administrative side of our football affairs.' He had a spring in his step, naming his cup final team to the press on the eve of the game. 'I have absolutely no fear about the game – well, no logical fears. The only thing is that a final is a final and I suppose anything can happen on the day.'

Back in Largs, John Greig had taken aside Davie Cooper, his wonderfully talented but inconsistent winger. He told Cooper he could be the man to win the cup for Rangers. Ferguson thought Cooper was a player of rich skills, with a wonderful left foot, but he liked the balance of his own midfield for the final: McMaster's intelligence and smooth passing on the left, the two young bulls, Cooper and Simpson, in the centre, and Strachan offering energy and menace behind the attackers. It was a quartet to worry Rangers and also protect the back four of Kennedy, Miller, McLeish and Rougvie. McGhee was partnered up front by young Hewitt and there was more youth on the bench in the shape of Eric Black.

Ferguson believed in his two young players in central midfield. Simpson was an uncomplicated, popular Aberdeenshire boy who was already in the club's youth system when Ferguson arrived. He offered midfield strength, drive and goals. Cooper had been a stand-out in Aberdeen schools football, his height and mop of curly blond hair adding to the sense that he was something different. He had trained with Aberdeen since the age of ten and signed for them at fourteen. A bubbly, boyish enthusiasm and sense of fun made him hugely popular with the other players, and with Ferguson and his staff. Hewitt had also come through from the Aberdeen schools scene, as a quiet, introspective lad blessed with speed and finishing ability. Black had been raised near Glasgow until his family moved to the Highlands so his dad could get work in an oil fabrication yard. All four of them had emerged under Ferguson and been indoctrinated by him. They shared two key character traits: each had a ferocious will to win and was nerveless. That allowed them to handle big occasions and large intimidating crowds without missing a beat.

Still, after fifteen minutes of the cup final, John Greig might have thought his judgment had been vindicated. Cooper began brightly and was involved in the build-up as John MacDonald got space behind McLeish and McMaster and glanced a deft header past Leighton. Rangers had the opening goal. Was it going to happen again? This, though, was a different Aberdeen. They harried and chased Rangers, aggressively going for the ball when Greig's defenders tried to build moves from the back. They were behind for only seventeen minutes before equalising with a memorable Hampden goal. When Simpson's shot was charged down, the ball rolled just out of the penalty box to McLeish. The ball actually stopped dead on the grass just before he hit it, as if it had been placed for a free-kick, and McLeish curled a shot inside the far top corner. Three days earlier in a training session he had scored with an identical shot.

At half-time the manager delivered one of his greatest performances. One by one he looked his players in the eye as he scanned the dressing room. 'Do you really want to win this cup? You're not here just to make up the numbers. Can you do it in cup finals? That's the question. You've won the league, you've done well in European games, but can you win cup finals?' They were the words of a man who had been dropped from the 1965 cup final by Dunfermline despite being their top scorer, a man who had been made a scapegoat when Rangers were thrashed by Celtic in 1969, a manager who had already lost cup finals with Aberdeen in 1979 and 1980. 'Three cup final appearances – all lost – may be all right for some people but it doesn't satisfy me. You only remember winners, not runners-up. I want Aberdeen to be winning: league, cups, competitions of any kind. We must be winners.'

In the second half Aberdeen were far stronger. They made chances and missed them. There were no further goals but Rangers looked out on their feet by full time while Aberdeen had plenty more in the tank. Ferguson had put Bell on for McMaster after fifty-eight minutes, playing him on the left of midfield and switching Strachan to the right. The changes clicked and Bell ran Rangers ragged. McLeish said: 'This was a new breed of Aberdeen players. There was mental strength. Fergie gathered us round at full time and said stuff along the lines of "We'll no' bottle this one". He said, "Look. Look at them. They're all lying down getting rubs, they're knackered." We were clenching our fists.'

Three minutes into extra time Strachan lofted a ball over the Rangers defence and McGhee powered in to bury a downward header at the near post. At last Aberdeen were winning in a cup final. Ten minutes later, McGhee reached the by-line and threaded the ball into the empty goalmouth for Strachan. The *Sunday Post* said: 'Strachan had so much time he could have taken the bladder out of the ball before putting it over the line.' And that was not the end of it. When Neale Cooper burst through on Jim Stewart he got a lucky break. The Rangers goalkeeper's attempted clearance cannoned into his chest and broke back towards the open goal. A disbelieving Cooper thrashed it in and performed an impromptu celebration. 'All I could see were thousands of Rangers fans behind the goal. So I scored and did a forward roll. I still don't know where the idea for that came from. I don't know why I did it, but it was funny.'

STV commentator Jock Brown summed it up: 'Suddenly it's a rout.' The significance of the win was impossible to miss. At 4–1 Aberdeen had not just beaten one of the Old Firm in a cup final, they had embarrassed them. Two years had passed since they had won the league but Ferguson now had his crucial second trophy. RANGERS BOW TO THE NORTH, said the *Glasgow Herald*. In the *Daily Record* chief football writer Alex Cameron wrote that Aberdeen had 'annihilated' Rangers. 'Extra-time was like a wake for Rangers fans. They had gone ominously quiet, as if they knew what was coming.' John Greig praised those supporters for their loyalty but in truth many left long before the end. They recognised Aberdeen's supremacy, albeit reluctantly, but plenty had no desire to linger as witnesses to it. Greig was magnanimous: '[For] the previous two years we have been winners at Hampden and I'd like to think we can behave in defeat as we did in victory. I don't want to take any credit from Aberdeen: they are a very good side and were worthy winners.'

Winning a cup final in Glasgow was a hurdle Aberdeen had to clear. The way they did it was enormously significant. Hammering Rangers at Hampden was extraordinary. It meant the league title in 1980 could not be written off as some sort of freakish one-off; it had now been followed with the first cup win of the Ferguson era. McLeish believed: 'That was the game. I know winning the league was something to behold after twenty-five years but I think some people still looked on it as a flash-in-the-pan. Folk might have said, "They went twenty-five years without the league and now it's gonna be another twenty-five." Winning that Scottish Cup so soon after the championship really gave us confidence.'

Ferguson was shaping a new unit of winners. Six of the players used at Hampden had never been in a cup final before.

Jim Leighton was twenty-three, Dougie Bell twenty-two, Neil Simpson twenty, John Hewitt nineteen, Neale Cooper and Eric Black both eighteen. Ferguson had built exactly what he wanted: a side who were getting used to lifting trophies and with young players whose style and character he could shape and dictate. When he went downstairs to speak to the press he was jubilant. 'The average age of the side is only twenty-three. Who is to say what they can achieve?' For Simpson, Cooper, Hewitt and Black it was their first trophy. They had shown that they, too, could handle Glasgow. 'To go to Hampden and dominate an Old Firm team gives you reason to believe you have a decent team,' Ferguson said later. 'The players sprouted wings then.'

In the two seasons since winning the league Ferguson had challenged all his players, the young ones and the seniors, telling them to their faces that they might be 'a one-trophy team'. McMaster said: 'He was always challenging us. He was always saying, "Are youse happy with this, are youse in a wee comfort zone? Do you want to be watching *Coronation Street* on a Wednesday night instead of playing European football?"' None of them realised what was about to unfold at Aberdeen. They were heading into a campaign that would leave no time for Ena Sharples, Ken Barlow and Bet Lynch in the Rovers Return. They were about to launch a massive assault on Europe.

THIRTEEN

THE MARCH TO GOTHENBURG

The European Cup Winners' Cup is slowly being forgotten. The middle brother of Uefa's three club tournaments – lacking the prestige of the European Cup but enjoying greater status than the Uefa Cup – it was discontinued in 1999 and its significance has eroded steadily ever since. Yet when Barcelona reached the 1982 final 100,000 Catalans packed in to the Camp Nou to cheer a 2–1 win over Standard Liège. And the following season the tournament featured a number of European football's most famous clubs: Spain was represented by both Barcelona (as holders) and Real Madrid (as Spanish Cup winners); Italy sent Inter Milan, Germany Bayern Munich; the English representatives were Tottenham, and Paris Saint-Germain were there for France.

Aberdeen had played in the European Cup Winners' Cup four times without making an impression, though the same could be said of their past attempts in all of the European competitions. In their first European game in 1967 they had scored ten unanswered goals past KR Reykjavík at Pittodrie, but the adventure still ended in the next round. In the 1970s there were glamorous ties against Juventus, Borussia

Mönchengladbach and Spurs. They lost them all. In eleven previous European campaigns they had never beaten more than two opponents and never survived beyond Christmas. When Uefa introduced penalty shoot-outs to settle drawn ties, Aberdeen became the first team to lose one, against Honvéd. Of their domestic rivals, Celtic had won the European Cup in 1967 and reached the final three years later. Rangers had lifted the Cup Winners' Cup in 1972. Hibs and Dundee had both reached European Cup semi-finals in the 1950s and 1960s, respectively. Aberdeen, however, had no comparable European pedigree; beating Ipswich and running Hamburg close in 1981 was by far the best they had done.

Aberdeen were forced to take the scenic route at the start of the European Cup Winners' Cup in 1982–83. They were drawn to enter in a preliminary round and had to come through that to reach the competition proper. They were paired with the unknown Swiss club Sion. Ferguson was irritated that the fixture cut short the players' summer holidays: they were playing European football almost a month before the competition's first round. He entered his fifth season at Aberdeen without signing any reinforcements; he did not think he needed them. Sion turned up at Pittodrie and were torn apart, losing 7–0 to six different goalscorers. When Sion won the Swiss Cup they had taken 20,000 supporters to the final in Berne. Only 2,400 had the stomach for their home leg against Aberdeen, a comfortable 4–1 win for Ferguson's men. 'I don't think we have ever seen a better team at our ground,' said Sion manager Leon Walker.

Ferguson was a meticulous compiler of information on opponents. He watched Sion once himself and sent Archie Knox to see them before the first leg. He hated being surprised by opponents. Consequently Aberdeen's next opponents, Dinamo Tirana, made him nervous. Albania was a closed shop, a Stalinist dictatorship under Enver Hoxha, and Ferguson and his backroom staff were denied entry visas to watch Dinamo in advance. 'I must be honest and admit that I don't think we have played against a team during my time at Pittodrie when we knew so little about them,' he said. 'The unknown is always a problem. It leaves a funny and peculiar feeling that there may be something we don't know about that will surprise us.' Information was so scarce ahead of the first leg at Pittodrie that there was a blank space in the programme where the Dinamo Tirana squad should have been listed. There was little to soothe Ferguson or his team as they ended the game with a narrow 1–0 lead. Dinamo dug in, defended in depth and wasted time whenever they could. Ferguson looked across to the away dugout and saw all the Tirana coaches staring back and chanting 'Albania, Albania'. It had the ring of a threat.

The return game became a test of Aberdeen's nerve and strength of character. The Albanian state remained resolutely difficult to deal with. Aberdeen's secretary, Ian Taggart, was among those refused an entry visa. Only twenty-two were granted to the club. Stuart Kennedy remembered the trip as a prolonged endurance test: 'They're putting alarms off at one in the morning, they're giving you crap food, the bus is late for training. They're not helping you.' There were even rumours that there would be a coup while Aberdeen were in the country, though those proved unfounded. Almost 20,000 packed into Dinamo's ground in the stifling, humid heat of Tirana. The locals felt the first-leg deficit could easily be turned over. Shortly before kick-off Kennedy turned to Ferguson and asked him where the referee came from. 'I was always into referees because I used to think "wars". Who has his country been at war with? I'm thinking, "This guy will give us a good deal here, everyone likes us, British, Scottish, we'll get a couple of decisions, especially when we're against a German team." I'd think stuff like that before a game. In Tirana the boss says, "He comes from Hungary." And I'm thinking, "Hungary . . . Hungary . . . I can't think of a war with them." I says, "Dougie, Alex, Willie, Simmy, watch your tackling because this referee will give a penalty from anywhere within ten yards of the box, then he'll just get into his car and drive back to Hungary." Simmy says to me, "Where's Hungary from Albania, Stuarty?" Now that's not an easy question with twenty minutes to go . . . Then big Alex turns to me and says, "What about watching your own tackling?" I tell him, "I don't give fouls away, I've not given a foul away this season." That got their attention. "All season?" "Yep. Think about it as long as you like. I don't foul people, they foul me. I don't need to foul people like youse do."'

It was typical Kennedy patter, and Ferguson loved it. His comic boastfulness emboldened and cheered the other players. If you believed him, he had never committed a foul in his entire career and no winger had got the best of him. 'I'd tell them, "This guy won't last ninety minutes. It'll be the usual, he'll last sixty minutes. Has anyone lasted a whole game against me?" I'd say to the boys, "Spend your bonus now. The game hinges on me against this winger? Phone home, tell your wife to spend the money, this guy'll no' last ninety minutes." The young boys would be thinking to themselves, "This is great." Fergie's winking at me. Mind you, I've put myself on the chopping block by saying all this stuff. I still have to go out and handle this winger.' Tirana's winger was handled. In the end the most comfortable aspect of the trip was the game itself. Aberdeen were composed and in control as they saw out the goalless draw that eased them through.

The second round also sent them behind the Iron Curtain, this time to face Lech Poznań in Poland. Again they took a narrow first-leg lead from Pittodrie, after a game they had dominated but which only produced second-half goals from McGhee and Weir. Black had hit the woodwork twice and Strachan once. Poznań were not dead yet. Almost 30,000 Poles clearly thought the same as they turned up intent on intimidating the Scottish visitors. What they witnessed on 3 November 1982 was an Aberdeen team who were becoming increasingly sure of themselves in Europe. It was the Dons' twenty-second game in Uefa tournaments under Ferguson and they had lost only one of the last eleven. Again they were calm and authoritative. When Bell scored in the second half it sealed the 3–0 aggregate win that took them into the quarter-finals. Dundee United had also survived in the Uefa Cup, but Rangers had been knocked out of that competition after a 5–0 defeat by Cologne and Celtic had gone out of the European Cup against Real Sociedad. 'Once again the wise men from the East – Aberdeen and Dundee United – are left with the responsibility of keeping Scottish interest alive in Europe,' wrote Jim Reynolds in the *Glasgow Herald*. The coverage was very matter-of-fact. No one speculated in print that they could go much further in their tournaments.

European football had more time to breathe back in 1983. Four months passed before the Cup Winners' Cup resumed. The draw for the last eight took place on 10 December and nearly all the heavyweights had survived. Ferguson took a deep breath. 'We shall be in an exalted group of world renowned sides who have more European trophies between them than we've got tea cups in the guest room.' Aberdeen drew Bayern Munich. This time there was no sense of the unknown. Bayern were footballing aristocracy. Only seven months earlier they had reached another European Cup final, their fourth, before losing narrowly to Aston Villa. Crucially, no foreign side had beaten them at home in Europe. In a team of international-class players there were three truly outstanding talents: Karl-Heinz Rummenigge was the 1980 and 1981 European Footballer of the Year, an explosive striker with pace, strength and intelligence; the dynamic midfielder Paul Breitner had won a World Cup, European Championship, European Cup and seven league titles with Bayern and Real Madrid; and by the time Klaus Augenthaler's career was over the classy sweeper had won the World Cup and seven Bundesliga championships. With the luxury of ample preparation time, Ferguson's dossier on Bayern was thorough. He told the press he would settle for a 2–0 defeat in Munich, reckoning that could be recoverable at Pittodrie. Privately he fancied his team to do far better than that.

Rummenigge was the one player who made him anxious. It was not Ferguson's style to focus on an individual, but he repeatedly sidled up to Miller in training and told him to stay on his feet against the outstanding West German. 'Don't dive in. Don't commit.' Cooper was instructed to mark Breitner. Simpson and Bell had to close down and harass Bayern. The defensive unit of Miller, McLeish, Kennedy, Rougvie and goalkeeper Leighton were up against the best side Aberdeen had faced since Liverpool in 1980. There was no room for passengers; everyone would have to deliver one of the performances of their career. But the key duel would be Rummenigge versus Miller. Franz Beckenbauer's experience with Hamburg made him an obvious person for the media to ask about the Dons' prospects. He was in no doubt that Bayern would win comfortably in Munich: 'As soon as the Scots set foot from their own country they are worth only half as much.' He felt that even the Bielefeld team recently beaten 5–0 by Bayern were 'technically superior to Aberdeen'.

The Olympic Stadium's spidery, Bedouin tent of a roof undulated over a vast bowl of 74,000 seats and gave Bayern the most iconic stadium in Europe. Ferguson liked it. A running track circled the pitch, which meant the stands were far back from the touchlines. It felt open and airy, and that meant Aberdeen would be able to play with calm heads rather than with a noisy German crowd breathing down their necks. As it turned out, only around 35,000 Bayern fans turned up on 2 March. The 2,000 who travelled from Aberdeen made a loud presence of their own. Commuters on Munich's U-Bahn had been bemused to hear 'The Northern Lights of Old Aberdeen' belted out on the way to the stadium.

On the eve of the game Aberdeen had put on a harum-scarum training session on the Munich pitch. Usually Archie Knox led the sessions, but at the last minute Ferguson stepped in and said he would take over. 'Archie's nose was out of joint straight away,' recalled McGhee, laughing. 'He went in a huff. He stood at the side, looking at the stand, not even looking at the pitch, petted lip, pissed off!' The players were instructed to use one half of the pitch with a group in each of the four corners and another group in the middle. They were told to fire long balls back and forth from the corners to the middle, and to swap positions. It was chaos. McGhee went on: 'There was a hollow round the edge of the trackside and within ten minutes we're running out of balls because they're all going in there. Five people have been hit; I get smacked with a ball on the side of the heid. It was an absolute shambles. It was supposed to be a passing exercise and folk are going off with bloody noses and black eyes. To be honest it was hilarious.'

It was not a deliberate attempt to look poor in front of watching German eyes, it was the real thing. Yet twenty-four hours later the same chaotic group delivered the most professional and high-class display in Aberdeen's history. Even in Ferguson's time nothing matched the defensive excellence of the master class they produced that night in Munich. Leighton, Miller and McLeish delivered their finest hour. Kennedy and

Rougvie stepped up with massive performances at full-back and Cooper, Simpson and Bell were outstanding across the middle. Ferguson's tactics were followed to the letter. Aberdeen constantly closed down the Bayern players and forced them to turn and look in vain for another route of attack. They were frustrated into shooting from a distance and that was easy for Leighton. Cooper shackled Breitner and Rummenigge got nothing out of Miller. 'I think if Rummenigge goes up to the refreshment stand Willie Miller would be up his back after him,' said Archie Macpherson during his television commentary. Rummenigge had a header and then a shot saved by Leighton, but the only lasting impression he made was to knock out one of Miller's front teeth when he attempted an overhead kick. To his credit, Rummenigge tried to help Miller find the missing tooth on the pitch and later admitted that he had been impressed by 'the one who lost his teeth and shouted a lot'.

A storm of whistling and boos met the Bayern players at half-time and again at the end. But the Bayern fans recognised how strong Aberdeen had been and Bell was notably picked out for applause. McGhee said: 'The football we played that night was as good as we ever produced in Europe. It was sublime. We passed the ball the way you'd expect Bayern to pass it.' Beckenbauer was startled by the performance: 'I just could not believe that this was the same Aberdeen team who played against us in Hamburg. In a tactical sense they have developed so much in a short time.' Jupp Derwall, the West German national manager, heaped on more praise: 'Bayern are by far the best technical side in the Bundesliga but Aberdeen matched them all the way. I have never seen a better performance by a Scottish team on German soil – either at international or club level.' The great Breitner said: 'They paced themselves quite brilliantly against us in Munich. They were still running strongly at the end.' Bayern's general manager, Uli Hoeness, felt vindicated: 'When I went to Scotland to watch Aberdeen I was rightly quoted in saying they were a better side than Real Madrid, Inter Milan and Barcelona. I do not think anyone believed me. I do not think the Scottish people believed me.'

For the two weeks before the second leg Aberdeen was at fever pitch. The club's travel agent gambled that they would not only finish off Bayern but reach the final in Gothenburg. He took the risk of booking 1,600 hotel beds in Sweden. After the debacle of the Liverpool tickets sale, the club introduced a system which gave priority to season ticket holders and then those who had collected vouchers distributed at domestic games. When the initial deadline passed, secretary Taggart phoned every season ticket holder who had not asked for a Bayern Munich ticket. He did so as a courtesy in case they had missed the deadline by accident. It did not take him long: there were only four who had not responded. On the black market tickets with a cover price of £3 were being sold for £30. 'People were scrambling for anything they could get,' said Taggart. Pittodrie held 24,000 and would be bursting at its seams.

There were two domestic games between the first and second legs, against Kilmarnock and Partick Thistle, and the defence who had been so impeccable in Munich failed to keep a clean sheet in either. The team's focus was on the second leg. Bayern flew into Aberdeen the day before the match looking cool and composed. Reporters jostled around Hoeness and asked if he thought Bayern could get the scoring draw which would take them through on away goals. 'Draw? I'm very confident that we have a real chance of actually winning,' he said. Ferguson was wary, determined to strike a balance between confidence and realism. The job was only half done. 'I'm certainly not over-confident, but I'm not worried. I would much rather be in our position than theirs.'

What happened on 16 March 1983 was marketed years later by Aberdeen on a DVD called *Pittodrie's Greatest Night*. It tends to be recalled as a cacophony of hysteria and noise, but that was not entirely the case. After ten minutes Bayern were awarded a soft free kick. Breitner rolled it to Augenthaler in a pocket of space and he took a couple of touches before striking a shot which rose into Leighton's top corner. Bayern had their away goal. Pittodrie hushed. Several minutes later Jock Brown, STV's commentator, said: 'Really now you could hear a pin drop.' Bayern looked in control and Aberdeen were being closed down. Nothing was coming off until McLeish hit the face of the crossbar with a header. It gave them a lift, and the goal they needed arrived six minutes before half-time. A cross was going out of play until Black stretched and twisted his neck to nod the ball back into the goalmouth. Augenthaler blocked it but the ball ran loose and Simpson barged in to force it home.

It was a niggly match with lots of fouls and interruptions. Both teams gave the ball away and made unforced errors, especially Aberdeen. Bayern indulged in some mild time-wasting in the knowledge 1–1 was good enough for them to go through. The Aberdeen support was unsure of itself. Brown picked up on the mood again. 'Pittodrie's a very strange ground in that there are moments of complete silence despite a full house being inside the stadium.' With just under half an hour left a cross into the Aberdeen box was flicked on by Dieter Hoeness, Uli's brother, and headed back out by McLeish. The ball dropped just inside the box and Hans Pflügler connected with a volley which whistled past Leighton. There was an audible gasp from the stands and then a ripple of gracious applause. It was surely all over now. Ferguson admitted: 'My gut feeling told me we had had it. I had to do something, because you are not going to sit back and accept defeat.'

Ferguson's full-backs were struggling against the wingers Pflügler and Karl Del'Haye. Five minutes after Bayern's goal he took off Kennedy and put McMaster into midfield. Rougvie switched from left-back to right to deal with Pflügler and Cooper concentrated on Del'Haye. The changes settled Aberdeen at the back, but time was running out. With fifteen minutes left Ferguson made his final substitution: John Hewitt for Simpson. Within seconds of the change Aberdeen were awarded a free kick just outside the Bayern penalty area. Strachan was about to take it quickly but had second thoughts. McMaster stood just behind him. Strachan turned and spoke to him. McMaster was nicknamed 'Spammer' because he came from Greenock where the locals were teased for spending so much on their houses that they had only enough money left to eat spam. McMaster said: 'The wee man's exact words to me were, "We're fucking it up, Spammer."'

Ferguson and Knox had always encouraged the players to experiment with set pieces. McMaster and Strachan were left- and right-footed, respectively, and sometimes they would both run towards the ball as if they were taking it, and then stop as if they had misunderstood and got in each other's way. There would be some gesturing and arguing. At first the crowd would groan or even shout at them. All of it was pure theatre. The thinking was that the defenders would momentarily switch off, then suddenly the kick would be taken with little or no run-up and the ball whipped into the box where only the Aberdeen players were still primed. McMaster said: 'We did it umpteen times. We practised this free kick, arguing with each other, and it came off a couple of times in Scotland. Big Alex knew when he saw the pair of us doing our run against Bayern. So did Black and Hewitt. I knew Gordon would take it because it was on his side. It worked a dream. The whole stadium was saying, "What the hell are they doing?" The Germans couldn't believe it.' Strachan spun and sent in a perfect delivery, and McLeish rose for a header which beat Manfred Müller's diving attempt to claw the ball away.

The game was broadcast live across Scotland and what happened next was almost too quick for the STV cameraman. A replay of the goal was shown, then the broadcaster cut to a close-up of McLeish in midfield. In the footage his eyes are clearly following a long diagonal ball from left to right. What the cameras had missed was a glorious cross-field pass by McMaster. Suddenly the camera switches to show Black leaping to flash a header which Müller dives to push away only for Hewitt to rush in and knock back through his legs. Aberdeen had scored twice in forty-eight seconds. It was as if a power surge had shot through Pittodrie. For the first time in the entire tie Aberdeen were ahead. The remaining thirteen minutes were bedlam. The noise was deafening as whole blocks of supporters bounced and leapt, sensing that something extraordinary was unfolding. Miller said: 'The atmosphere was quite amazing considering it was all Aberdeen supporters. It was packed. They stuck with us at 2–1 down and when it turned in that two-minute spell they went over the top in a way that they wouldn't normally.' McMaster regards the end of the Bayern game as 'the best fifteen to twenty minutes of my life'. When the final whistle went at 3–2 it was pandemonium.

McGhee said: 'If you edited the goals out and watched the game, and asked someone who won, they'd say Bayern Munich every time. They had the possession and the technique. But we won. They would have looked at us and thought, "How the hell did we lose to them?" It was like a circus act. Smoke and mirrors.' Miller added: 'I don't think Bayern took it too well. You know how the Germans are, arrogant and confident.

They certainly didn't take the messed-up free kick well. They claimed it was a fluky goal. Little did they know . . . They expected to beat us. You could tell that from the way they walked on the pitch, the way they handled themselves. They were a bit like Ipswich, stunned that we could play that well and beat them. They didn't take it too graciously.'

Staff at the airport hotel where Bayern stayed after the match saw the Germans sitting in muted disbelief, bickering about the 'confused' free kick. More than thirty years later Rummenigge, by then chief executive of Bayern, could still instantly recall the Aberdeen games. 'It was a very, very big surprise for us and for the football world. The Aberdeen supporters pushed them like hell. They deserved it. They fought like hell, to the last second. That became typical of Alex Ferguson all the way through his football career. Alex was a very young guy. It was quite clear from the very beginning that it would be the start of a very successful story for him. My memory from 1983 was not so good but I always had a great respect for him.' Those number-one writers Ferguson affected to disdain had been at Pittodrie for the second leg. They were invited back to the ground the following afternoon when they hung on his every word as he reflected on the most startling result of his managerial career thus far. He insisted that the players take the plaudits. 'It will be to their eternal and undying credit how they salvaged what I thought was a lost cause and came out on top.'

The quarter-finals had been a riot of dragon-slaying: Bayern, Barcelona, Inter Milan and Paris Saint-Germain were all eliminated, leaving Real Madrid, Austria Vienna and Waterschei to join Aberdeen in the semi-finals. The Bayern games had been such an adrenalin rush that when the Dons were drawn against Waterschei, the Belgian club, the sense of anti-climax was palpable. No one had heard of the part-timers from Genk who had just knocked out Paris Saint-Germain. They had Dutch international Adrie van Kraay, who had won the Uefa Cup with PSV Eindhoven, Belgian internationals Eddy Voordeckers and Lei Clijsters, and Lárus Guðmundsson was a lively young Icelandic striker. But there was no way of dressing it up: there was no Rummenigge or Breitner in their ranks. Beating Bayern Munich instantly transformed the way the football world thought about the last British club left in any of the three European competitions. 'We wanted to avoid Aberdeen,' admitted Waterschei manager Ernst Künnecke. 'They deserve to be favourites for the cup. I'm a little bit afraid of their strength.'

After the emotional peak of the Bayern second leg Aberdeen lost three of their next four league games, a sequence which cost them the championship. It was the sort of run which often befalls a club distracted by Europe. Ferguson and the team were pent up, waiting to be unleashed on Waterschei, and it showed as soon as the first leg began on 6 April. It turned into a pounding. After four minutes Aberdeen were 2–0 up, and two goals in two minutes made it 4–0 in the second half. When hapless Waterschei pulled one back, Aberdeen added another for 5–1. The 700 Belgian fans in Pittodrie were shell-shocked. 'A quite magnificent display by Aberdeen,' said Alan Green at the end of his Radio 2 commentary. 'Britain's last representatives in European competition, so much hoped from them, so much expected from them, and they haven't let anybody down.'

Black, Simpson, Weir and McGhee (twice) had scored but the architect of the night was Bell. When Ferguson used Simpson and Cooper in central midfield there was no room for Bell's balance, individualism and dribbling runs. The hurly-burly of Scottish football did not suit him quite as much as Europe, where he was given more room and time to dictate the play. He had been wonderful in Germany and was hurt to be left out of the home game against Bayern Munich. Bell said: 'Fergie was on my case a bit because every time the team got beat I felt as if I was the scapegoat. I think it was because of the way I played, very individual. If that works, it's great. But if it doesn't come off . . . I was given man of the match in the 0–0 game in Munich and then he left me out of the second leg. I wasn't big-headed; I was quite shy. At Kilmarnock the weekend before Bayern at home I wasn't in the team or even on the bench. Then I was an unused sub at home against Bayern.'

Waterschei at home was Bell's finest hour. He ripped into them from the start, his first stylish run ending with an outside-of-the-boot pass across the goal which Black tapped into the net. Waterschei's resistance had lasted eighty-five seconds. Bell continued to run at them, teasing and tormenting, and set up the third for McGhee, too. The crowd enjoyed Bell's virtuoso display so much there were boos for Ferguson when he took him off in the closing stages. Miller said: 'Waterschei just couldn't handle Dougie Bell. They were like rabbits in the headlights. He tore them apart.' The instant aggression and pressing sent Watershei into a tailspin. They had wanted to ease themselves into the game but were blitzed. Aberdeen chased and harried them as soon as their defenders got the ball. Miller said: 'They couldn't cope with the style of play we put on that night. There wasn't any complacency from us, maybe the opposite. We'd done the hard bit in beating Bayern Munich, so there was no way we were going to let Waterschei take away the opportunity of playing in the final.'

Even Ferguson was stunned by the margin of victory. What might have been a tense second leg thirteen days later had been reduced to a little more than a working holiday. By the time they arrived in Belgium they had been through a Scottish Cup semi-final against Celtic which deteriorated into a brutal kicking match. They lost Bell to severely torn ankle ligaments and Cooper to concussion and a broken nose. Strachan and Black also had ankle injuries. Usually Ferguson would have seethed about his men being booted around Hampden, but Aberdeen had won the semi-final and their European lead was unassailable. Life was good. When the squad arrived at their Genk hotel Ferguson was cracking jokes: 'Some of you have a room with a view of the river. They didn't give me one just in case we lose the tie.'

Wasterschei managed one unanswered goal but not the four they needed to survive. Aberdeen's slightly makeshift team held out until the seventy-third minute when Voordeckers scored. McGhee said: 'No one gave a toss about that one; there was no way we were going to go out. No one gave a monkeys.' Ferguson offered the press pack a different version: 'The boys are all in there absolutely sick at having lost their unbeaten record in the tournament.' They had lost a lot more than that, though. One of the great pillars of Ferguson's team, one of his most trusted lieutenants for the past five years, finished the ninety minutes against Waterschei and never played football again. Stuart Kennedy had also been injured in the ugly game against Celtic three days earlier. His right knee had taken a knock and he told Ferguson he did not feel ready to play in Belgium. But Ferguson did not want to change his back four. Kennedy recalled: 'I said I wasn't 100 per cent fit and in front of everybody he said, "You could play this game with your suit on and not break sweat." My ego liked that, so I played.'

Fifteen minutes from the end his studs caught in the ground right at the outside lip of the playing surface and a Waterschei player fell on the injured right knee. Straight away Kennedy knew he was struggling. Aberdeen had used all their substitutes so he played on. 'I finished the game – your system's still warm so you can keep going – but I could hardly move my legs. Their guy attacked me down the wing a couple of times and I couldn't shut him down. I got a hairdryer for that. An injury that finished my career and he gives me a hairdryer for not shutting the guy down. I couldn't fucking run.'

Ferguson would later show Kennedy the compassion and sympathy the player richly deserved, but for the time being things were moving too fast for him to stand still. On the morning after the second leg he left his players and boarded a flight for his first look at Real Madrid.

FOURTEEN

REAL MADRID

Alex Ferguson was eighteen when he first set eyes on Real Madrid and the great Alfredo Di Stéfano. As a young player at Queen's Park he received the invaluable perk of a complimentary ticket for the schoolboys' enclosure at Hampden to witness one of football's classic games: Real Madrid versus Eintracht Frankfurt in the 1960 European Cup final. Just about every Scotsman of a certain age claims to have been one of the specks in the 127,000-strong ocean of heads as Real beat Eintracht 7–3 to win the cup for a fifth successive year. But Ferguson really was there that night, and watched in undisguised awe as Di Stéfano hit a hat-trick only to be outscored by Ferenc Puskás, who weighed in with Real's other four goals.

In 1960, Di Stéfano was a man at the peak of his powers. He was one of the four players who had appeared in all five previous finals for Real, as well as winning multiple league titles. Born in 1926 in Argentina, he had become an iconic, patriarchal presence at the club, renowned the world over as a phenomenal goalscorer with power, touch and vision. The consensus was that he was one of the greatest footballers to grace the game. Di Stéfano played a central role in the evolution of Real, dapper in their pristine white kit, into a club of vast international appeal. Though his glittering playing career ended in 1966, and he then served other clubs, his emotional bond was always with the Bernabéu.

Nearly quarter of a century later, the great man would be sitting in the opposite dugout to Ferguson for the final of the 1983 European Cup Winners' Cup in Gothenburg. By then, Di Stéfano had been a manager for sixteen years in Argentina and Spain. While Ferguson was still turning out for Falkirk in 1971, Di Stéfano was winning La Liga with Valencia. In 1980, he won the Cup Winners' Cup when Valencia beat Arsenal in a penalty shoot-out.

He had returned to Real at a particularly fallow period in their history. The club was still emerging from the era of Santiago Bernabéu, the formidable president whose reign lasted nearly quarter of a century. Since his death in 1978, aged eighty-two, Real's dominance had waned and they would fail to win the league for six years between 1980 and 1986. In the 1982–83 season when they faced Aberdeen, they played arch-rivals Barcelona in five league and cup games and could not win any of them. More to the point, the club who were *nonpareil* in the early years of European competition had not won a trophy on the continent since their sixth European Cup in 1966. Like the man he was about to come up against, Di Stéfano had something to prove.

When Ferguson took his seat in the Bernabéu for Real's semi-final against Austria Vienna on 20 April, he was able to watch his opponents with a cool, dispassionate eye. Real won that second leg 3–1 for a 5–3 aggregate but it had been level at 1–1 on the night with twenty minutes left. One more Austrian goal would have swung the tie on its head. Ferguson saw flaws and weaknesses in the Real team; they were certainly not as strong as Liverpool, Ipswich, Hamburg or Bayern Munich. Later that evening he phoned Dick Donald and said: 'I think we're a certainty.' The old chairman was not quite ready for that; he wanted Aberdeen to be heading for Sweden as underdogs. He told Ferguson firmly: 'For God's sake don't tell anybody.'

Someone else had reached pretty much the same conclusion, though. Vienna's coach Václav Halama walked into the Bernabéu press room after the match and refused to indulge the Madrid media with the platitudes they expected. 'I would like to wish Real Madrid well with the final,' said Halama. 'But I think Aberdeen will win. Player for player they are the better side, and much stronger.' What Ferguson did say publicly about Aberdeen's chances was less bullish than his private words to his chairman, but not by much. 'We have reached the final of this tournament by being brave and we'll have to be brave in Gothenburg. Remember, Celtic won the European Cup in Lisbon in 1967 by showing a bit of bravado all through that tournament and that is something my players must keep telling themselves. I haven't seen anything from Real Madrid yet which should frighten us.'

Aberdeen's directors knew they were in completely uncharted territory. History warned there was a danger the occasion would prove too big for the club, and not simply on the pitch. They needed help in the boardroom and employed a Glasgow-based sports promotion agency to handle the commercial side and create a revenue pool to maximise the players' earning potential. 'There was little to be done commercially because it was a short time-frame from semi-final to final,' said Alan Ferguson, the sports marketing expert who travelled to Sweden with the club. He was known as 'Fingers' because his connections were so broad he seemed to have a digit in every pie, and he had negotiated the Scotland players' off-field deals at the 1982 World Cup finals. But Aberdeen was different. 'Regrettably, the very annoying attitude of Corporate UK was that it was a wee team from a wee town up in the north of Scotland. Who cares? My view was it was a remarkable achievement and especially to be meeting Real Madrid managed by Di Stéfano. So we said, "Let's enjoy it."'

The window of opportunity was short, so planning had to be swift. The players recorded a surprisingly catchy cup final single, 'The European Song':

We're the Dons from Aberdeen
And we're the finest that's ever been
And we're gonna do it for you
And we're gonna do it for you
Mcleish and Miller and Strachann too
They'll lead us forward and take us through
And we're gonna do it
We're gonna do it
We're gonna do it for you!
We've taken our team into Europe
Yes we have, Ooooh yes we have
All the way every night and day, singing a European song
Ooooh
All the way every night and day, singing a European song
We can sing, and we can play
And Alex Ferguson, he knows the way
And we're gonna do it
We're gonna do it
We're gonna do it for you!

Suddenly the media was asked to pay for exclusive interviews and photographs. Ferguson had already announced that his senior players would be attending fewer social functions until after the game. Satisfying the sudden national and even international media interest in the club would take priority for the meantime. Gothenburg had the compelling narrative of a mighty footballing superpower being challenged by an unknown club from a supposed backwater. Ferguson knew the game tapped into the David versus Goliath archetype. 'There will be millions of people seeing Aberdeen for the first time through their televisions,' he said. 'Winning a major European trophy would give the club the kind of publicity money can't buy. And we want it.'

The weekend after the semi-finals Di Stéfano journeyed to Pittodrie and watched Aberdeen beat Celtic 1–0. After qualifying for the final, Aberdeen played five league games, winning four and drawing the other. The unbeaten run meant they could still win the league on the final day even though Dundee United and Celtic were first and second. Di Stéfano went home impressed by Aberdeen's aggression, strength, vigour and resilience. The old man was shrewd enough to recognise that Real Madrid would have a game on their hands. He described McGhee as 'a born fighter, unpolished, rough and tough, like the classic British tank'. His classy Dutch centre-half Johnny Metgod had watched them, too: 'Aberdeen are like lions. They hunt their opponents through every minute of a match. Strachan is the eyes of their team, their intelligence.'

At the same time, Ferguson and his players had cast a spell over Scotland. The *Daily Record* said: 'It's football's biggest night for years.' Aberdeen estimated there would be around 14,000 supporters making the 530-mile trip from north-east Scotland to south-west Sweden. Almost fifty flights were booked including some leaving from Inverness and the Scottish islands. Airport staff handed out rosettes and pennants and many of the flight crews wore red and white. The duty free shop sold a month's worth of alcohol in three days. Almost 500 supporters travelled on the passenger ferry *St Clair*, leaving Aberdeen at 1pm the day before the match and arriving in Gothenburg twenty-six hours later. Over the course of the round trip they put away 14,000 cans of lager. Several trawlers were commandeered by fans who worked in the fishing industry. Another couple of fans took a week to make the trip by motorbike. Aberdeen versus Real Madrid became one of Scotland's lead news items. In the north-east the *Press & Journal* and the *Evening Express*, the two local newspapers, devoted page after page to the final. Rougvie remembered: 'Aberdeen was bubbling. Everywhere you looked it was "Cup Winners' Cup". It was just a fantastic time for the whole city. We were verging on stardom. Everyone knew it had been eleven years since a Scottish team had won anything in Europe.'

For the official club flight the plane had its nose painted with the phrase 'The Flying Dons'. Everyone officially connected to the club, from reserves, ground staff, office workers, players' wives and girlfriends, to friends and family, was invited on one of the flights. Politicians and Scottish football figureheads were on the guest list; most importantly for Ferguson, it included his managerial mentor, Jock Stein. It was impossible to miss the sense of fun and anticipation. Willie Miller's wife, Claire, secretly organised a singing telegram girl who turned up at the airport departure lounge dressed in Aberdeen kit, stockings and suspenders to give the players a good luck message. Ferguson had given the wives and girlfriends a spoof itinerary: the plane would depart at 4am and they were to bring their own sleeping bag and a knife, fork and spoon as accommodation would be in dormitories. It was all part of a concerted attempt to do as much as possible to maintain a relaxed atmosphere around the players. If Ferguson, Archie Knox, Teddy Scott and the rest could remain calm, there was less likelihood of the team being spooked by the enormity of the occasion. But Ferguson also called the ladies in for a meeting and urged them to do whatever they could to ensure their men had no domestic stress to contend with until the final was out of the way. If any of them had any issues they were to come directly to him. And that included Dougie Bell's pregnant wife.

On the way to a game against Dundee the players were given their first sight of Real Madrid when Ferguson slipped a tape of their recent match against Barcelona into the bus's video machine. Rougvie said: 'It was so boring I fell asleep halfway through . . .' Ferguson might not have minded such a display of indifference from his men. He was wary of them being intimidated by the name, the very aura, of Real Madrid, and remained studiously unmoved when discussing them. Kennedy said: 'Usually you could be playing Inverurie Locos and he'd build them up as if they were Brazil. He never, ever said, "This is an easy game today, boys." But he had watched Real and – inwardly, without expressing it to us – I think he felt, "We'll win this game, we've got better players than them, and we've got more to offer." He got the balance right between letting you know you were up against a hard team, but always that he still felt you could beat them.'

There was no saturation coverage of overseas football in the 1980s. In fact full, live coverage was restricted to very few fixtures each season: Scotland international games, occasionally one of the club's major European ties, and the cup finals. Fans knew far more about Real Madrid's past than their present. The same knowledge deficit applied to the Aberdeen players. 'It wasn't as if Real Madrid were on the telly every week in those days,' said Eric Black. 'You didn't know their team inside out. You knew them as bigger names, but not as you would know Barcelona or Real Madrid these days. So we needed a little dossier. But with Fergie it was more about ensuring we didn't get overawed by the Real Madrid badge or the white strips. He didn't talk them up too much. They were good at this, they weren't so good at that, this is how we can win the game. He tried to calm it down a bit.'

McGhee was impressed by Ferguson's clear determination to puncture any sense of awe his players might have about Real Madrid. 'I don't ever remember having a feeling of even knowing who we were playing,' McGhee said. 'It was all played down. Maybe it was just me, but I'm sure he was aware and played a part in that. Fergie was incredible. If he watched a team like Argeș Pitești once he would come back and talk to you about their players as if they were as familiar as Ayr United or Partick Thistle. Maybe he was making it up, but he'd say, "The central midfielder's left-sided, he's weak on the turn," or whatever. We'd be going, "How the fuck does he know that?" It was as if he could say, "The striker's got five children but he's a bad father." Eh? What? He'd claim to know all that! But he genuinely was thorough. He always had the knowledge.'

Despite the lack of television coverage, there was no mystery about Real Madrid, nor any shortage of information on them. Their key men were German midfielder Uli Stielike, Spanish international left-back Antonio Camacho and forwards Juanito and Carlos Santillana. Stielike, compact and hard, had won multiple titles in Germany and Spain, lifted a Uefa Cup and faced Liverpool in a European Cup final. He had even played in the 1982 World Cup final. Juanito was a squat, dribbling winger, temperamental and exciting. Santillana was a Real veteran who led the line for the Spanish national team. Though not tall, he was good enough in the air to be a major threat to McLeish and Miller. It was not a vintage Real side, but not a weak one either. Losing to Valencia on the final day of the league season meant they finished one point behind champions Athletic Bilbao. Di Stéfano told the Spanish media that meant beating Aberdeen had become 'doubly important'. They lost fewer La Liga games than any other club that season, and they won fifteen of seventeen league matches at the Bernabéu. Just before the final they beat Gijón 6–0 in the first leg of the Copa del Rey semi-final. Ferguson was still sure he had the men to deal with them even if Kennedy was out and, cruelly, Bell had failed a fitness test two days before the flight to Sweden.

Ferguson's confidence was buoyed with the discovery that Real Madrid players were taking ten penalties each during their training session on the eve of the game. Real Madrid were evens with the bookmakers and Aberdeen 2–1, but Di Stéfano was evidently expecting a difficult night. The Dons manager did not carry the same sense of awe he had twenty-three years before. 'We are dealing with the present Real players, not the side who last won a European trophy seventeen years ago. Spanish football is not totally convincing at the highest levels. Real's back four are not as disciplined or as talented as Bayern Munich's. And Santillana as a penalty box player isn't in the same class as Rummenigge. I doubt if Stielike is fully fit after being out injured for five weeks. We will soon find out when he's had Neil Simpson breathing down on him. There is no sign of excitement [for me] although that will come. No doubt I'll be reaching for the Valium nearer the time.'

Real Madrid would be taking only around 3,000 supporters to the final but that number was misleading as any sign of indifference. Fans travelling in big numbers to away games has never been a part of Spanish football culture; support in Spain is intense and local. At the second leg of Real's semi-final against Austria Vienna 75,000 flooded into the Bernabéu to see if their club would get through to meet Aberdeen. And on the night of the final itself, the Plaza de Cibeles, the focal point of Madrid where Real fans congregate to celebrate their great triumphs, would be primed for a long-awaited party.

Venues for the European finals were not chosen years in advance back then, as they are now. It was only when the quarter-finalists were known that Uefa announced the showpiece would be in Gothenburg's Ullevi Stadium, a distinctive ground with an undulating, clam-like roof. With a capacity of 52,000, one potential problem was removed right away: there would be more than enough tickets to satisfy demand. The place was familiar to Ferguson. In 1964 he had played his first European game there when Dunfermline faced Örgryte in the Fairs Cup. Aberdeen had chosen to stay in a complex fifteen minutes' drive to the north of the city in the Fars Hatt Hotel. In 'Doric', the Aberdeenshire dialect, 'far's 'at' translates as 'where's that?' The coincidence amused Ferguson and his players. He felt the secluded location, beside a river and woodland, was more appropriate than the faded grandeur of the city-centre hotel Real Madrid had chosen.

On the day before the game Ferguson conducted the two biggest media events he had faced as a manager. The first was for the British journalists who had been invited out to Fars Hatt, the second for the international reporters among the 200 accredited by Uefa at the Ullevi. As well as doing the commercial deals, 'Fingers' was also on the payroll to act as Ferguson's media advisor for the final. As soon as Aberdeen beat Waterschei, Ferguson had phoned Stein and asked: 'What will be my biggest problem?' Stein, who had won the 1967 European Cup with Celtic and reached another final three years later, gave an unequivocal reply: 'Dealing with the media.' When the British reporters congregated at the team hotel, Ferguson was charm personified, even handing out the biscuits. Fingers recalled: 'The English lads didn't know him so they were thinking, "Gee, this guy really knows how to treat us." All the Scottish press corps are going, "Eh, what's going on? We don't recognise this guy." I travelled to Gothenburg believing I would be there to kinda cool him down a bit, with a word in the ear or an arm around the shoulder or whatever. But he was calm throughout the whole thing. It was like an out-of-body experience, as if he was looking down on the whole thing. There weren't a lot of the main English "number ones" because it was Aberdeen and it was Real Madrid, a foregone conclusion. Why go? But there were a few. They didn't know Alex at that point and they were taken aback by the courtesy they were shown.'

David Begg would go on to become a huge figure in Scottish football broadcasting, but in 1983 he was an inexperienced radio commentator unsure of how he would be treated by a manager with an intimidating reputation. 'The thing I remember most about Fergie was how he was around Gothenburg. He could not have been more helpful. Every single journalist was met, warm handshakes: "Come in boys, nice to see you, sit down." He was absolutely fantastic. He said to me, "Is there anything you need?" I said, "I'll tell you what would be handy, Alex: your team. And also if you would tell me how you think Real Madrid are going to play." He looked at me and said, "Come on then." We sat down for five minutes. He gave me his Aberdeen team, his tactics, how they were going to play, and I wrote it all down and had it for my notes. That was on the day before the game. He trusted me. It was fantastic. He did trust people.'

As far as Ferguson was concerned it was simple: injuries apart, his team had picked itself. Yet the openness was so unfamiliar that when he repeated it at the second press conference the Spanish media politely dismissed what they were being told. Even when Fingers distributed a printout of the Aberdeen team to all the reporters they did not believe it. 'There was a Spanish reporter who said, "I thank you for your courtesy in providing us with this information, but can you tell me when you are naming your real team." Fergie said, "I've got nothing to hide. This is the team who got us here and this is the team who are going to win it."' The printout even gave the foreign press a little line by including the Aberdeen captain's middle name: by coincidence he was William Ferguson Miller.

Ferguson's managerial career spanned thirty-nine years and 2,133 competitive games. Only once did he make an individual selection which was not intended to help his team win. The uncompromising pursuit of victories was not compatible with picking a player or a substitute who was literally useless to him. Occasionally he would bring a prominent favourite off the bench, maybe to involve him in a league or cup triumph, or to make a farewell to supporters before a planned departure. But these players were always still able to make some sort of contribution. There was only decision that was based entirely on sentiment. And he made it in Gothenburg.

Stuart Kennedy had been around the block often enough to know the trouble he was in after Waterschei. His knee was swollen, angry and painful. The only chance of getting any game time against Real Madrid would be if he could fool Ferguson: a few white lies and downplaying the seriousness of the injury which was causing him agony. It was his one hope. When Kennedy was in the Pittodrie treatment room in the weeks leading up to the final Ferguson would walk in and start asking some gentle questions. It became a game of cat-and-mouse. Ferguson knew his player might try it on because he was desperate to make the final. Kennedy knew a brilliant act of deception was required to outfox a streetwise manager he had served for five years. Ferguson would point at Kennedy's knee:

'That looks a bit swollen.'

'Whereabouts?'

'There, that big huge swollen bit there.'

'That? Oh no, not at all. That's fine.'

Kennedy missed all five games between the Waterschei second leg and Gothenburg. The days ticked by without real improvement. The time came to make a decision. Ferguson asked him to come out to the Pittodrie trackside and told him to make a run to the halfway line. Kennedy put on a 'can-do, no problem' face while trying to hide the numbing pain. When he got to the 18-yard area Ferguson shouted at him to stop and come back. Kennedy walked towards him. 'Fergie says, "How do you think that went?" I said, "It felt great." Actually it was a nightmare. He said, "Come here . . . in you come . . . closer . . . come right in here." It was almost a cuddle. He says into my ear, "I'm putting you on the bench, guaranteed, you can stop the charade with your knee. Right, how is it really?" I looked at him and said, "Where do you want to amputate?" Now that's man-management. There was nobody else there, just the two of us. I loved him saying that. He's ruthless, we know that. He doesn't make kind gestures in terms of team selections. But he showed a lot of compassion to me.'

Uefa struck sixteen winners' medals for the 1983 final. One for each of the team and the five named substitutes. At that time only two substitutions were allowed during a game and Ferguson figured that he had enough cover and versatility in the squad to sacrifice one of the five places and give it to a player who was unfit. He explained his thinking to his assistant Archie Knox. 'He just said to me, "Stuart deserves to be there, what's the point of putting a young boy on the bench who doesn't deserve to be there?" He took the risk of not needing to bring all the substitutes.' The decision was useful to Ferguson in another respect: it went down extremely well with the other Aberdeen players. Kennedy was one of the boys, extremely popular in the dressing room, and it was grotesquely unfair that he had been cut down by serious injury so close to the greatest occasion of his career. Putting him on the bench showed a different side to Ferguson. It was his thank you to Kennedy.

At one point Kennedy thought Ferguson's kindness might go even further. It has sometimes been suggested that he was on crutches on the Gothenburg bench, but with the aid of cortisone injections he was able to move freely and even run, almost to his usual full speed. Only quick twisting and turning was beyond him. 'I thought if we got two- or three–nil up he might put me on with five minutes to go, up front or something. Late in the game he sent me out to warm up. The fans are shouting, "On you go, Stuarty." I actually believed I was getting on! I'm saying to the fans, "I'm going on to sort this out," having a bit of craic with them. Then I get back to the dugout and he says, "Right, Johnny, get stripped." He was putting Hewitt on! I said, "Hey, I'm warmed up here," and he says, "I was just giving you a run in front of the fans, you stupid cunt." Ach, deep down I knew he couldn't put me on. When Johnny got the winner I said to him, "Not a bad substitution, boss."'

If he had been fit Kennedy would have started the final, probably at the expense of John McMaster. It has often been suggested that Dougie Bell might also have started had he been fit, possibly instead of Neale Cooper or Neil Simpson. But the muddy midfield would not have suited Bell's running with the ball even though Ferguson did tend to prefer him in the big games. What Ferguson could not do was have two injured players on the bench. The kindness shown to Kennedy was denied Bell. Ferguson took Bell aside to break the bad news. He told him he had decided Kennedy would have a place among the substitutes but he could not do anything for him. Bell offered to take painkillers for his damaged ankle, but Ferguson insisted he could not take the risk. Bell said: 'He told me Dunfermline had left him out when they won the Scottish Cup final, but I wasn't caring about that. I could see he was genuine, though. It wasn't bullshit. He wanted me to play.'

There were eleven games in the European run. Andy Watson appeared twice and Ian Angus once and both received medals as unused substitutes in the final. Reserve goalkeeper Bryan Gunn was awarded a medal without playing a single minute. Bell started eight of the games, was man of the match in Munich, and was the architect of the semi-final rout of Waterschei. He was a central figure in the campaign, but for 40 years he was the only 'Gothenburg great' not to have a medal to show for it. The injustice of that was a source of regret within the team. When Gordon Strachan wrote his autobiography in 1984 he said the likes of Gunn and Angus had nothing to feel guilty about, but 'they would be the first to agree that they made virtually no contribution to the victory and were less deserving of the award'. Bell recalled: 'After the game we went back to the hotel, the wives were there as well. Somebody, it might have been Archie Knox, read out the team that had played and said, "You will always be legends." I felt it a wee bit then. I always remember that. There was talk for years of them getting a medal for me and I've been to a few things half-expecting a medal, but it never came. Strachan put it in his book that Andy Watson offered me his, but I can't remember that. I wouldn't have taken it anyway. I'm just glad to be associated with it all. Every time Gothenburg comes up I get quite a lot of mentions, whether I was sub or not.'

Putting Kennedy on the bench showed a different side to Ferguson, at least for those outside Aberdeen who had him pigeonholed as a despotic sergeant-major. The simultaneous rise of Ferguson and Jim McLean at Dundee United led to them being bracketed as similarly intense and uncompromising figures, men who ruled by fear. In truth, Ferguson's management was more nuanced than that. McLean's temper was such that it could darken the whole of Tannadice and he kept his players at arm's length. Ferguson had a warmer relationship with his squad. He knew when to joke and join in the fun, using humour to relieve stress as they prepared for big matches. There was always plenty of laughter around Pittodrie. It was a crucial difference between the two managers and one vindicated by Aberdeen's superior record in cup finals.

The eve-of-final visit to the Ullevi served two purposes: the press conference and a late afternoon training session to allow the players to familiarise themselves with the surface and its surroundings. There was one additional little incident. Stein had told Ferguson that he should take a bottle of Johnnie Walker Black Label whisky and present it to Di Stéfano as a gift. That act entered Aberdeen folklore as a classic example of Ferguson's mind games; a gesture calculated to portray him and his club as grateful and awed to be in the presence of the mighty Di Stéfano and Real Madrid. McMaster remembered: 'He took Jock Stein to the ground. Fergie thought we would be in awe of Di Stéfano at training. But the boys didn't care, didn't even give him a look. The next minute all the Real Madrid boys are staring at Jock Stein. Fergie was miles ahead in his thinking.'

Back at Fars Hatt that night the players were divided into two teams for a quiz session. The contest became so engrossing they were still arguing over the outcome at breakfast next day. As an exercise in taking their minds off Real Madrid it worked brilliantly. Fingers had banned Ferguson from taking part on the grounds that he would be too competitive. Instead the manager agreed to act as referee. On that Tuesday, Ferguson also found time for a team talk. He warned that the ball would stick in the mud and any passes back to goalkeeper Leighton should be lifted slightly above the surface. Miller had looked at the Ullevi pitch and felt the grass was a little long for his liking. No one realised quite what a factor the weather, and the pitch, would become. It had rained on and off during the morning and early afternoon of Wednesday, 11 May, but around 3pm the sky over Gothenburg truly opened. Around 3,000 Aberdeen fans converged on a city-centre shopping mall, drawn initially to gain shelter and then by the word-of-mouth news that the European Cup Winners' Cup itself was temporarily on display in a jeweller's shop window.

Meanwhile, the Aberdeen players and management were taking their afternoon nap, unaware of the rain lashing down. Ferguson woke around 4.30pm, took a look out of the window and muttered, 'Oh, Christ.' A quagmire of a pitch would do nothing to help ball players like Strachan, Weir, Black and McMaster. Stein was on the team bus from Fars Hatt to the Ullevi. During the journey he turned to the players: 'Lads, I prayed for rain for you because I thought it would give you a better chance, but I think I've overdone it.' For a while there were fears that the game would not go ahead at all. Rumours spread about the need for a 24-hour postponement and they intensified when the deluge continued after the Ullevi's covers were taken off. Fingers said: 'The big issue was the weather. All this indecision, was the game on or off? If you're building up to a game and there's the prospect of it being off, and then it's on, that can play on your mind. It wasn't the best preparation.' Occasional thunder and lightning added to the drama but both teams wanted the game to go ahead. So, crucially, did Gianfranco Menegali, the Italian referee.

The occasion was too big for the rain to dampen the atmosphere. Fans stood in the Ullevi bowl and got soaked. It was cold, too, and plenty cursed themselves for not checking the weather forecasts and packing the right gear. But drink had fortified thousands of the Aberdeen supporters. Their excitement was palpable. The lightning was not the only electricity in the air. The team selection was already public knowledge: Leighton in goal, Rougvie, Miller, McLeish and McMaster across the back, Strachan, Simpson, Cooper and Weir in the middle, Black and McGhee up front. By kick-off the incessant rain meant their red shirts were dark with water. The strips stuck to their skin, their hair was plastered to their heads.

Ferguson thought Real Madrid would not vary their short passing game and would want Aberdeen to come on to them so they could counter-attack. He trusted his boys to cope. Aberdeen went for them from the start. When Strachan sent a cross to Black in the third minute the 19-year-old leapt to connect with a glorious volley only for it to smack off the crossbar. It served as a declaration of intent. When Strachan floated in a corner McLeish came powering in to connect with a header. A Real defender took a swipe at it and the loose ball broke for Black to pounce and sweep it across the goalkeeper into the net. Black said: 'The goal? It was just a reaction really. It just fell and I was first to react. I wish the earlier volley had gone in. Now that would have been remembered.' The goal was a move Aberdeen practised in training: an out-swinging corner, McLeish making a late run to smash it into the box, confusion with the chance of something breaking to Black or McGhee around the goalmouth. Real had been caught out by a set piece, just like Bayern.

And still it rained. There were pools of water around the edge of the pitch. When players ran into the corners water splashed up around their feet. Leighton tried to bounce the ball and it died on the ground. Unfortunately, it would be the team from rainy Scotland who fell foul of the conditions. McLeish undercooked a long pass back to Leighton which slowed in the mud and allowed Santillana to get there first. Leighton could only claw the striker's feet away to concede a clear penalty. McLeish was horrified at his mistake. 'Well, that's a shocker,' said Ian St John on the ITV commentary. It could have been worse. The rules had yet to be changed, otherwise Leighton might have been sent off automatically. Juanito sent him the wrong way from the spot. 1–1. Ferguson stared darkly at McLeish from the dugout. A few yards away, Di Stéfano smoked a cigarette.

Ferguson was relieved to reach half-time without further damage, not least because Real had followed the equaliser with their first spell of ascendancy. McLeish knew what was coming when they reached the dressing room. 'I came in and I thought,

"He's going to start." It's the European Cup Winners' Cup final. I'm highly strung as well. Then I'm giving it back to him. Archie's involved. I think he then realised he'd better back off. Let's just say he wasn't saying to me, "Alex, what were you thinking, my dear boy?"' The crucifixion of McLeish was abandoned. Ferguson had more important points to press home in the brief time available. He reprised a message he had used at half-time in the 1982 Scottish Cup final. Rougvie recalled: 'He said, "Do you want to win the cup? Are you feart to find out how really good you are? Get out there and do it."' Specifically he wanted the midfield to get closer to Stielike, who had surprised him by being more influential than he had expected for a player just back from injury. Crucially he told Weir and Strachan to push up and act more as wingers than deeper midfield men. McGhee and Black had been cut adrift and were taking some punishing treatment. They needed support.

Aberdeen had started the final brilliantly and then gone quiet. But in the second half they looked a different side. Weir and Strachan lit them up. Strachan almost scored a volley. Black forced a terrific save with a powerful downward header to the bottom corner. Then he put a far easier chance over the crossbar after Weir beat four Real defenders in a thrilling run. Aberdeen were getting closer. They even tried the messed-up free-kick routine a couple of times, though they came to nothing. Still the rain poured down, water collecting in the trophy itself as it stood unclaimed on an exposed table beside the pitch.

Tension steadily rose. Suddenly Di Stéfano and Knox were embroiled in a shouting match across the few yards between the dugouts. Knox said: 'It was a foul or something and he's gesticulating away. I'm wound up to the heavens. I'm across, shouting at him. It's Alfredo Di Stéfano and I'm saying, "Shut the fuck up, you." Even as I was saying it I'm thinking, "I remember watching you playing at Hampden, you're one of the greatest players there's ever been, and I'm telling you to shut the fuck up." We just got carried away with it all.' The pitch sapped the strength from the players' legs and Black and McGhee also had to contend with bruising attention from Real's back four. Black tired visibly. When he went up for yet another header he landed heavily and hurt his ankle. He hobbled on for a few more minutes but clearly needed to be substituted. After eighty-seven minutes his final was over and John Hewitt's was about to begin.

On the bench Hewitt was so cold he wore two Aberdeen tops and still had both on when he replaced Black. He struggled to pick up the pace of the game and irritated Ferguson by dropping too deep as he chased possession. The cameras caught Ferguson howling at him from the edge of the pitch: 'John . . . you fucking stay up!' In the twenty-second minute of extra-time, Hewitt was twenty yards inside the Aberdeen half when he started to make a run straight up the middle of the pitch. Real Madrid were attacking but Weir intercepted the ball when Juanito tried to go past him. Weir turned to give himself space in front of a Real player and then lofted the ball over another one to find McGhee up the left wing. Hewitt was still running. Real were stretched. A defender came over but did not do enough to close down McGhee before he hoisted a left-footed cross just over the head of Stielike and the hands of the diving goalkeeper. Augustín had hesitated for a fraction of a second before deciding to come for the ball, a fatal decision. No one had tracked Hewitt. The ball landed perfectly and he dived in to connect with a glancing header deep into the corner.

In that moment everything changed for him, forever. He had become the third and, for the time being, last man to score a Scottish club's winner in a European final. Only sixteen months earlier he had scored that 9.6 seconds goal on a January afternoon at Fir Park that started the Scottish Cup run and took Aberdeen into the European Cup Winners' Cup competition in the first place. Now he had popped up again to clinch their place in history. Hewitt's goals bookended a run which took Aberdeen past Motherwell, Celtic, Kilmarnock, St Mirren, Rangers, Sion, Dinamo Tirana, Lech Poznań, Bayern Munich, Waterschei and now Real Madrid.

When Aberdeen celebrated their centenary in 2003 permanent messages were engraved on concrete slabs in the shadow of Pittodrie's newest stand. Most were placed by supporters, but one stood out for its three-word message: 'I scored it.' Underneath was Hewitt's name. Hewitt stressed the club was responsible for the wording because he worried it made him look big-headed. But no one was in any doubt what 'it' was. That header, which left him landing on his hands and knees in a muddy goalmouth, transformed his life.

The move and the finish are still shown regularly, yet they are often misremembered. Weir eventually gave up correcting people who congratulated him for putting in the cross. The run and the delivery from the left wing looked like classic Weir, yet it was McGhee. 'It's amazing how many times I've been described as – or told I was – the guy who crossed for the winning goal in Gothenburg. I remember when I later worked at Celtic I went with Danny McGrain to present a trophy at a school in Glasgow. There were three or four hundred kids there. I was introduced as "The guy who played for a great Aberdeen team and who made the cross for a boy called John Hewitt to score the winning goal against the great Real Madrid". I just looked across the audience and thought, "Ach, I'll just milk it this time." Sometimes I let it go, other times I'll say, "You know what, you're wrong, it wasn't me."'

The final was over. There was one late scare when Real Madrid took a free kick just outside the Aberdeen area. The players in the defensive wall heard Weir saying, 'Please, God, don't let them score,' before the kick fizzed inches wide. The full-time whistle sparked mayhem. Aberdeen fans leapt and surged forward, not caring about the risk of hurting themselves on the wet and slippery terracing. Those on the bench exploded out of the dugout: Ferguson, Knox, Teddy Scott, Black, the unused substitutes, the doctor and the physio, they all ran to the pitch. As they did so, Ferguson cut across the big reserve goalkeeper, Bryan Gunn, who accidentally clipped the manager's heels. Ferguson went sprawling. Gunn said: 'Everyone else ran over the top of him. I was in the middle of the pitch looking for Johnny Hewitt and celebrating with the rest of the lads. I have this vision of the boss running towards me with this red ash from the track streaming down his face and over his Adidas coat. I have a memory of Alex doing his first interview with this red ash and water coming out of his hair.'

Ferguson was delirious. Archie Macpherson's job was to grab him for an immediate BBC interview: 'He was incoherent. I was the first to hug him coming off the pitch. All you can do is take what he babbles. What he'd done was a phenomenal achievement. Why? Because he was a Glasgow man. He exported the street fighting qualities of Glasgow into this prissy atmosphere up there where Aberdeen had lovely managers but they didn't know how to win.'

As supporters chanted 'Fergie, Fergie' he darted between one player and the next, not sure who to celebrate with first, reacting as he had when the league was won in 1980. McLeish's head was still a mess because of that first-half pass back, and he was struggling to put it in perspective. 'It ate me up. I was thinking, "Nobody will be focusing on us winning the cup, it'll be all about my mistake." You start to magnify things in your head. If we'd lost that could have affected my career because it was a mistake at the highest level. I was the last player in the shower after the game, still feeling sorry for myself. I was cuddling the boys and so excited but in my head

The revolution begins: a thirty-six-year-old Alex Ferguson stands front and centre before the 1978-79 Aberdeen squad at Pittodrie. *Mirrorpix*

The twin pillars of the Aberdeen board: chairman Dick Donald (left) and vice-chairman Chris Anderson (right) flank Ferguson in 1980. *SNS Group*

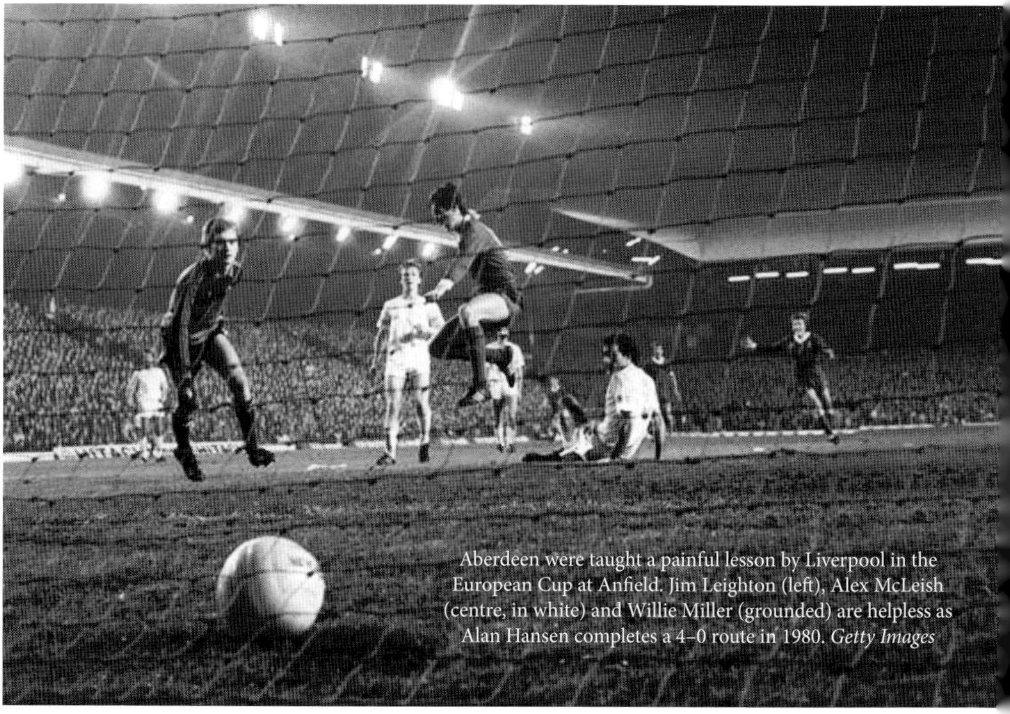

Aberdeen were taught a painful lesson by Liverpool in the European Cup at Anfield. Jim Leighton (left), Alex McLeish (centre, in white) and Willie Miller (grounded) are helpless as Alan Hansen completes a 4–0 route in 1980. *Getty Images*

Two Glasgow hard men show their emotions moments after Aberdeen win the league at Easter Road in 1980: Miller and Ferguson. *Eric McCowat Photo Archives*

Champion! Ferguson displays the 1979-80 Scottish league trophy during an open-top bus tour of Aberdeen. *Mirrorpix*

Gordon Strachan, Neale Cooper, Mark McGhee and Alex McLeish were cornerstones of the Ferguson era. *Mirrorpix*

Ipswich manager Bobby Robson (centre) upset Aberdeen fans and the Scottish press with provocative comments before a 1981 UEFA Cup tie, but he remained a respected friend and ally to Ferguson. *Getty Images*

Real Madrid's legendary coach, Alfredo Di Stéfano, was wrong-footed when Ferguson presented him with a bottle of whisky. *Eric McCowar Photo Archives*

That's number one! Eric Black scores the opening goal against Real Madrid in the 1983 European Cup Winners' Cup final. *Getty Images*

John Hewitt celebrates as he beats Real Madrid's goalkeeper Agustin to score the winning goal in extra-time. *Getty Images*

The on-field leader and icon, captain Willie Miller with the European Cup Winners' Cup. *Eric McCowat Photo Archives*

The 'bad cop-bad cop' combination: Ferguson and assistant manager Archie Knox (right) celebrate at full time in Gothenburg. *Alamy*

Ferguson's trusted aides: Knox (left), trainer Teddy Scott (centre) and chairman Dick Donald (peering over his shoulder) on the jubilant return flight from Gothenburg. *Mirrorpix*

Ferguson felt that Aberdeen touched true greatness when winger Peter Weir was on form: he was the perfect balance of pace, strength and skill. *Getty Images*

The ultimate Aberdeen team? The line-up for Gothenburg and the 1983 Scottish Cup final (from left to right): Ferguson, Willie Miller, Jim Leighton, John McMaster, Mark McGhee, Gordon Strachan, Eric Black, Neil Simpson, Doug Rougvie, Peter Weir, Neale Cooper, Alex McLeish, John Hewitt, Andy Watson. *Colorsport*

Aberdeen-Rangers became the ugliest fixture in Scottish football in the 1980s. Referee George Smith hauls Ally McCoist to him, with Stewart McKimmie, Stuart Munro and Brian Mitchell nearby, during the most ill-disciplined match of all, at Ibrox in 1985. *Bob Thomas Sports Photography*

Mentor, inspiration, confidant: Jock Stein hand-picked Ferguson as his assistant manager for eight Scotland games over thirteen months, from 1984 to Big Jock's death in 1985. *Getty Images*

Feeling the heat: Ferguson was Scotland's manager and Graeme Souness his captain at the 1986 World Cup finals in Mexico. They were about to clash as the rival bosses of Aberdeen and Rangers.

Heading off into the sunset. Ferguson grips the last trophy he won north of the border, the Scottish Cup, in 1986. *Eric McCowat Photo Archives*

Above and below: Ferguson returns to Pittodrie in 2022 to unveil a statue cast in his honour. *Alamy*

I'm still thinking, "What a mistake." I cared. Fergie came into the shower, his suit soaked, and said, "I'm proud of you. A lot of guys would have crumbled but you stayed strong."'

Real Madrid were gracious losers. The beaten Di Stéfano delivered a classy quote which Pittodrie still cherishes: 'Aberdeen have what money can't buy: a soul, a team spirit built in a family tradition.' Early in 2014, having taken a coaching job with Colorado Rapids in the United States, Real Madrid's centre-half in Gothenburg, Johnny Metgod, cast his mind all the way back to 1983. Metgod's distinguished career included spells with Nottingham Forest, Tottenham, Feyenoord and, of course, Real Madrid. 'If you play for a club like Madrid the only thing that counts is winning,' he said. 'To say that people were disappointed in 1983 is an understatement. What do I remember? It was pissing down. Strachan did me a couple of times. He went past me as if I wasn't on the pitch. It was sort of the start of Alex Ferguson as a manager, but for me it wasn't about Ferguson that night, it was more about McLeish and Miller and Black and McGhee and Strachan. The emphasis wasn't on the manager. He was young and upcoming. Real weren't complacent. Absolutely not. Any team who reaches a final hasn't done it by being lucky. Aberdeen had something. Players like Doug Rougvie, Alex McLeish and Willie Miller typified them. They were just a really good team who fought for every yard on the pitch. As a reasonably smaller club in Europe they were in a final against Real Madrid and they beat them. I don't think it can get any sweeter if you're an Aberdeen fan.'

The euphoria and chaos continued. Some of the players went to find their family and friends, others headed to the Real Madrid dressing room to swap shirts. Weir went in and found the right-back he had tormented, Juan José, in tears. McGhee was derailed by press interviews. 'By the time I got back there was hardly anyone left in the dressing room. All I could hear was Archie Knox singing at the top of his voice, "What becomes of the broken-hearted? Paid a penny and only farted." Totally random! He was just happy, just letting it out.' At a celebration party back at Fars Hatt the drink and speeches flowed. Ferguson made a point of thanking the wives and girlfriends for playing a huge role. The boozing continued long into the night and there was more of it when the cup was filled with champagne and passed around on the flight home the following afternoon.

The Granite City came to a standstill. An open-top bus carried the team and the cup from the airport to Pittodrie. An estimated 100,000 lined the streets, especially the city's grand Union Street, with a further 20,000 waiting at the stadium. It took the team two hours and forty minutes to get from the runway to Pittodrie. The city had never seen anything like it. There was red and white everywhere. The local authority refused to close the schools early but most of the kids skipped classes anyway to stand with their pals or their mums and dads. The bus inched its way through the city, through the beaming, cheering crowds. Players waved, held the cup aloft and pointed to familiar faces on the streets. Supporters had started flooding into Pittodrie from 2pm. It was three-and-a-half hours later before the team arrived. Ground staff tried to keep younger fans off the pitch but they kept vaulting the barriers before being herded back. Some kissed the centre circle. When Miller emerged with the cup he and the other players were engulfed. 'It was like trying to keep quicksilver under control,' said Grampian Police chief superintendent John Gordon, who was in charge of controlling the crowds. 'They were here, there and everywhere.' The players did laps of honour, each taking their turn with the cup. They posed for photographs and hugged fans, staff and each other. The celebrations went on and on. At last, finally satisfied, the numbers began to thin. The players began to leave, each with family and friends. They were absolutely drained.

After nearly twenty-four hours of backslapping, partying and general hysteria, a weary John Hewitt eventually reached home. He checked his video recorder and discovered it had stopped taping after the first ninety minutes with the score at 1–1.

It was a local triumph but one which registered on a national, even international level. In Glasgow the city's *Evening Times* carried an editorial in its news pages: 'We really are the greatest. Aberdeen proved it again last night when they slaughtered the pride of Europe Real Madrid and claimed the Cup Winners' Cup for Scotland. The football was superb and so were the fans. We were all Aberdonians.' Uefa had sold television rights for the final to sixty-eight countries and the estimated audience was 200 million. Ferguson had made his first impression on an international stage. 'Ferguson is a winner,' wrote Alex Cameron in the *Daily Record*. 'His only defeat of the European tie was by his wife. He lost a bet with her on the game and it will cost him a £3,000 fur coat.' A motion was tabled in the House of Commons congratulating the club. Messages arrived from the president of Bayern Munich, Liverpool manager Bob Paisley and other football figures. The Queen Mother, whose Birkhall estate south-east of Aberdeen was in natural Dons-supporting territory, sent a telegram: 'I was delighted to learn of Aberdeen's splendid victory in the European Cup Winners' Cup and I send my warmest congratulations to all concerned. Elizabeth R.' The *Press & Journal* reported that Prime Minister Margaret Thatcher sent 'congratulations and well done'. On BBC *Breakfast Time* the morning after the game, presenter Selina Scott, who had begun her broadcasting career in the north-east, wore an Aberdeen scarf.

In Sweden the biggest-selling morning newspaper summed up the way everyone felt. On 12 May 1983, the headline in *Aftonbladet* said: A NEW TEAM IS BORN IN EUROPE.

FIFTEEN

THE HAIRDRYER AND THE BASEBALL BAT

For ten days after Gothenburg there was unprecedented attention and hubbub around Pittodrie. Aberdeen still had the chance of pulling off the club's first league and cup double. Having drunk long into the early hours of Thursday, with a few top-ups during the flight home, it was a contented but delicate group of players who took on Hibs that Saturday afternoon. Aberdeen were third going into the final day and they had to win, with leaders Dundee United losing and Celtic dropping a point, for the dream to be realised. 'I really believe Dundee United will win the title,' Ferguson told the newspapers. 'But we will be much more relaxed than United or Celtic. We have done our week's work by winning in Gothenburg.'

The Hibs players lined up to applaud the heroes on to the pitch. Adrenalin carried Aberdeen to a 5–0 rout but a bigger story unfolded sixty-six miles south, where Dundee United secured the victory they needed to claim their first league title. It was the week when the 'New Firm' really arrived. A European trophy and a championship were the greatest achievements in Aberdeen and Dundee United's histories and, four decades later, they remain so. For Ferguson, if the championship was not to go to Aberdeen, he was pleased that it went to Jim McLean. He felt a symbiotic relationship between the clubs and saw United's triumph as helpful in suppressing the Old Firm.

Ten days after Gothenburg, the 1983 Scottish Cup final threw Aberdeen and Rangers together yet again, but now the landscape had changed. No one questioned the temperament or 'bottle' of Ferguson's team this time. The Rangers striker Sandy Clark said in a match programme that Aberdeen still had 'something to prove', but this was wishful thinking. For the first time Aberdeen took on one of the Old Firm at Hampden as the bookmakers' clear favourites. Close to 30,000 descended on Glasgow to roar them on. 'The whole of the north-east is coming to support us,' said Ferguson. The final was Rangers' last chance to salvage something from a dreary season. They had finished eighteen points behind the champions and been beaten by Celtic in the League Cup final. In the Uefa Cup they had lost 5–0 to Cologne. Manager Greig was under growing pressure after five bleak seasons. 'I have never wanted to win a match so much,' he said ahead of the cup final. 'Underdogs? That's a laugh. Well, if people want to think that, let them.'

Hampden was Aberdeen's sixtieth fixture of the season. They had played thirty-six league matches, eight League Cup ties, eleven European games and four rounds of the Scottish Cup. Miller, Strachan, McLeish and Leighton had barely had a break since the previous summer's World Cup finals in Spain. Even during the domestic season they had continued to play for Scotland. Gothenburg had been the team's physical and emotional peak, but Hampden demanded that they crank themselves up one more time. They were more vulnerable than they seemed.

Rangers delivered a proud and eager display. Their midfielder, Jim Bett, was excellent and almost scored with a long-range shot which Leighton somehow pushed over the crossbar. Billy Davies had the ball in the net for Rangers but was ruled offside. The game stayed goalless over 90 minutes and then deep into extra time. Aberdeen had been flat and one-paced but four minutes from the end, when the game seemed bound for a replay, they scored. Rangers gave the ball away in midfield and as Aberdeen flooded forward McGhee's cross spun up off a defender for Black to leap and head it into the corner. Aberdeen became the third team in the twentieth century, after Rangers and Celtic, to retain the Scottish Cup. They had won two trophies in a season for the first time in their history. What followed was all the more remarkable.

Ferguson had torn into Leighton on the pitch between the end of the ninety minutes and the start of extra time, telling him he was 'Rangers' best fucking player'. In fact the goalkeeper had made important saves from Bett and John MacDonald and he was not slow to put Ferguson straight. The exchange was merely the first spit of lava ahead of the volcanic eruption which came after the cup was won. On-the-pitch interviews with managers who have just won a trophy are easy. The beaming boss is asked to describe how happy he is or to praise the wonderful fans. There has never been another interview like the one Ferguson delivered that day. And he did it all more than once, not only to STV and the BBC, but in another version in the Hampden press room for the newspaper men. When it was STV's turn the camera fixed on his face. He was visibly seething and bulldozed over the reporter's questions. 'We're the luckiest team in the world,' he said with a face like thunder. 'It was a disgrace of a performance. Miller and McLeish won the cup for Aberdeen. Miller and McLeish played Rangers themselves. A disgrace of a performance. I'm no' carin' – winning cups disnae matter – our standards have been set long ago and we're no' gonnae accept that from any Aberdeen team. No way can we take any glory from that.' Archie Macpherson received a similar outburst for BBC viewers. 'He went mental. His first answer was, "That was a disgrace." I thought he was talking about Rangers. He fulminated. "How could they play like that?" Suddenly I realised he was talking about the team who had won the Cup Winners' Cup and now beaten their bitter rivals. I didn't get it. I still don't get it.'

The players returned to the dressing room with the cup, unaware of what was about to hit them. When Ferguson walked in they were told, 'Sit on your arses,' and ordered to listen to what he had to say. Weir said: 'He started shouted and bawling. We were looking at each other going, "Is this a wind-up?"' In the past eight weeks they had overcome Bayern Munich, strolled through a European semi-final, beaten Real Madrid, taken the league title race to the final day of the season and beaten Celtic and Rangers at Hampden to win the cup. Neale Cooper kept looking at the trophy sitting in the middle of the room. 'I turned to Johnny Hewitt and quietly said, "Did we just win that?" It was brutal. He hammered us.' When Dick Donald walked in with bottles of champagne Ferguson told him there was no need.

Managers often give more measured interviews to the newspaper journalists than to the cameras. In those precious few minutes between the dugout and the press room they cool off, step back, take control. That day Ferguson's line barely wavered. He was asked why Aberdeen had been below par. 'You'd need to open up their heads and look into their minds to find out. The team looked tired, dead. There was no spark or movement about them. It was all square passing stuff. Nothing football. The only excuse I can make is that they looked knackered, as if they need a holiday. But I'm still not prepared to accept it. If Aberdeen players think I will accept that standard of performance I will be looking for new players next season.' When he left the press room the reporters looked at each other in disbelief. He had just filled their front pages, let alone the back. But he had also crossed a line. The *Sunday Mail* wrote: 'Plain Lucky! Boss puts the boot in. Aberdeen manager Alex Ferguson launched an amazing verbal assault on his players yesterday.' Under the headline WHAT'S THE POINT? chief sportswriter Allan Herron had quickly penned a critical comment piece. 'I am astounded that Fergie should blast his players publicly after winning the Scottish Cup at Hampden. What does it achieve?'

On the evening of the final the team was driven to a celebration party and overnight stay in St Andrews but the mood was sombre and strained. Ferguson had made the biggest misjudgment of his Aberdeen career. He had publicly criticised the players who had delivered so much, spoiling what should have been one of the happiest nights of their year. They could not understand his behaviour and for the first time since his early days at Pittodrie there was real tension between team and manager. Worse, it was shared by even his most loyal lieutenants. Strachan was so fed up that he and his wife walked out of the 'party' and drove off to visit his parents. Some players joked that if Miller and McLeish had won the final on their own the club could dispense with a bus for the next day's victory tour through Aberdeen – a tandem would suffice. The wisecracks were for their ears only; they were not for Ferguson's.

While the Aberdeen players were going through the charade of 'celebrating' their cup win, Alan 'Fingers' Ferguson was receiving calls from some of the newspaper men telling him what had happened after the match. 'He's done them in,' they told him. The following morning he rose early to get the Sunday papers and saw the negative headlines, reading criticism where there should have been adulation. 'I phoned him at St Andrews and said, "What have you done?" He goes, "What are they saying?" "They're saying you've done your team in." You know the boys left their legs in Gothenburg. I know you want to win in style but the records show they won two cups in ten days.' By then Ferguson had already reached the same conclusion as the press. After breakfast he gathered the players together in the hotel. He stood in front of them and apologised. The Monday newspapers happily relayed his contrition. 'I asked the players to understand that the comments were made at a vulnerable time. I'm tired and in need of a holiday and I haven't slept properly since coming back from Gothenburg. I feel terrible about the criticism of the players. I am not very proud of myself when I look at the coverage we got on television and in the Sunday papers. It happened because managers – particularly me – are vulnerable immediately after a game. Sheer courage won us the trophy. On reflection, I could see that the team had hit its peak in Sweden. That should have been the finale to the season.'

The apology was grudgingly accepted but the damage was done. For many of the players, the episode continues to rankle. Even those whose allegiance to him is beyond question, and whose respect borders on reverence, have struggled to disguise the hurt they felt. Peter Weir said: 'That is one of the worst memories. As much as I loved Alex Ferguson and all the things he did for the club, he was totally wrong there. No one could believe the great man had done that. The next day he apologised before taking the cup around Aberdeen. But we couldn't really forgive him. Even taking the cup around Aberdeen – which were always big days, the people turned up in their thousands – inside it hurt us guys, it really did.' Others were more sanguine, though, seeing in his outburst a kernel of truth. The two men exempt from his criticism, Miller and McLeish, have always credited Ferguson for swiftly apologising to the team. Miller, in particular, remembered the episode with mild amusement: 'I thought he was spot on, to be honest.' McGhee was similarly unperturbed: 'I don't remember it really hurting me. Looking back on it, it was another great Aberdeen moment. Hilarious. Wee Gordy stomped off out of the party! Big Alex and Willie were perfectly fine! I wasn't offended at all. We were shit in that final.'

In the two autobiographies which cover his time at Aberdeen Ferguson wrote briefly of his regret over what happened without explaining quite what had made him so angry. One of the beaten Rangers players that day, Davie McKinnon, suspected it might have been triggered by the Aberdeen players' reaction at the final whistle: 'Their players were saying to us, "The better team lost," and "You didn't deserve to get beaten," . . . until Alex Ferguson went out on the pitch. I don't know if he was too enamoured with that sort of attitude from his players. Maybe he saw it as a sign of weakness.' McKinnon's theory gains some credibility from the observation that during the game and extra time Ferguson behaved quite normally in the dugout. Assistant Archie Knox said: 'I had no idea what was coming. He was fine on the bench. There was nothing like that, absolutely nothing.'

In the years that followed, Ferguson never succumbed to another public outburst as ferocious as the one unleashed at Hampden in 1983. But two traits would remain constant: his angry assertion of control and his unpredictability. The players became used to coming in at half-time or after a match believing they had played well, only to be slaughtered by him. Or feeling they had played badly only to be overlooked, or even praised. What later came to be known as the 'hairdryer' – the loud, expletive-laden, nose-to-nose vilification of some unfortunate player at Manchester United – was no doubt a fearsome experience, but for those who remember Ferguson at Aberdeen the fury of its prototype was of a far greater magnitude. Stuart Kennedy said: 'It wasn't a "hairdryer" when he was thirty-six or thirty-seven years old. It was a blast furnace. Brutal. A total examination of an individual's failings – according to Alex Ferguson – delivered in front of his team-mates. Over the years it reduced to the level of a hairdryer.'

Hampden 1983 was different only in that the evisceration of the players was delivered in public, covering almost all of them, and came after a major victory. Otherwise the intensity and the anger were familiar. Being an Aberdeen player under Ferguson was the equivalent of occupying a place on a fairground's moving shooting gallery: it was only a matter of time before everyone passed into the crosshairs and took a hit. Players became experts in the treatment. Those delivered at half-time were preferable to the ones at full time because at least they were guaranteed to end quite swiftly. Those after a game could last far, far longer. One secret was not to catch his eye when returning to the dressing room. Sometimes that was all it took to become the victim. Ferguson would stand at the door eyeing them all as they came in.

Anything could set him off. Once, during the players' routine pre-match lunch in an Aberdeen hotel, McLeish walked in and from across the room told McMaster that his wife wanted him to drop off the pram for their baby. McMaster was aware that Ferguson and Knox's eyes were burning into him. He remembered: 'I had a nightmare in the first half that day. At half-time Fergie says, "Spammer, you just sit on your arse, you're not going out again. Fucking prams. That's all you have in your heid. You're too much of a family man, ya cunt."' Black, then just nineteen, received an angry mouthful after scoring a hat-trick against Celtic at Parkhead, a feat no player equalled until Sparta Prague's Lukas Julis in 2020. Black said: 'It was frightening, embarrassing, uncomfortable, all of those things. Your fellow players are watching. We always knew somebody was going to get it. You just had to look at your boots and hope it wouldn't be you.' What had he done wrong? That was never made clear. In all probability the tirade was simply an act calculated to ensure he would not let his prodigious talent go to his head.

Dougie Bell made his debut in a 1979 friendly against the Tottenham midfield of Glenn Hoddle, Steve Perryman, Ossie Ardiles and Ricky Villa. 'I thought I'd done okay. After the game he showed me the video – I'd never seen myself on video before – and he slaughtered me. "Look. Where the fuck are you? What are you doing up there?"' Defender Tommy McQueen similarly had every aspect of one performance stripped down to the bone: 'He said, "See you . . . I don't know what it was you did out there. You didn't run with the ball, you didn't pass the ball, you couldn't control the ball. In fact, you're a non-descript." I actually felt like laughing but I knew he'd kill me.' Before one game in foul weather at Morton, Ferguson asked if any of the team wanted to play in long-sleeved shirts. Defender Doug Considine said yes, he'd take one. Ferguson was livid. He wanted to take Considine straight out of the side and play Rougvie instead, but the official team line-ups had already been submitted to the referee and it was too late to change.

No incident, it seemed, was too trivial to attract his wrath, and occasional misinterpretation. Weir was once given the man-of-the-match award after an Aberdeen victory at Ibrox. The reward was a case of a dozen bottles of Moët & Chandon champagne handed to him in one of the corporate lounges. He carried it down the stadium's famous marble staircase to the Aberdeen bus which was waiting at the front door. As he was about to step on to the vehicle Weir spotted his father, sister and team-mate

Billy Stark's father waiting to congratulate him. Instinctively he handed each of them a bottle before putting the rest on a spare seat. A few minutes later Ferguson boarded and quickly spotted the champagne. Weir recalled: 'He doesn't ask me where the missing bottles are or what happened, he just starts shouting and bawling. "Who gave you the right to open those bottles? Who said you could drink on the bus?" This was in front of everyone. I sat there biding my time to try and explain what had happened. It went on and on, non-stop. "Just 'cos you had a good bloody game today disnae give you any right to bloody open the bottles and gie everybody a drink of champagne." He was right up to my face. He stormed away back down the bus and I see him talking to Archie, still going on about it. Then he comes back up and he goes, "What the hell happened to the bloody champagne anyway?" So I says, "Can I get a word in? When I came out of Ibrox I saw my dad, my sister and Billy's dad and I gave each of them a bottle of champagne." He looked at me. There was a pause. Then he shook my hand and said, "Bloody brilliant! Look after your family. In fact, get another three bottles open now. I'll get the plastic cups and we'll all have a drink."'

The young players were especially vulnerable because Ferguson saw it as an important tool in the manipulation and shaping of their character. He was constantly on their case. On one occasion, Hewitt was called into his office and fined £20 for overtaking Ferguson in his car on the way back from training. Hewitt said: 'Fergie was in front of me doing about 20mph. I had a car full – McGhee, Simmy, Cooper – and they're going, "Get past him." So I pulled out to overtake. McGhee's waving at him, egging him on. We get back to Pittodrie and about twenty seconds later the door bursts open. "Bloody hell, Hewitt, what were you bloody well doing? You've got millions of pounds' worth of talent in that car, you could have caused an accident, you're fined." McGhee's winding him up, going, "You're right, gaffer, in fact I'm worth at least two million."'

Another fine came Hewitt's way when he delayed signing a new contract and the local press named him in speculation about moves to other clubs. He went to see Ferguson after discovering a £100 deduction in his pay. 'He told me, "I'm sick of reading about you in the *Green Final*. You're getting fined, now get out." The following week, another £100 deduction! The same again. I was furious because I'd done nothing wrong. That ate away at me for weeks.'

Steve Cowan and Ian Angus once told Ferguson they intended to move out of the club's digs into a flat. He stood in front of them and said: 'How do you make a pot of soup?' They looked at each other. Neither knew. Ferguson snapped: 'Right, you're no' getting a bloody flat.' Even the older players were policed. Strachan, married with children, once saw Ferguson driving past his house on a Friday evening, obviously checking he was home. Kennedy recalled a team meeting in which Ferguson praised the importance of family life, talked with regret about how little time he had spent with his children because of work, and of how he had missed them growing up and left too much of the responsibility to Cathy. And then he said: 'I'd like some of youse to do the same. We've got this big European game. Shut them out. Concentrate totally on Aberdeen Football Club.'

When Pat Stanton was assistant manager the players could turn to him for a bit of understanding and compassion. Another assistant, Willie Garner, was similar. But Archie Knox was a different character. He was popular with the players, but they knew he was a gruff disciplinarian whose attitude and style was close to Ferguson's. None of them mistook him for a shoulder to cry on. Knox admitted: 'People used to ask if we were a good cop-bad cop sort of combination. It looked to me like we were just two fucking bad cops. If Alex got on to somebody I would be feeling the same way. They just had to put up with it.'

The pair of them kept a baseball bat behind the door of Teddy Scott's room. Ferguson would sometimes grab it and threaten some of the younger players while they played snooker. It was done in jest, but was unnerving nonetheless. Knox was prepared to go further: 'I'd take it to the boot room and I'd say to the young boys, "I'll meet youse in the boot room, any of you that fancy it?" I'd put the lights out and wave this baseball bat around. Sometimes you would clout them . . . not hit them properly. Maybe jab them a bit. Some of the things we did then, you'd get jailed for now.' One of Ferguson's later signings, Robert Connor, laughed as he remembered that period: 'Considering some of the things he used to get up to with the players it's a surprise the European Court of Human Rights never sat in Aberdeen.'

All the players have their tales. Now, forty years later, most laugh and shake their heads when asked to recall the times Ferguson turned on them. Their personal hairdryer anecdote is worn like a badge of honour. After one game Joe Miller returned to the dressing room later than the other players because he had been collecting the man-of-the-match award. Miller said: 'I could hear him going ballistic. Maybe we'd conceded a goal. He had been banned from the dugout and was using the walkie-talkies. I just walked in the dressing room right at the moment when he hurled this walkie-talkie. The aerial hit me in the face and the rest of it smashed against the wall. He knew he'd done something wrong, but he just went, "And you . . . sit on your arse. You think you've done it all but you could have scored four, five, six. It's not good enough!" I've seen him kick a wee coffee table and the whole teapot came back at him and scalded his legs. He's got his trousers down at his ankles in the middle of the dressing room, standing there with his pure white legs all scalded. The physio's trying to treat him. All the boys were laughing into their towels! I've seen the hairdryer umpteen times. For not holding the ball up, not trying hard enough, whatever. What he was really doing was testing me: could I handle it or would I curl up and cry like a wee boy? And I saw some boys doing that.'

Ferguson could also show his disapproval silently. A player passing him in the narrow corridor between Pittodrie's reception and the dressing rooms might be totally ignored if he had just contributed to an Aberdeen defeat. Weir said: 'He'd just walk by you. You'd be looking at him as if to say, "Well, nod your head at least . . ." But he was mentally letting you know you hadn't done the business. He'd just ignore you in that wee corridor.'

The capacity to induce obedience stretched beyond the players. During Garner's spell as assistant manager Ferguson sent him to watch a Hearts-Hibs derby. It was a dreary match and with five minutes remaining Hibs were winning 1–0. Garner decided he had seen enough. 'Just as I'm going out I hear this roar and I think, "Aw shit, I've missed a goal, well, I'll get it on the radio." So I get to the car and switch on the radio and it's 2–2. I've missed three goals in the last five minutes! In the morning, being naïve and instead of just getting a report and telling him about the goals, he asks me what they were like, and I said, "I never saw three of them, I left." He goes, "You left? You fucking left? Before the end of the game?" Oh, he slaughtered me. Slaughtered.'

Even supporters could be brought to heel. Billy Stark's tall, languid-looking presence in midfield often received a cool reception from Aberdeen fans, for no obvious reason other than that he was not Gordon Strachan. Stark said: 'If I was playing well I was "elegant". If I wasn't playing well I was "a big lazy bastard".' This lack of appreciation irked Ferguson: Stark worked tirelessly and was a prolific goalscorer. When he scored a hat-trick in a cup tie against Alloa, Ferguson used his post-match press conference to criticise Dons supporters for jeering him. In the very next game, at Dumbarton, Stark scored the opening goal. He said: 'There was a wee knot of Aberdeen supporters and suddenly I could hear them chanting my name. It was so bleedin' obvious! Basically Fergie had given them a row and they'd followed the party line.'

Ferguson appreciated the fact that the majority of his players – Miller, Kennedy, Strachan, McLeish, McGhee, Leighton, Weir, Bell, Rougvie, McMaster – were married with young children. That spared him worries about them being out on the town. The most prominent exceptions were Neale Cooper and Bryan Gunn, the midfielder and goalkeeper, both instantly recognisable for their mops of curly blond hair. Neil Simpson said: 'He was always getting on to the pair of them. "I know what you were bloody up to this week!" It would be, "Cooper, Gunn . . . in my office!" He wanted players settled down, eating well, getting rest at the right times.' Gunn said: 'We were always getting hauled over the coals for something. "You've been seen speaking to my friend's daughter!"'

Hairstyles proved a particular source of irritation. When he ordered the younger players not to follow a fashion of the time by having perms done, one of them, teenager Alan Lyons, unwisely did so anyway. Ferguson made him train wearing a balaclava. Cooper and Gunn were inevitable focuses of his attention. After a defeat away to Hibs the squad was ordered in to Pittodrie for a Sunday-morning dressing-down. Gunn said: 'We were in the boardroom, actually sitting on the floor because there weren't enough seats. We were the first two he picked on, "Gunn and Cooper, get your hair back to its bloody original colour". Me and Neale were single so we spent a little bit longer getting our hair done with hairdressers who were quite happy to add a bit of colour now and again. Every so often we would come in with blond streaks. It was always noticed but never mentioned . . . until the next defeat. Our hair colour got blamed for that defeat at Hibs. It was back to its original colour that afternoon. We had to follow orders.' Another time Cooper returned from a holiday with highlights. 'I had this big mop of curly hair. So I walk in and he says, "Take that stupid thing off." It took me a second to realise he thought I had a wig on. I said, "But this is my hair." He came over and felt it, then he goes, "Right, up to the hairdressers, get a beige tone put through it." For a while I was going around with a beige barnet.'

Cooper was the most effervescent character among all the Aberdeen players, with an infectious laugh and an endearing sense of fun and mischief. As a young boy he had grown up without his father. He was born in India and raised there by his mother and sister until the family moved to Aberdeen when he was two and a half. Ferguson felt protective towards him even if he did more than most to push the boundaries. All the lads called him 'Tattie' (as in tattie peel: Neale). Cooper said: 'You were always feart of Fergie. But he was also a nice guy. I used to get the bus from where my mum lived and he would pass most days. I used to hide behind the bus stop in case he stopped and gave me a lift. He'd listen to Terry Wogan on the radio. The boys would wind me up if they saw me getting out of his car: "teacher's pet" and all that. But he was very likeable. There was a Celtic game in Glasgow when Tommy Burns smashed me in the face. I had to get my nose reset. Fergie was straight to the hospital to see me after the game, straight into the theatre: "How's my boy?"'

McMaster savoured the level of attention Ferguson gave him when he was ruled out for a year by the knee injury suffered against Liverpool. The manager ensured McMaster continued to receive the team's win bonuses while he was out. 'Fergie looked after me. Brilliant. He kept encouraging me. He made sure everything was all right with the family.'

There was, of course, an element of manipulation in such kindness. Not all mind games are intimidating. Now and again he would have a quiet word in a player's ear to give him the impression he was a little more special than the others. He would tell McMaster: 'They could have played music to your performance today.' When he passed Simpson in a corridor he would say: 'How's my favourite midfielder doing?' That alone would leave Simpson with a spring in his step for a day or so. And when Ferguson passed Cooper he would say exactly the same thing. It was years before the two players realised they were both being fed the same line. Similarly, Ferguson would approach a player privately and tell him he had been given a bonus, saying, 'Here's a wee bit extra in your wages, but don't tell anybody, don't say a word, or they'll all be chapping my door.' Joe Miller remembers a ploy Ferguson used as he was going about his chores as a teenaged member of the ground staff. 'Sometimes Fergie would have a word with you, saying, "You can't be happy putting his gear out? He's not half the player you are and you're here washing his strip and cleaning his boots?" Little did I know he said the same thing to everyone. But it made you feel great.'

Ferguson's use of psychology may have been devious, but the camaraderie around Pittodrie was genuine nevertheless. The manager would occasionally be the butt of the joke as well. When he was getting himself fit for the Aberdeen half-marathon he did lap after lap of the pitch, checking his time by glancing at a stopwatch he hung on a nail at the mouth of the tunnel. After one of the laps he saw the stopwatch had been swapped for a calendar, the less-than-subtle implication being that he was far too slow.

It was rarely a good idea to sit next to Ferguson on the bus going to a game, especially when he joined in the card school, playing for £1 a hand. Striker Steve Cowan said: 'He would mutter and moan at you for the cards you'd given him. Mental torture.' On the way to a match at Partick Thistle, Cowan knocked Ferguson out of the card game. 'I was due to be a substitute and by the time we got there he had changed the team-sheet and put in Andy Harrow. Maybe it was a wind-up, I don't know. But half an hour before the game it was, "Right, fucking Cowan, get stripped, you're back in."'

Neither were the players safe when they were out of the manager's sight. Aberdeen is not a particularly large city and Ferguson's network of contacts and informants, which included publicans and nightclub staff, allowed him to keep close tabs on their extra-curricular activities. A 1984 interview in the *Daily Star* suggested that he did not object to them enjoying themselves in moderation: 'I don't expect them to be goody-goody monks. A pint after a match or a little lovemaking beforehand doesn't do any harm.' The likes of Cooper and Gunn, however, as young, single men, had a slightly different interpretation of what counted as moderation, and they saw going out without getting caught as a challenge.

Cooper recalled being in a bar with a Bacardi and Coke, thinking himself safe, when Ferguson suddenly appeared as if from behind a pillar. 'He said, "What's that you're drinking, Cooper?" I get a sweat on. I said, "It's Coke." He came really close to me and he took my drink and he smelled it. He just looked at me and said, "That doesn't smell like bloody Coke to me." I says, "It is, it's Coke." So he tasted it and he looked at me. He came closer and he just said: "You're dead." I said, "What?" and he said, "You're dead." Quietly, he said, "Monday morning I'm going to run the bloody bollocks aff you. You won't know what's hit you."'

Over time some of the senior players became bolder. The likes of Strachan, McGhee or Leighton would occasionally answer back when Ferguson got going. Sometimes whoever was on the receiving end of the hairdryer would look over the manager's shoulder to see his team-mates making funny faces or hand gestures, trying to make the helpless player laugh. Rougvie said: 'If you laughed, you were dead. If he turned round really quickly they were all suddenly as still as statues. It was hilarious.' Garner remembered the sense of excitement among the risk-takers: 'Strachan used to sit behind Fergie making gestures with his hands while he was letting rip on somebody. I'm thinking, "Oh wee man, don't do that, he's going to erupt at some point."'

There were occasions, however, when the manager's confrontational style could push a player too far. While heads were clouded by alcohol the day after Gothenburg he had an angry clash with McGhee. The players were lined up in the tunnel, about to show off the cup to an adoring Pittodrie, when McGhee spotted the trophy lying on its side on the floor. As he went to pick it up Ferguson suddenly appeared and snatched it from his hand, saying, 'Willie's taking that.' McGhee was incensed by the implication that he wanted to usurp his captain or hog the limelight. The red mist fell and he grabbed Ferguson by the lapels, pushed him through a doorway and took a swing. Others rushed in to grab his arm and Ferguson landed a retaliatory blow of his own before they were separated. McGhee was taken away to cool off in the boardroom and missed the players' lap of honour and team photograph. He sobered up and spent a sleepless night fearing he had blown his relationship with Ferguson and ended his Aberdeen career. Ferguson forgave him instantly and the incident was never mentioned again. If a player was important to him, Ferguson was enough of a pragmatist to turn a blind eye.

Nor was the provocation one-sided. On one occasion, when Aberdeen were down at half-time, things threatened to boil over between Ferguson and Stewart McKimmie, the tough and competitive full-back signed after Kennedy retired. Garner said: 'Fergie had a go at a lot of them, and then had a go at McKimmie. McKimmie said something back, Fergie grabs him, McKimmie's trying to stand up, getting off the seat, and Fergie's still got a grip of him. I come across and pull Fergie away and say, "Woah, this isn't doing us any good." Some of the boys got McKimmie away and it settled down. Fergie then switched just like that, straight back to the game: "Right, this is what we have to do . . ."'

That ability to move suddenly from apparent fury to clinical analysis gives credence to the theory that Ferguson's hairdryers were acts of premeditated theatre designed to assert control. Having shredded some poor soul it was not uncommon for him to turn away and wink at one of the other players. The tactic even extended to the younger and emerging players. On 7 May 1985, Aberdeen's teenagers played Celtic in the BP Youth Cup final at Pittodrie and were 2–0 down at half-time. Garner was in charge and was trying to lift them when Ferguson suddenly appeared. The left-back, David Robertson, was sixteen at the time: 'The dressing room door burst open. Hairdryer treatment. Up in people's faces. It was amazing. We had some guys there fourteen, fifteen years old and he just completely crucified everybody. We were 2–0 down and not playing well, but we beat them 5–3 after extra time. I know for a fact if he hadn't come in at half-time we'd have lost.'

Some figures in the dressing room, such as Miller, Kennedy and McLeish, were generally spared his rants. And to them, the few occasions when they were singled out felt like token exercises. Kennedy said: 'I did get some. Maybe one a season. I got my hairdryers on trumped-up charges. I was framed now and again just to show I wasn't exempt.' For the rest of the team, though, Ferguson's verbal assaults on his most senior, talismanic players were all the more astonishing for their rarity. They were taken aback one Friday afternoon when he started angrily criticising Miller, McLeish and Leighton following two consecutive losses. Stark said: 'We were all looking at each other. I was sitting there thinking, "If those guys are getting it, this must be serious." It was only much later I found out he'd taken them into his office beforehand and said, "Listen, on Friday I'll lay into you so just sit there and take it." It was all for show.'

SIXTEEN

EUROPEAN TEAM OF THE YEAR

In the autumn of 1983 Aberdeen were contacted by France Football and given some surprising news: the prestigious magazine had voted them European Team of the Year. An invitation arrived for a club delegation to attend the awards ceremony in Paris. Ferguson, Chris Anderson and Ian Donald, Dick Donald's son who had replaced Charlie Forbes on the three-man board, made the trip over. The trophy was small, gold and in the shape of the logo of the award's co-sponsors, Adidas. Ferguson was thrilled to lay his hands on it. The runners-up were Hamburg, despite the German club having won the European Cup two weeks after Aberdeen's triumph in Gothenburg. During the evening Ferguson had detected coolness from Hamburg's general manager, Günter Netzer. 'Netzer was certainly none too pleased when we received that Adidas award,' he said. 'It rankled with him.' Netzer confirmed that in comments to the German media: 'The wrong team got the award. What more can we do? We won the European Cup as well as lifting the Bundesliga title. We should have had that award. No doubt about it.'

Hamburg were back on Ferguson's radar. In the two years since putting Aberdeen out of Europe they had reached the 1982 Uefa Cup final, won the European Cup and been back-to-back Bundesliga champions. Now it would be Hamburg versus Aberdeen over two legs for the European Super Cup. Ferguson took the event so seriously that he broke off from a summer holiday in Florida to watch the German club play a pre-season friendly against New York Cosmos. Fixture congestion briefly cast a doubt over whether the Super Cup games would go ahead at all, but eventually dates were found with almost a month between the two legs. Aberdeen travelled first to play on a November night of rain and biting cold in the Volksparkstadion. The awful weather and live coverage on German television meant fewer than 15,000 fans turned up. Those who did saw Aberdeen give another sound defensive performance. Miller and especially Leighton were resolute in a goalless draw. They had not looked like winning it, though, and Ferguson was unmoved: 'Okay, a draw against the European Cup holders away from home must be classed as a good result. But I didn't think we played that well.' Hamburg were still coached by the great Austrian Ernst Happel, as they were for the clubs' previous meetings. 'There is a big difference in Aberdeen from two years ago,' he said. 'They are now a much more aggressive side.'

The first leg had left the Super Cup in need of a revitalising return game in Scotland. It got one. All 24,000 tickets were sold. Ferguson placed such huge stock in the Super Cup because, for many onlookers, the rise of the New Firm still seemed fragile. If Aberdeen failed to build quickly on the peak of Gothenburg the old questions, doubts and jibes would soon return. 'I don't want people saying we were just a flash in the pan. I would like to think that we can build a reputation like Liverpool's. That's what we're aiming for. The structure of this club is perfect for that kind of thing. We're financially sound with a first-class ground, and in a trouble-free atmosphere the fans, entire families, are turning up in their thousands.'

On the rainy night of 20 December, 1983, Aberdeen became the first Scottish club to win a second European trophy and the first to win the Super Cup. After a sleepy first half they scored through Simpson, then pummelled Hamburg and added another from McGhee's tap-in. By full time they had shown too much strength, stamina and guts for the champions of Europe. Pittodrie roared its approval. As captain, Miller already knew he would not be getting an actual Super Cup; there wasn't one. Vice-chairman Anderson had visited Uefa's Swiss headquarters and been stunned to make the discovery. 'I was told that no one had ever asked for one before. It's ridiculous.' The best Uefa had to offer was a commemorative plaque, like something they had taken down from the president's office wall.

Trophy or no trophy, Netzer had decreed that whoever came out on top over the two legs could regard themselves as the best team in Europe. That team was Aberdeen. But acknowledgement of Aberdeen's second European trophy has always been given grudgingly, even in Scotland. Stewart McKimmie said: 'Others called it a Mickey Mouse trophy, but for us it was a major trophy. Hamburg didn't like it when they got beat.'

Kennedy provided a characteristically colourful defence of Aberdeen's twin European triumphs. 'The Cup Winners' Cup lifts Aberdeen, along with the fact it was against Real Madrid. If anyone's trying to get the better of me I'll go, "We won that trophy, that European trophy, I'm trying to remember who we beat again? Was it Roma? Nah. Real Zaragoza? Nah. Bayer Leverkusen? Nah. Oh . . . it was Real Madrid, the club of the Millennium, how could I forget? It was Real Madrid, pal, Aberdeen beat Real Madrid. If you want to beat anyone in a final it has to be Real Madrid. The Super Cup? That's two European trophies. What kind of cup was it again? Super. And we beat the European champions, easy, over two games. You've got tankers and you've got super tankers. Why are they called super tankers? Because of how big they are."'

By the time they won the Super Cup Aberdeen were making good progress towards becoming the first team to successfully defend the Cup Winners' Cup. The bookmakers had them as joint second favourites with Barcelona and Juventus to go all the way and win the final in Basle. Manchester United were 11–4 favourites, with Porto 12–1 outsiders. As holders, Aberdeen had enjoyed a straightforward path to the last eight. They had beaten Akranes of Iceland more comfortably than the 3–2 aggregate scoreline suggested and then looked convincing against Beveren. The Belgians had reached the semi-final of the competition in 1979, knocking out Inter Milan en route before losing to Barcelona. They were top of the league when they faced Aberdeen in 1983 – and would go on to win the championship – but after a goalless away leg, Pittodrie savoured a comfortable 4–1 win.

In the quarter-final, the Dons were drawn against the Hungarians Újpest Dózsa. Again there was a long gap between European rounds, and in between Aberdeen extended their unbeaten run in all competitions to twenty-seven games. They were still involved in four tournaments but a major wobble was coming. Újpest Dózsa seemed humble. 'Aberdeen are the best team we have met since I came here,' said Temesvári Miklós, who had been their coach for three years. He also said his men were not yet fully fit after Hungarian football's winter shutdown. If it was all an act it was very well performed. In the first leg their snow-lined Budapest stadium was crammed with 25,000 fans for a bitterly cold afternoon kick-off. They saw a startling 2–0 home win. The goals came in the second half and Aberdeen were guilty of bad misses by Black, Strachan and McGhee, though his team-mates contended that McGhee's shot had gone over the line before it hit the goalkeeper. Long after full time the Scottish reporters found Ferguson in a corridor outside the Aberdeen dressing room, predictably furious. 'I can't trust myself to go inside,' he told them.

Dougie Bell knew he had been slightly more complicit than most in the defeat and hoped Ferguson's hawkish eye for detail had, for once, let him down. Újpest's opening goal had come from a free kick when Bell was placed on the edge of Aberdeen's defensive wall. He thought Sándor Kisznyér's shot was going wide, but it bent around him into the top corner. This looked like sure-fire hairdryer material. 'I thought, "He's going to kill me." But after the game he didn't say a word. Next day, plane back, he still hasn't said a word. I thought, "That's no' bad, maybe he didn't realise." So then it was Celtic on the Saturday in the second leg of the League Cup semi-final. I was playing okay but went for the ball and Tommy Burns just dived over my leg. Celtic got a penalty and they scored. 1–0. That put us out. 'We get back into the dressing room and Fergie says, "Who pulled down Tommy Burns in the box?" I said, "It was me, boss, but I never touched him, he dived." He looks at me and goes, "You fucking bastard . . . you've knocked us out of the Cup Winners' Cup and the League Cup in a week." He'd seen me in that bloody wall after all.'

Aberdeen were not out of Europe yet, though. A mighty effort in the second leg was required and Ferguson was determined they would deliver. The fans responded by filling Pittodrie again on 21 March and Ferguson used his programme column to whip them up: 'There is no doubt about it, anyone among the capacity crowd in the ground tonight will be watching one of the most exciting and competitive matches ever seen at Aberdeen. As far as this club is concerned, it is the challenge of a lifetime. Újpest Dózsa are going to have one of the hardest matches in their entire history.' In three seasons of stirring European football at Pittodrie, the supporters had seen sixteen Aberdeen goals in wins against Ipswich, Hamburg, Bayern Munich, Waterschei and Hamburg again. Now they needed to see at least two more to stand any chance of keeping their hold on the Cup Winners' Cup. They got them. Újpest were battered. McGhee buried a header just before half-time. The visitors held on, wasted time and got within two minutes of going through before McGhee scored again. Extra time was a formality because the Hungarians were dead on their feet. McGhee completed a hat-trick and Újpest's goalkeeper was sent off for butting McLeish.

The semi-final draw looked kind towards Aberdeen. Now 2–1 favourites, they avoided Manchester United and Juventus and were paired with Porto. Ferguson sent his assistant to watch Porto play at Sporting Lisbon. Waiting for Willie Garner at the airport was a man Ferguson had asked for a favour: Sven Göran Eriksson. The Swede was the manager of Benfica at the time and turned up with an attractive girlfriend. Garner remembered: 'We went to the game and we were so high up in the stand I couldn't make out what was going on. Eriksson says, "I can't help you here; if I'm seen to be helping you against a Portuguese club I'll get shot." His girlfriend took the pen and wrote down the players' names for me.' Nonetheless, by the time of the first leg in Oporto on 11 April, Ferguson had enough information on the opposition to claim that Porto knew 'every trick in the book'. In conditions thirty degrees warmer than Scotland, the vast bowl of the Antas Stadium was packed with 65,000 enemy fans. Fireworks and chanting created precisely the intimidating atmosphere Porto intended. Their star was the captain, Fernando Gomes, a Portuguese international striker with great penalty-box instincts and a terrific goalscoring record. After fourteen minutes he headed the ball past Leighton from a corner. Later he miskicked another chance and forced a fine save. Porto were well worth their 1–0 win.

Ferguson reproached himself for picking Bell after a hamstring injury had kept him out for weeks. He substituted him at half-time. After the game he told reporters: 'I took a chance against my usual principle by playing Bell after a month's absence. It didn't work. Dougie felt the pace too much.' It was a classic example of Ferguson's belief that an individual member of the team should never be criticised publicly. What he said to Bell in private, however, was merciless. Bell recalled: 'He played me wide in a four. Porto's right-back was a flying machine, bombing on. I hardly touched the ball! At half-time he went ballistic at me: "This game's live on the TV, you're a disgrace to Scottish fitba." I felt like saying, "I've no' played."'

More than twelve years later the game in Oporto was at the centre of a baffling allegation that Porto's chairman, Jorge Nuno Pinto da Costa, had bribed the Romanian referee to guarantee a win. In November 1996, when Ferguson was long gone from Aberdeen, a former coach and club official called Fernando Barata claimed he had acted as Porto's intermediary to bribe referee Ioan Igna. Barata said he had been asked by Pinto da Costa to 'mediate with the referee, arranging the result and everything'. Uefa investigated the allegations but nothing came of them. Besides, they did not square with Aberdeen's own recollection of the game, or Igna's refereeing; Porto had even had a penalty claim rejected. 'The Romanian referee, close up to the action, refused the frantic Portuguese claims for a spot-kick,' wrote Ian Paul in his report for the *Glasgow Herald*. The following day he mentioned Igna again:

'Aberdeen were impressed by the fairness of the Romanian referee, Ioan Igna, who refused to be overwhelmed.' McGhee had no sense of anything untoward: 'I have to say that in the game I never had any sense that referee was bribed. They only beat us 1–0, but they really stretched us. It never felt like there was anything wrong. We were beaten by the better team.'

Pittodrie was full again for the second leg. By now Aberdeen's home support had forgotten how it felt to be denied in Europe. But Porto's visit was different and Ferguson knew exactly how dangerous they would be. Before the game he sounded almost Churchillian: 'It will require the greatest effort any and all players in the team have ever made in the cause to put this club on the map.' Fog enveloped the stadium during the game and its effect was deadening. Pittodrie was packed but ghostly and quiet. Fans could hear the players' shouts. Aberdeen played without urgency. With fifteen minutes left they gave the ball away and Vermelhinho chipped Leighton to give Porto a late and unassailable lead. Whatever Pittodrie electricity Aberdeen had tapped into against Ipswich, Hamburg and Bayern Munich had drained away. McGhee said: 'Those European games used to give you an edge. When I ran out of the tunnel I would do a sprint and jump as if heading a ball. On nights like Bayern you felt like you could jump over the stand. But I ran out against Porto and felt like my boots were full of lead. That energy and that explosiveness just wasn't there. There was something missing. The bubble had burst. It wasn't just me. Willie said he felt it before the game, too. It was as if we had run our course.' Porto, though, were outstanding. Six of their team at Pittodrie were still playing when they won the European Cup in 1987. Ferguson thought their midfield was exceptional, though he also admitted that Aberdeen had run out of fuel. 'Last year it was a glory, glory run when we did not even contemplate defeat. During this game, I sensed we would lose.'

It was a bleak day for the New Firm. Dundee United had been within touching distance of the European Cup final and Ferguson admitted he was 'praying' they would defend their 2–0 first-leg lead against Roma. But in an ugly, vicious atmosphere in Rome the Italians won 3–0. Despite the desperate disappointment, Aberdeen and United could be proud. They had, again, lasted longer in Europe than the Old Firm. Rangers had gone out of the Cup Winners' Cup (also to Porto) in the second round and Celtic tumbled out of the Uefa Cup in the third. Aberdeen and United's European campaigns in the 1980s ran in tandem: United reached the Uefa Cup quarter-finals in 1982 and 1983, the European Cup semi-finals in 1984 and were Uefa Cup runners-up in 1987. Maurice Malpas, the United and Scotland full-back, can remember a joke that used to do the rounds at Tannadice. 'When all the papers' main writers appeared to cover our European trips we'd say, "Oh, it must be the third round already . . . Rangers get knocked out in the first round and Celtic in the second, so the reporters start coming with us."'

After Ferguson's arrival at Aberdeen the only time Celtic made an impression in Europe was in 1980, when they reached the last eight of the European Cup. Rangers had done the same the previous year and then deteriorated into a series of dreary first- and second-round exits. This dismal record on the international stage mirrored their decline at home. In a sequence of seven consecutive seasons, from 1980 to 1986, Rangers never finished higher than third, never finished above Aberdeen or Celtic, and were never within ten points of whoever won the league.

Celtic were Glasgow's main power in the early 1980s. 'I think we are now at the stage when Aberdeen versus Celtic, or vice-versa, has taken over from the traditional Old Firm games,' said

Ferguson, though in his 1985 autobiography, *A Light in the North*, he used the same line about Dundee United, writing: 'The intensity at Aberdeen-Dundee United matches is now greater than at an Old Firm game.' Aberdeen-Celtic games were given more flavour by the apparent tension between their managers. Initially Ferguson had to prove himself to a set of Aberdeen players who continued to admire Billy McNeill, even after he defected to Parkhead. The two men were born twenty-one months apart and were natural competitors. And neither could be mistaken for a good loser. Way back in 1969, when Ferguson was made the scapegoat for Celtic's opening goal in the cup final, McNeill had scored it. When their teams clashed the pair regularly descended into shouting matches.

In matches against Aberdeen, both United and Celtic had to contend with Ferguson's predisposition to intensity. He revelled in it. If there was no intensity, he would create it. By 1984 he had built a team who could comfortably handle anything thrown at them. Talented, attractive sides with pretensions to take on the Old Firm had risen periodically in Scottish football. None had been able to maintain a sustained challenge by complementing skill with swaggering confidence and insatiable hunger for battle. For all the similarities between Ferguson and Jim McLean, and their teams, it was these mental characteristics that elevated Aberdeen above United and made them true contenders.

The Celtic winger, Davie Provan, faced both teams in their prime. 'You had kicking teams who couldn't play, and you had teams who could play but couldn't kick. Dundee United come to mind. United could play but they weren't nasty with it. Aberdeen could play and they could be nasty as well. They had both elements that you need. United weren't going to go over the top or try to do you. It was different against Aberdeen. If Paul Hegarty or David Narey fouled you in a

United game they would hold out a hand to pull you back up. If Miller or McLeish fouled you they'd stand on your fingers on the grass.' The Celtic players heard rumours that even Black, the baby-faced striker, was encouraged to lead with his elbows when jumping for high balls, just to make defenders' lives difficult. They believed them.

Between 1980 and 1983 Ferguson had admired, but felt threatened by, the exhilarating young Celtic striker Charlie Nicholas. Good looks and a playboy image gave Nicholas an air of early celebrity, but his talent was the real thing. He had great control and balance, was a prolific finisher and played with terrific flair. Nicholas quickly formed the opinion that Aberdeen's players were instructed by their manager to stop him by any means necessary. One of the chapters in Nicholas's 1986 autobiography was titled: 'The Time I Hated Fergie.' At Pittodrie he felt they were 'lying in wait for me'. When Celtic entered the stadium he would sit in the away dressing room, skim through the match programme and find a piece by Ferguson or Miller praising how dangerous he was. Some players would have taken that as a compliment. Nicholas knew better: he interpreted it as a warning.

Ferguson knew his younger players were impressionable. Before a league game against Celtic at Pittodrie in the 1982–83 campaign he decided to rewire Neale Cooper's attitude to Nicholas. The indoctrination began at training on Monday. Ferguson and Knox would shout 'Cooper' and he was told to shout back 'Nicholas'. He was force-fed a diet of 'Nicholas, Nicholas, Nicholas. Everyone loves Nicholas'. 'Nicholas likes to drop into the middle.' 'Nicholas is the guy you have to be tight on.' By the Saturday he had endured a week of it. Celtic took the kick-off, Frank McGarvey touched it to Nicholas and . . . smash! Cooper hit him in the centre-circle at roughly the same time as the ball left it. Cooper said: 'It's still one of the quickest tackles ever. It had been like a build-up in the week before. The manager had me in most days. He drilled it into me. I was like a man possessed. I caught Charlie on the knee. It wasn't a good tackle. The Celtic boys were going mental, Roy Aitken, Billy McNeill in the dugout shouting and swearing. I just looked across to the manager and he's giving me big thumbs up, both hands.'

Nicholas also remembers it well: 'It wasn't the hardest tackle I ever received but it was just so fast. You could sense a real anger in the crowd because it was so quick. It was the obviousness of it: he was coming to nail me. It was just a take-out, American Football stuff.' Ferguson's aim was not that Cooper should maim or seriously hurt Nicholas, just 'give him a dull one'. Nicholas recovered to open the scoring, but Aberdeen won 3–1. Cooper was not even booked. Ferguson took great pride in the low number of yellow and red cards Aberdeen collected, and especially that they went through the marathon 1982–83 campaign without a single suspension. Players would be fined if they were booked, even if the referee had been harsh or simply wrong. Even so, Ferguson wanted a team who sent out an unequivocal message: don't mess with us. Aberdeen would not be bullied or pushed around by anyone, anywhere.

Provan said: 'There was an arrogance about them. And there was also the fact that at Celtic we found it hard to beat them. That wasn't easy for us to accept and our resentment boiled up into a real dislike and brought several grudge games between us. The Old Firm didn't like it, the Old Firm players didn't like it and the Old Firm fans didn't like it.' There would be scuffling and shoving in the tunnel, insults flying back and forth. Bad blood would carry from one fixture to the next. And with four league games a season, and the possibility of Scottish Cup and League Cup ties, there were numerous opportunities for things to flare up. McGhee said: 'We were never intimidated. Never. Quite the opposite. I remember big Roy Aitken saying that they used to say we were on drugs. They'd stand in the tunnel and look at us, guys like Rougvie, nae teeth, in your face, kicking the walls, twitching.' Provan added: 'Aberdeen was "the" game. By the time you got on the pitch both teams were sky-high with adrenalin. They wanted to kill each other. It was as physical and aggressive as you will ever get on a football pitch. And Aberdeen could play. They'd come to Celtic Park and sit back, the crowd would be driving us forward and Aberdeen would just pick us off.'

Aberdeen's ability to get under the Old Firm's skin extended to the fans, sometimes inciting violence. In two different games lone Celtic supporters tried to attack Strachan. The darting wee fella with ginger hair seemed to drive them up the wall. The first attempted assault happened during a 2–0 Aberdeen win at Parkhead in 1980, the second ten months later after he scored a penalty two minutes into a match at Pittodrie. The intrusions resulted in the nearest enforcers, Bell and Rougvie, springing protectively into action. McLeish said: 'Gordon wasn't trying to wind them up but he was definitely a focal point. When the fan ran on the pitch at wee Gordon that flicked the switch for big Dougie.' Rougvie said: 'I was his bodyguard. We had to protect our match-winners. If any bastard went near them we were going to give them a doing, weren't we? We needed Strachan and Weir to win our bonuses for us.'

When Davie Hay became Celtic manager he decided they had to get tougher with Aberdeen. He introduced the combative Peter Grant to give his midfield steel and aggression. The plan was soon apparent. As Miller tried to usher a ball back to Leighton in a typically robust Celtic game, Grant came smashing into both the goalkeeper and Cooper. Grant said: 'Aberdeen was full-on. It was like going to war. If you booted someone, then five minutes later you knew you were getting done, because you'd done him. You were waiting. People talk about concentration so you don't lose a goal; it used to be concentration so you didn't lose your legs.'

Aberdeen's commitment to standing their ground extended to a strategy of challenging, pressurising and questioning referees. Jim Duffy, the Morton defender, remembers his startling introduction to the ploy: 'If you tackled any of their players, by the time you got up, or the referee had approached you, you had about six of them round you. You were literally isolated. They completely surrounded you: Miller, McLeish, Rougvie, Simpson, Cooper. In your face, really aggressive, intimidating. It was like a swarm of bees. And they're saying to the referee, "You need to make a decision here." The ironic thing was that if anyone dished it out to them – especially to Strachan, Weir or any of the young ones – they were on you like the house Mafia. They would sort you out.' It was not spontaneous. McGhee said: 'We were instructed, "Claim for everything." If the ball was going out for a throw-in you saw eleven hands going up.' The hand likely to shoot up fastest was Miller's. It was said that if football had rugby union's ten-yard retreat rule for dissent Miller would have spent most of his career in Norway.

Miller would regularly approach a referee and argue forcefully that Aberdeen should be getting more protection, or had been harshly penalised, or were generally not getting the rub of the green. When Miller was in full flow, haranguing an official, it could look as though the Aberdeen captain was the man in charge. But he has never felt apologetic. Miller said: 'My view was that Rangers and Celtic had all these fans who influenced referees so we needed something too. I would think, "This ref's getting influenced by their fans, I'm going to do something about it." Of course, Fergie encouraged us to apply a wee bit of pressure. You have to stand up to injustices and that's what we did. Besides, you have to show belief when you're going down to these places, and perhaps a little bit of arrogance.'

In one game at Pittodrie, a linesman Ferguson was berating snapped back at him to 'sit down'. Ferguson turned to trainer Teddy Scott: 'Who is that?' Scott knew the man personally: 'That's the Reverend Roger. He's my minister up in Ellon.' Ferguson said: 'You're not going to his church tomorrow.'

Aberdeen's nerveless attitude to the Old Firm and their pressurising of referees defined the force Ferguson had created. They had gained respect from other players, managers and, even if given grudgingly, many rival supporters. For Aberdeen's own fans it was liberating to follow a team who had unshakable belief in themselves. There was nothing Celtic or Rangers could do to intimidate them. If this combative streak went against the Aberdonian grain, against the gentle nature of men like directors Donald and Anderson, they said nothing about it. Ferguson had reinvented Aberdeen as the equal of the very best Old Firm teams in history, and that meant they were consistent winners.

Dundee United had a fine side, but they did not have a Willie Miller. Paul Hegarty and David Narey, their centre-halves, were quiet and undemonstrative. And despite his own thunderous temper Jim McLean did not approve of his players mobbing a referee. Ferguson did not mind, though, and in the final game of the 1983–84 campaign the tactic would lead to renewed animosity at the season's showpiece occasion.

Aberdeen had reached their third consecutive Scottish Cup final. This time Celtic, not Rangers, awaited them. In the twenty minutes before kick-off referee Bob Valentine walked into the dressing rooms and warned both teams that he had been ordered to clamp down on indiscipline by SFA secretary Ernie Walker. After twenty-three minutes Aberdeen took the lead. Black scored a goal like the one he put away in Gothenburg: Strachan corner, McLeish header and a loose ball converted in the goalmouth. Celtic claimed Black was offside, but the real controversy came seven minutes before half-time. McGhee broke into space and was running between the halfway line and the penalty area when Roy Aitken ran square across and brought him crashing down. McGhee was not hurt but took a bang on his elbow and lay on the ground until the muscle relaxed. He looked up to see Valentine holding a red card.

Provan said: 'I remember Gordon Strachan being in the referee's face to get Roy sent off. Wee Gordon had to get his bit in.' Valentine was an experienced and accomplished referee. Whether he was influenced or not, Aitken became the first player sent off in a Scottish Cup final since 1929.

Celtic responded brilliantly. They regrouped and played with terrific heart before equalising through Paul McStay four minutes from the end. There were no histrionics from Ferguson this time, no vilification of his players. They still had the extra man and though Celtic had taken the final into another half-hour the Glasgow team had nothing left in their legs. Aberdeen were revitalised, and after Bell crashed a shot off the post Strachan crossed and McGhee volleyed home the winner. Not since Rangers in 1950 had a team completed three straight Scottish Cup victories. To boot, Aberdeen had bagged their first league and cup double: after three years behind Celtic and Dundee United they reclaimed the league title in 1983–84. This time, there was none of the drama of the 1980 run-in. They went top of the table in October and were never supplanted. Celtic were four points behind when they went to Pittodrie on 4 February and Hewitt's winning goal stretched Aberdeen's lead to six. Ferguson thought it was the decisive result of the campaign. The twenty-one goals conceded during the season was the lowest total since the Premier Division was formed in 1975; in eighteen away games they let in only nine. As they had four years earlier, the league celebrations came in Edinburgh, this time with two games to spare after McKimmie's goal delivered a 1–0 win at Hearts on 2 May. When he spoke to reporters the following day Ferguson was relaxed, happily pondering what the seasons ahead held in store: 'A European Cup final with Liverpool would be ideal.'

The New Firm was in its pomp. The last time two non-Old Firm clubs had won consecutive Scottish titles was eighty years earlier, when Hibs and Third Lanark did so in 1903 and 1904. Now Dundee United and Aberdeen had cemented Scottish football's new order. Ferguson still indoctrinated his players with the mantra that the Glasgow press was biased against them, but in truth the praise for both east coast clubs was generous. Ferguson and Jim McLean were colourful and opinionated and their sides played admirable, entertaining, winning football. The Glasgow-based newspapers held them up as the standard to which Celtic and struggling Rangers should aspire. The Old Firm still drew the country's biggest average crowds, but only just. Rangers averaged 21,996 for league games in 1983–84, Celtic 18,390, Aberdeen 17,138 and Dundee United 10,894. In 1984 the newspapers had every reason to believe that Scottish football's natural order, of unchallenged Old Firm supremacy, was a thing of the past. 'Aberdeen's success this time is far more commendable than when they won the premier title for the first time in 1980,' wrote Ian Paul in the *Glasgow Herald*, arguing that competing on five fronts proved the depth and quality of their squad. They had been involved 'in everything bar the Calcutta Cup'.

Aberdeen's magnificent campaign had yielded the Super Cup, the Scottish Premier Division and the Scottish Cup, plus runs to the semi-finals of the European Cup Winners' Cup and the League Cup. It had been the most successful season in the club's history. But surrendering the trophy won against Real Madrid still hurt. Years later Doug Rougvie was working in the oil industry. One of his colleagues told him a story from 1983, when he had been a 15-year-old fan. His father had said they should go to Gothenburg but the boy had just started a relationship and wanted to spend time with his girl. Rougvie said: 'The boy said, "Dad, I'm no' going, I'll go next year . . ." Back then people didn't realise Gothenburg was a one-off. They didn't realise there'd never be another one.'

SEVENTEEN

SUMMER 1984: THE REBUILD

One morning a hand-written letter arrived in the post at Pittodrie addressed to Alex Ferguson. Club secretary Ian Taggart read its contents: 'The letter was from a patient at Gartnavel Mental Hospital who wrote to Fergie saying, "It should be you who's in this hospital, not me".' The author suspected mental illness because Ferguson had the chance to sell Rougvie – a cult hero, but not to every fan's taste – to Middlesbrough but turned it down. In fact, one of Ferguson's great triumphs at Aberdeen was that he kept his team together for so long. Between 1978 and 1984 he sold only one player against his will: Steve Archibald, who had made up his mind to leave. All other departures were on the manager's terms.

Success was the adhesive that held the component parts together. There was no point leaving for Celtic or Rangers because there was a greater chance of winning with Aberdeen. Besides, the money on offer there was no better. In England, only Liverpool and Manchester United had the combination of size, history and financial muscle to make irresistible offers. It was the era before Sky Sports, the English Premier League and the Uefa Champions League, and before the Bosman ruling ushered in freedom of contract. Aberdeen were not a rich club but they were financially competitive. Crucially, they could afford to keep their key men. In the early 1980s player salaries were closely tied to how much money came in through the turnstiles. The average league attendance in England's top division in 1983–84 was 18,856; Aberdeen's was close to that, at just over 17,000. Add to that the very real prospect of going the distance in the European competitions, and a high quality of life in one of Britain's most affluent cities, and no one was in a rush to leave.

It had not always been like this. When Aberdeen appointed McNeill as manager in 1977, Miller heard the news while doing summer joinery work for a friend to supplement his club wage of £50-a-week, worth around £370 in today's terms. In Ferguson's first seasons the salaries had been so low Strachan had to request a loan from the club simply to buy a modest house. Garner remembered: 'The money was awful. They only stepped it up once guys became internationals. Until then you weren't getting a lot.' Low basic wages left the players reliant on appearance money and win bonuses to make a decent living. That gave Ferguson immediate control over them. It was not the ferocious hairdryer that the likes of Rougvie and Strachan feared, but their manager's ability to dictate their finances by dropping them. Rougvie said: 'Fergie realised early doors what power he had. If you didn't play, you didn't get appearances money, only your basic. If you played, you got your appearance money and a possible win bonus. That was your wages. We had to play. There was no way I was going to do anything to him. Fergie could just put you out of the game. I had a wife, a kid and a mortgage. If you're out of the game, I'd be out bloody labouring to make money. It was one of those things where if

Fergie said, "Jump!" the boys had to say, "How high?"' Strachan admitted: 'We all had a fear of him. He could make or break your career. When I wasn't playing I had to say to my wife, "I'm not getting my bonus money this weekend." It might mean you couldn't go on holiday or something.' The players had a phrase for how much money they could expect to take home in any given week. 'If we played and won it meant chocolate biscuits. If we were dropped, it was digestives.'

The size of the bonus payments was an enduring game of cat-and-mouse with the players on one side and the manager and directors on the other. At one team meeting Ferguson told them he had consulted Dick Donald and the bonus for a tournament would be the same as the previous season: £300. Some of the players remembered it had been £400 the previous year. No, he said. He had checked. It was definitely £300. Neil Simpson had still to become one of the senior dressing room figures and was not expected to voice an opinion. 'I was listening to all of this and I knew it had actually been £500. Now £500 was a massive amount to me. So I piped up, "Actually it was £500." Woof! Fergie was right on top of me. "Who the fuck do you think you are? There will be no fucking bonus." He went out the door and slammed it! I never played for about three months after that. But to give him his due, in the following seasons he would ask me what I thought the bonus should be!' Stewart McKimmie was on £35 a week at Dundee. He moved to Aberdeen in December 1983, too late for the first leg of the Super Cup against Hamburg, though he did play in the return game at Pittodrie. 'Let's say the bonus for winning it was £1,000. I looked at my payslip after we beat them and it was only £500 up. So I chapped on his door. That was the first time he'd stung me. He said, "The £1,000 was if you played in both games, you only played in the second leg."

Well, I couldn't argue. He had an answer for everything.' The bonus for winning in Gothenburg had been £2,000-a-man.

The players accepted Aberdeen's parsimonious attitude to money with a mixture of exasperation, fatalism and amusement. McMaster remembers how the players were once 'looked after' by Donald, the Pittodrie patriarch: 'Dick was the best chairman ever. Board meetings would last four minutes and then the meal would last three hours. He'd say, "Whatever you do, Alex, don't put us into debt." I remember going to his house at Rubislaw Den, a lovely part of Aberdeen, the granite wall alone was worth £100,000. We're playing cards and the chairman comes in – soft hat, a wee shuffle – and he takes out a big brown envelope and says, "That's a wee treat for the boys." We're looking at it. It was sweeties. Actual sweeties.'

The success at home and abroad brought in more money than the club had ever known. Increased attendances, prize money, sponsorships and commercial revenue saw cash flowing into the Pittodrie bank account. There had been £800,000 for selling Archibald, £45,000 for Ian Fleming and £82,000 for Dom Sullivan. The only significant money spent by Ferguson to that point had been the £300,000 paid for Weir, £87,500 for McKimmie, £70,000 for McGhee and £70,000 for Stark. Ferguson was a chairman's dream: a winning manager who made money. The Bayern Munich and Waterschei games cleared £300,000, and Aberdeen returned profits of between £200,000 and £300,000 in every year between 1981 and 1984. The club could not wait to open the mail every morning. Taggart said: 'In the year after the Cup Winners' Cup every delivery of the post seemed to contain a cheque from somebody for something. Money attracts money. It went on for months. A cheque from Uefa for this, a cheque from somebody else for that. We just thought, "Bloody hell, this is great."'

Shirt sponsorship had still to catch on among British clubs but in 1979 Aberdeen struck an exclusive deal with Adidas to manufacture the team's kit and boots. McKimmie turned up on his first day of training with his trusted pair of Nike boots. 'It had taken me ages to break them in. I arrived there on the Monday morning, Archie Knox took my boots, threw them in the bin and said, "You'll nae be needin' them, we wear Adidas."' On one occasion a representative from Puma approached Black, Cooper and Hewitt about switching sponsors. Tentatively, they went to run the idea past Ferguson. Hewitt said: 'We knew he was friendly with the guy from Adidas, but we went to see him anyway. "Gaffer, we've been approached by a guy from Puma." "Get fucking out!"'

But no one had any illusions about what really drove the manager. Ferguson reminded his players that Aberdeen gave them a platform to earn respect and admiration not just in Scotland, but across Europe. He told them it was ambition, not money, that tempted Scotland's best players across the border to England. 'But how many clubs, apart from Liverpool, can offer players such a good chance of being in Europe? I'm not looking for people saying, "Fergie's done this and he's done that." I owe the players everything and I'm sure they'll show loyalty to me. I want Aberdeen to be a club no one wants to leave.' He understood the allure of the big English teams, though, and knew the risk they posed.

Aberdeen players picked for Scotland were encouraged not to socialise with any Anglos, those Scots playing for the big English clubs. When Strachan submitted a transfer request after the 1982 World Cup, Ferguson said: 'This has happened to Aberdeen before. A player goes with the international squad and then comes home unsettled.' Miller can recall being advised 'not to be listening to nonsense that these Anglos talk about money, it's not all about money'. Miller, the rock at the centre of the great Aberdeen team, was an obvious target and he had two serious opportunities to move. In 1980 he was offered three times his salary to join Sunderland. He travelled to Wearside only to leave unimpressed that the manager, Ken Knighton, was acting on a recommendation from Jock Stein and had not personally seen him play. The second opportunity came in 1982 when he was out of contract. Rangers offered him a take-home wage of £200 a week, the same as he was earning. With an understanding that the Rangers captain also inherited a £40-a-week column in the *Scottish Daily Express*, he would have been better off. But only marginally, given that he could expect to earn more bonuses with a powerful Aberdeen than a weak Rangers. Miller said: 'I didn't think they had a particularly good team. We did, and it looked like we were going places and were maybe capable of doing something special.' He asked Aberdeen for £220 a week to stay. Donald refused but offered £210. Miller accepted.

Few of the players had agents and Ferguson tended to keep them in the dark if he received a phone call asking if someone was for sale. Even so, it was only a matter of time before the unit began to split. The first player to break ranks was Strachan. When he submitted his transfer request Ferguson said he would not sell him for less than £2 million. Strachan was talked into staying, and he continued to make a major contribution while patiently awaiting the chance to leave. By midway through the 1983–84 season, though, he had had enough. It was his sixth season in the north-east and his fifth under Ferguson. He told the manager he would be leaving in the summer. Ferguson said Strachan's explanation was that he was 'bored', a statement the manager thought ridiculous. 'My advice was uncomplicated, "Go and get yourself un-bored."' Relations between the two soon deteriorated. Strachan said: 'I felt there was a bit of tension because I was the first one to leave him. He felt that was a slight against him as a coach, and it wasn't. I couldn't speak more highly of him. I just wanted to move on. I just wanted to see other places. Willie Miller has always said to me it's easier for defenders to stay at one club, the game comes to them. Forwards have to reinvent themselves and that's what I was having to do. So there was friction, an underlying friction. My transfer request used to come into play now and again, every time I had a bad game. "Who's going to buy you?"'

Strachan had his own weekly column in the *Scottish Daily Express*. When Ferguson left him out for a game against Hearts on 2 April 1984, he immediately retaliated in print. Under the headline 'Wrong, Fergie: Hearts match wasn't the time to drop me', he fired off an astonishing opening salvo: 'I am livid with my boss, Alex Ferguson. He dropped me against Hearts on Monday night and that hurt. But what has made me really angry is his timing.' Strachan claimed Ferguson had forced him to play for two months with a hamstring problem only to drop him when he was fully fit. Ferguson reacted against caricature. He had not cut his nose off to spite his face when McGhee swung for him after Gothenburg, and he did not do it when Strachan stepped out of line either. Strachan was brought straight back into the team five days later – he scored the winner against Motherwell – but was told his lucrative newspaper column was finished.

Cologne had sent a representative to the Motherwell game and over the following weeks Bernd Killat, a German agent already known to Aberdeen from organising pre-season tours, helped negotiate a deal. Strachan signed a pre-contract agreement. Unaware of that, Ferguson was trying to drum up interest from England because Aberdeen would receive a higher transfer fee. He secured an agreement with Manchester United. When Strachan then told him about the written deal with Cologne, Ferguson was incandescent. In his first autobiography, *A Light in the North*, Ferguson wrote: 'I said, "What do you think you're doing going to a club like Cologne? Last year they played to crowds of about 3,000 in some games. You need a big platform. That's why you're leaving Aberdeen in the first place." I told him there was no bigger platform than Manchester United.' Strachan did recognise that he had made an error. He was still leaving, but not to go to Germany. Cologne were furious and the transfer became an ugly, drawn-out mess. On 29 July, Strachan was even banned from playing by Fifa until there was a resolution. Eventually, after the involvement of the SFA, Uefa and Fifa, Aberdeen paid Cologne a sum to invalidate the deal Strachan had signed, and he went instead to United for a far higher fee of £500,000. The transfer was concluded on 8 August.

Strachan was unapologetic about leaving but felt guilty that he became distracted during the second half of the 1983-84 season. 'I wasn't proud of my behaviour. I didn't upset anybody; I was still best mates with them. But my mind wandered at times. I'd never had an agent, this was new to me. I was hoping I'd get a hand from people in the club but I didn't. Me and Mark [McGhee] would be sitting about fifteen minutes before a game, turning to each other, saying, "Has that guy from Hamburg phoned you back?" "Aye, I don't know what I'm going to do." "I might go to Cologne or Man United." This was going on for a long time. I hope it didn't affect the club too much. We did win a double.'

Strachan and McGhee were two of the dressing room's big characters. Intelligent, strong-willed and quick-witted, they were among the first to answer back if they felt Ferguson was taking liberties. They were also close friends. While Strachan was negotiating with one German club, McGhee was in talks with another. But the move which took McGhee to Hamburg went through without any complications or controversy. There had been no prospect of keeping him. During the closing weeks of the 1983–84 campaign, when he first heard what the Germans could offer, he was stunned. His personal Adidas sponsorship alone would be bigger than his salary at Aberdeen. The transfer fee was £280,000.

A third blow struck Ferguson. If he was resigned to losing Strachan and McGhee, the departure of Rougvie was a bitter setback. Ferguson was furious to discover that Rougvie, out of contract, had gone for talks with newly-promoted Chelsea. Rougvie has always maintained that he wanted to stay with Aberdeen but the club were inflexible about his request for a modest rise. He felt at the top of his game. He was twenty-eight and he had just won the Super Cup, a league and cup double, and had been capped for Scotland by Stein. 'All I was wanting was a decent wage and Ferguson said, "You've been down speaking to Chelsea, you mercenary bastard." Unbelievable! He slaughtered me in the papers. He left me without a name and that was the biggest disappointment. I had wanted to stay but he wouldn't pay what I was looking for. When I think of Fergie, I think, "He didn't give us a bag of money, but he did give us a bag of medals."'

Rougvie felt Ferguson was trying to please Dick Donald by keeping wages down, with the result that the Gothenburg team broke up unnecessarily when they could have been appeased with reasonable rises. In truth, the financial gulf between Aberdeen and Europe's elite clubs was such that Strachan and McGhee's transfers were inevitable. According to Strachan: 'I made a huge leap in money when I went to United. I was getting five times what I was getting at Aberdeen. They couldn't compete with that. I wouldn't have embarrassed them by asking.'

The trio's departures left enormous holes in the team. Chunks had been taken out of the defence, midfield and attack. Strachan was an impish magician, capable of turning even the biggest matches, and in six seasons under Ferguson he had weighed in with eighty-eight goals from midfield. McGhee's total was 100 over the same period and he had been the club's top scorer in three of the previous four campaigns. Aberdeen needed a lift. It seemed to come when a story broke that they had opened talks to land the outstanding Juventus and Poland midfielder Zbigniew Boniek. 'At first they were prepared to let him go and the player was keen to come,' said Ferguson. 'But then Juventus changed their mind.' The deal, if it had happened, would have been sensational. Boniek had just won Serie A and the European Cup Winners' Cup with Juventus. But nothing did happen, and Ferguson made no mention of any move for him in his two autobiographies that included the Aberdeen years. Instead he found replacements on his doorstep. Fearing that Strachan might leave earlier, as he wanted to, Ferguson had signed one of his former St Mirren players, midfielder Billy Stark, in the summer of 1983. To replace Rougvie he went to Clyde for their hard-working left-back Tommy McQueen. As for a goalscorer to fill McGhee's boots, he raided St Mirren for the fifth time in six years to land their squat, powerful and prolific striker Frank McDougall.

That great team, the Gothenburg team, had become so familiar that the fans were shaken by the departures. Here was the first confirmation that the club did not exist in some sort of never-ending fairy-tale. The consequences of Aberdeen's new profile and status were not all positive. Manchester United, Hamburg, Chelsea and others had hovered over Pittodrie, sensing easy pickings from a comparatively small club.

For the first time Aberdeen had become fashionable. Everyone wanted a piece of them. Ferguson and director Ian Donald returned to Paris for another award from Adidas, this time a bronze prize for being Europe's third-best team in 1983–84, behind Liverpool and Juventus. The manager attended the Midland Soccer Writers' Player of the Year dinner in Birmingham. The Variety Club of Great Britain named him their first 'Scottish Sports Personality of the Year'. He was invited to Buckingham Palace to receive an OBE. At the end of the year, Ferguson and Miller were invited to London for the BBC Sports Review of the Year. It was thought Aberdeen might be named as the Team of the Year. They were beaten by Olympic ice dancers Torvill and Dean. Miller was a guest on BBC's *A Question of Sport* and took his place with snooker star Terry Griffiths on Emlyn Hughes's team. Miller said: 'I'm sure I've got the footage somewhere on a VHS in a box in the cellar. That all came from what Aberdeen were achieving. At first nobody knows you. Nobody had any idea who Aberdeen were at first. Who Willie Miller or Alex McLeish or Jim Leighton were. Not a Scooby. Then Scotland went to Wembley and we beat England in 1981 and they start to take notice of you. From then on they recognise you as being a player. That was unusual, for anyone who played for Aberdeen to be noticed in England.'

No one was generating more attention than Ferguson. He had toppled the Old Firm to win the league title aged thirty-eight, got the better of Bobby Robson's Ipswich at thirty-nine, and beaten Real Madrid in a European final at forty-one. Around the north-east of Scotland he was constantly in demand for public appearances and promotions in schools, businesses, pubs and clubs. When programmes like *Football Focus* did features on what was stirring up in Scotland, there were shots of seagulls circling above Pittodrie and boats in the city's harbour. It gave the impression that Aberdeen was detached from football's mainstream, and resulted in a sharp contrast whenever the club's young manager, with his captivating energy and charisma, appeared on screen.

The first club who tried to lure Ferguson south were Wolverhampton Wanderers. An approach was made in January 1982, and he was sufficiently interested to travel to the Midlands and meet their chairman and directors. He thought Wolves uninviting and lifeless, just as Miller had felt about Sunderland. Molineux was in a state of disrepair and Ferguson was appalled to realise that no one other than a secretary was working at the stadium on a weekday afternoon. At the World Cup finals in Spain that summer Ferguson told Strachan: 'I don't want to leave Aberdeen.' Wolves had been easy to dismiss. The first real test of his commitment came in 1983 when Rangers twice approached him about taking over at Ibrox. That was an opportunity which appealed to Ferguson's heart and soul. Rangers was in his DNA, the club he had supported and the stadium which towered over the streets where he had grown up. The first approach was made after the 1983 Scottish Cup final, which Ferguson ignored out of respect for his friend and former team-mate John Greig, who was still employed as manager. If he gave a private hint that he would be more receptive if and when the job became available again, Rangers took note. Four months later Greig resigned after bleak opening results. Within hours Ferguson took telephone calls from a journalist asking if he was interested in the Rangers job and then from the club's vice-chairman, John Paton, making the same inquiry. Paton was given sufficient encouragement to detail what sort of offer Rangers could make, and to follow up with several calls over the following few days.

In *A Light in the North*, Ferguson talked of wrestling with a decision for two or three days and discussing the matter with Cathy long into the night. He called his old Rangers manager, Scot Symon, for advice. Symon had been sacked abruptly by the club in 1967. Ferguson was a player then, and he said: 'The minute Scot Symon left Rangers they seemed to lose their greatness.' Symon, however, was unequivocal in his view that Ferguson should leave Pittodrie for Ibrox. He then made a subsequent call alerting Ferguson to division among the directors at Ibrox. Hanging over Rangers like a bad smell was the question of whether or not the club would allow their next manager to sign Roman Catholics. Publicly Rangers said whoever was appointed would have the freedom to sign whoever he wanted. But the matter was deeply contentious and an unwritten policy of not knowingly signing Catholics divided the Rangers support.

Ferguson's friend Jimmy Reid, the legendary Clydeside trades union leader, tackled the issue in an interview with him for the *Sunday Mail*. 'To put it bluntly, football is about football in Aberdeen,' wrote Reid. 'There is an absence of the religious hatred and bigotry which has scarred the otherwise generous and human face of my beloved Glasgow for so long. I am convinced this view is shared by Alex Ferguson. He is a warm-hearted, outgoing intelligent man who brings up his family in a spirit of tolerance. Any team that Fergie manages will recruit players exclusively on ability.'

There has long been an unspoken rule that prominent figures in Scottish football say little in public about religious bigotry, and even less about it being prevalent at certain clubs, or among a certain set of fans. That does not imply acceptance, only pragmatism. Ferguson had abhorred sectarianism since his youth. 'A glance at my family tree suggests why bigotry never had any chance of spreading its pollution among the Fergusons,' he explained in *Managing My Life*. Ferguson was a Protestant married to a Catholic, as was his father. 'Through all its branches, and for as far back as we can trace, there have been mixed marriages. Perhaps it doesn't always breed religious intolerance out of the later generations, but it certainly did so in our case.' Such hatred troubled him when considering the Rangers job, though. 'I was already reluctant to entertain exposing my family to the risk of a recurrence of the bigotry I had encountered at Ibrox in my playing days,' he wrote. 'Cathy's religion would probably have been enough in itself to convince me that returning to Rangers was not a good idea.'

There was also a powerful reluctance to leave the club he had built. Ferguson arranged a meeting with Dick Donald, Chris Anderson and their respective lawyers. The following morning's newspapers reported 'Fergie set to stay'. Details of a deal were revealed in which Ferguson would receive £50,000 a year plus bonuses over a five-year contract. In fact, he had been on these improved terms since the start of the 1983–84 season but only now had he formalised them by signing a contract. Manager and chairman had believed that the strength of their relationship meant they did not need one. 'If I asked my chairman for a contract he'd think I didn't trust him any longer,' Ferguson had said after the Bayern Munich game. 'I do, so I don't need a piece of paper.' Seven months later, because of the Rangers approach, he had one. Donald and Ferguson's relationship was as close as ever but a contract protected the club and entitled them to compensation if and when the manager left. 'It's been a trying time but I know I have made the right decision,' said Ferguson. 'I'm remaining with the club who have brought me any success I've had in football.' The *Daily Record*'s chief football writer, Alex Cameron, told his readers: 'The very fact he is staying underlines the attraction of Pittodrie where the chance of being in Europe is at least as good as it is at Liverpool or Manchester United.'

Ferguson's rejection of Rangers was further confirmation of Scottish football's new hierarchy. Previously it would have been unthinkable for a manager at another club to reject a call from the Old Firm. And Ferguson was not the only one. The following Sunday, Dundee United's Jim McLean had three hours of talks inside Ibrox but turned them down as well. Four days later Rangers appointed their former boss, Jock Wallace, giving him £65,000 a year and the supposed freedom to sign whoever he wanted. In fact, it would be another six years, with another manager in place, before Rangers made a point of signing a high-profile Catholic.

The club who came closest to taking Ferguson from Aberdeen at that time were Tottenham Hotspur. Keith Burkinshaw had given notice that he would leave at the end of the 1983–84 season. Spurs targeted Ferguson. He liked the mood and ambition at White Hart Lane and was impressed by the charismatic chairman, Irving Scholar. 'I liked the principle of the way the club was run in the sense that they admired pure football,' he said. Wages, terms and even accommodation were agreed over a series of phone calls and two meetings, held in Paris to maintain privacy. 'Alex Ferguson and I finally shook hands on the agreement that he would become our next Spurs manager,' Scholar claimed in 1999. Scholar said the plan was that Ferguson would tell him when to make a formal approach to Aberdeen, and that the move would be announced early in the summer of 1984. But Ferguson got cold feet and changed his mind. Why?

He told Scholar he felt it would be disloyal to Donald to leave Aberdeen. After all the discussions they had had, Scholar felt there was another reason, namely that Cathy Ferguson could not be persuaded to move the family to London. Ferguson's own explanation was that he wanted a five-year contract and Spurs would offer only two. They improved that to three, but he needed more: 'I was not convinced that was long enough to do the job,' he explained later. 'Once again I opted to stay with Aberdeen.'

It was a close shave for the Scottish club: Ferguson and Scholar had impressed each other hugely. Spurs promoted Peter Shreeves, their assistant manager, instead. He went on to finish third in his first season, ahead of Manchester United.

Ferguson cleared his head and prepared for 1984–85, his seventh season at Aberdeen. The campaign, without Strachan, McGhee and Rougvie, included a return to the European Cup for the first time since they lost to Liverpool four years earlier. This time they went into the competition without the injured Weir and could not play Frank McDougall because he carried a European suspension from his time at St Mirren. In the first round they were drawn against Dynamo Berlin, the East German champions for the last six years in a row. Aberdeen were coasting in the first leg at Pittodrie on 19 September, 1984, when Berlin pulled a goal back eight minutes from the end to lose only 2–1. Two weeks later in Germany, with Bell added to the injury list, another late goal gave Berlin a 2–1 win, which took the game into extra time and then penalties. Aberdeen were 4–2 up in the shoot-out but Miller and Black had their attempts saved and the East Germans converted their last three for a stunning win. A crack at the European Cup, the one tournament in which Ferguson was desperate to make an impression, had been tossed away cheaply. There was not even the consolation of going out to a good side. All of Aberdeen's previous European runs had ended with huge credit. Any team who beat them rubber-stamped their credentials: Fortuna Düsseldorf went on to reach the Cup Winners' Cup final in 1979; Eintracht Frankfurt won the Uefa Cup in 1980; Liverpool became European Cup champions in 1981; Hamburg reached the 1982 Uefa Cup final, and beating Aberdeen took Porto into the 1984 Cup Winners' Cup final. Berlin, meanwhile, were immediately knocked out in the next round. 'It's particularly disappointing to lose to a side who were inferior to us,' said Ferguson.

There was trouble at home, too. Aberdeen had crashed in the League Cup against lower-league Airdrie on 22 August.

Airdrie were managed by Ally MacLeod, Ferguson's larger-than-life predecessor at Pittodrie, and inflicted a 3–1 defeat at their Broomfield ground. 'Aberdeen were made to look an ordinary side,' wrote the *Glasgow Herald*. Weir, Black, Cooper, Hewitt, McMaster and McDougall had been unavailable, but it was still a heavyweight team: Leighton, McKimmie, McLeish, Miller, Simpson and Bell all started. 'I have to hope that what the young players saw in the dressing room after Airdrie, when top men were shattered by the result, will teach them something,' Ferguson told the newspapers. 'They have had a nice, easy baptism here. Now they have to turn into men.'

Aberdeen had lost three of their key players to other clubs, been robbed of Cooper, McMaster and Weir through worrying injuries, been knocked out of the League Cup by a team of part-timers, and had gone out of Europe at the first hurdle. The season was eleven games old and already two tournaments were dead. MacLeod was sympathetic to his former club: 'When you lose the players they have through injury and transfers you can't be the same team.' After six years of Fergie momentum it looked as though Aberdeen had stalled.

EIGHTEEN

'THIS SEASON'S TARGET IS TWO TROPHIES . . . MINIMUM'

Anyone who suggested Aberdeen's power was on the wane was liable to be put right by the manager in no uncertain terms. Ferguson was eager to assert that it was business as usual at Pittodrie. If he thought someone was sowing doubt, he sorted it out. Just before the 1984–85 season started, the experienced television commentator Jock Brown heard from friends in the game that Ferguson was unhappy with him. 'They were saying the same sort of things,' Brown recalled. '"Ooh, Fergie's gunning for you." When I asked what the problem was they said, "Your cup final commentary."' Brown had no qualms about telephoning Ferguson to confront him. Ferguson got straight to the point: the issue was indeed his commentary for STV during the Aberdeen-Celtic cup final at the end of May. 'He said to me, "Aye, aye, you were biased in favour of Celtic. And I can prove it. Did you or did you not say that it was against the run of play when Eric Black scored the opening goal?" I said that yeah, from memory, I think I had. He said, "I can tell you that it wisnae." I was getting more intrigued. I can't remember the exact numbers now, but he said something like, "In the first half of that game we were in their box for fourteen minutes twenty-two seconds, they were in our penalty box for nine minutes sixteen seconds, so that proves it, we were on top." So I said, "But what was the count after ten minutes when Eric Black scored?" There was a pause. He goes, "Oh, you smart bastard . . . how are you doing anyway?"'

Brown later discovered that Ferguson had also filleted Archie Macpherson for his cup final commentary for the BBC. 'What that told you is that he had recorded both outputs, studied carefully both outputs, so that he could identify "the west of Scotland bias", and then he could tell all his players, "What about those cup final commentaries? Even when you win the cup they don't give you any credit."'

Ferguson was bitterly disappointed, in particular, by the European Cup exit to Berlin. 'I began to feel that events were piling up on top of me,' he admitted in *Managing My Life*. 'I was actually beginning to think that maybe I should have taken one of the recent job offers I had received from Rangers and Spurs.' He said his mind was reeling. A calm look around the dressing room would have reassured him. He had built a squad and an ethos that could survive the loss of Strachan, McGhee and Rougvie and overcome the early setbacks as their replacements settled in. 'It still felt like a winning machine,' said Simpson, who was only twenty-two at the time but in his fifth season as a first-team regular.

A 'winning machine' was an apt description of their form in the Premier Division. The first eighteen league games brought fifteen wins, two draws and one defeat. A little wobble at the end of 1984 offered the chasing pack some hope. Over nineteen days they drew against Dundee and St Mirren and lost home and away against Dundee United. 'One or two people think we're crumbling,' said Ferguson dismissively. Sure enough, they came again, finishing with eight wins and a draw from their last nine league games. Aberdeen's three previous championships, in 1955, 1980 and 1984, had all been clinched by a result in the central belt. In 1985 there was the pleasure of crossing the finishing line at Pittodrie. When Celtic arrived on 27 April they needed a victory to maintain any hope of catching Ferguson's team, while a draw was enough for Aberdeen. Just before half-time Celtic were awarded a penalty when Stark nudged striker Mo Johnston as they went for a cross. Miller led an instant delegation berating referee George Smith, but the decision stood. Roy Aitken thrashed the penalty straight down the middle to give Celtic the lead. In the sixty-first minute Aberdeen were awarded a free kick on their right wing. Ian Porteous swung the ball into the area and Miller connected with a downward header which went in off the post for the precious equaliser. 'All credit to Aberdeen, they have done the business,' said Celtic manager Davie Hay.

Aberdeen had lost just four of their thirty-six league games and their fifty-seven points was a Scottish Premier Division record. The former Newcastle, Arsenal and England striker Malcolm Macdonald was a guest at Ibrox when Aberdeen won there in November. Later he was effusive: 'Aberdeen are the best British team I've seen in the last five years, with the possible exception of Liverpool.' That day he had watched a winning goal from the player who lit up Aberdeen's 1984–85 season. Frank McDougall was a former amateur boxing champion from a tough Glasgow housing scheme. He played snooker, liked a pint and was not averse to the odd cigarette. He worried that Ferguson would be turned off by his reputation as a lad who enjoyed a night out. But what Ferguson saw was an instinctive, cool and fearless finisher who could score with either foot or head. The most goals McDougall had scored in a season had been eighteen for St

Mirren; Ferguson told him he wanted thirty. He went pretty close. Despite a slow start, and later missing eight games because of injury, he scored twenty-two times in the league, including a hat-trick at Pittodrie against Rangers. There was a run of goals in eight consecutive league games and his final total earned him third place and a trip to Paris to collect a bronze boot in the European Golden Boot awards.

Supporters embraced McDougall as a vibrant new force in their team. He was a natural who reminded them of Joe Harper. McDougall revelled in playing on the biggest stage of his career, and produced superb football, but he remained a street fighter who could test Ferguson's patience. Whenever his lifestyle caused strain between them, Ferguson would say: 'I'll put you on the dole, McDougall. You'll be signing on if you don't get your act together.' The potential for conflict was constant and it boiled over when McDougall disguised a groin injury because he was desperate to face Hearts in the Scottish Cup quarter-final. When he took a free kick in the first half Ferguson saw him grimace in pain and immediately realised what was going on. When the game ended in a draw all the players were ordered in for Sunday morning training. Ferguson burst into the dressing room and marched straight up to the striker. McDougall panicked and the old boxer in him emerged: he swung a punch which caught Ferguson on the face and knocked him down. When he published his autobiography, McDougall wrote: 'Of all the stupid things I had done in my life, putting Fergie on his arse had just stormed straight into the charts at number one.'

McDougall was convinced he had just ended his Aberdeen career eight months after it began. Ferguson bounced back to his feet and shouted at Teddy Scott: 'Get him out of here, he's fucking finished.' McDougall went home and agonised over what to do. When he next saw Ferguson he blurted out a desperate apology. Ferguson stared at him and then calmly replied: 'Make it up to me on the pitch. I want you back in the team.' Curiously, Ferguson's physical altercations with Aberdeen players all involved strong-willed strikers: Joe Harper, Mark McGhee and McDougall. He had been one of those himself in his playing days. McDougall was forgiven because he was invaluable: a familiar Ferguson trait previously demonstrated with Archibald, McGhee, Strachan and others. His goals had won Aberdeen the league. The punch was not mentioned again and the pair's mutual respect, and eventual friendship, deepened.

McDougall made an incredible impact in his debut season, bringing a fresh look to the team with the promise of further success to come. Tommy McQueen was not the iconic big figure Rougvie had been at left-back, but he was steady and reliable, a valuable ally to Leighton, McLeish and Miller at the back. Stark had continued to blossom as an outstanding presence alongside Simpson and Cooper, when fit, in midfield. And Stark scored twenty times over the season. He was stylish on the ball and had the ability to change the pace of the team's play.

At the end of the campaign Ferguson used his programme column to celebrate Aberdeen becoming league champions for the third time in six seasons and to underline how rewarding that had been. Stark said: 'At the start of a season he would have an idea about how many points we would need, how many defeats we could take, how many goals we'd need to score. And he was never far away. When you looked at the table at the end of the season you'd see how close he was and you'd think, "That's spooky." He not only knew the strengths of his own squad but the strengths of the others. And he'd say this to us, "The target this season is two trophies . . . minimum."' By that unforgiving standard 1984–85 was a failure. Aberdeen won the league, but their record in the cup competitions was the poorest of Ferguson's time at the Dons: first-hurdle exits from Europe and the League Cup had been compounded by a loss to Dundee United in the Scottish Cup. He had been determined to secure an historic fourth consecutive Scottish Cup triumph but, after a four-year sequence of twenty-three games without defeat, the run ended in the semi-final. He wished his old friend Jim McLean luck in the final against Celtic. 'We supported them just as they would have given their support in a similar situation. The two clubs, after all, have done so much together for Scottish football in combatting the consistent dominance of the Old Firm.' United, though, could not follow in Aberdeen's wake, and Celtic won the cup.

Finding ways to beat Celtic and Rangers was the flame that never went out for Ferguson. The Old Firm managers he faced most often were Billy McNeill and Davie Hay at Celtic and John Greig and Jock Wallace at Rangers. When they tried to outwit him or apply psychological pressure he would usually pull off a successful counter-punch. He began to notice that when the Aberdeen bus pulled up to Parkhead a member of Celtic's staff would scuttle inside. Moments later the foyer would be packed with members of Celtic's legendary Lisbon Lions side, the 1967 European Cup winners. Ferguson reckoned it was an attempt to unnerve his players as they walked in. On the way to one Parkhead game Ferguson flagged it up to his players. Walker McCall remembered: 'He said, "You watch, as soon as our bus pulls in the doorman will run inside. I don't know who he goes to but he talks to someone." Sure enough we pull up and the doorman disappears. As soon as we were through the front doors you had what seemed like all the Lisbon Lions standing there. It was Celtic trying to intimidate us. Fergie said, "We're not going to be intimidated." We marched in there with our heads held up. We weren't disrespectful, we'd say a hello or whatever, but we were never going to be intimidated by them.' Ferguson would include injured players in the travelling party so that Aberdeen would walk in mob-handed. More than twenty first-team players coming through the doors of Parkhead or Ibrox gave an impression of strength in numbers.

There was one stunt Celtic pulled so many times that Aberdeen started having fun with it themselves. Around fifteen minutes before kick-off at Parkhead there would be a knock on the away dressing room door. It was the Celtic chairman, Desmond White. He was sorry, it was out of his hands, but the police had asked for the kick-off to be delayed because there were so many Celtic supporters still outside the ground waiting to get in. It happened every time they played there, to the extent Ferguson and his players could set their watches by White's arrival and would joke among themselves as if counting down the seconds until they heard the knock. Ferguson decided to show White he was wasting his time. Archie Knox explained: 'Alex said to the boys, "Fuck this, don't get ready." Desmond chaps the door and looks in. He started giving it the usual . . . then noticed all the boys were still sitting in their suits, looking like they didn't have a care in the world! Fergie wouldn't let them change until Desmond had gone out.' White never knocked on the door again.

Ferguson retaliated by playing the Old Firm at their own game. He sought every little advantage. Remembering how Stein had operated at Celtic, he built a network of spies and informants. A couple of days before the 1983 Scottish Cup semi-final, Celtic's Charlie Nicholas suffered an ankle injury in training. It was obvious he would not recover in time for the game but McNeill was desperate to keep the fact secret. The press did not get wind of it. Having a police escort to Hampden usually meant the Celtic bus arrived before their opponents. This time they turned up only to find Aberdeen already there and Ferguson standing watching from behind the main glass doors. Nicholas said: 'Big Billy wanted me to walk in as naturally as I could, looking as fit as usual. But it was quite a jump down from the step on the bus to the ground and when I landed on my bad ankle I grimaced and started hobbling. I looked up at Fergie: I was the one he'd been watching. He just smiled right at me and then turned to go inside and tell his team, "Nicholas is injured."' Ferguson had made sure the Aberdeen bus arrived earlier than usual, so he could confirm the information he had been given that Celtic's star man was out.

On another occasion, in the build-up to one Rangers-Aberdeen game at Ibrox, Jock Wallace told the newspapers his squad was desperately depleted by injuries. Two or three of his key men were out. When the Aberdeen bus pulled up to the stadium Ferguson was quick to jump off. Wallace, who was a friend, was one of the first people he saw near the door. Ferguson handed him a piece of paper. Wallace was nonplussed. Ferguson told him he had written down the team Rangers would have on the pitch at the start of the game. Wallace looked at it and pretended to scoff, asking Ferguson why he had included all the players who were injured. Didn't he read the papers? Ferguson laughed and said the charade was over. The previous day he had visited his mother-in-law who lived in a block of high-rise flats overlooking Rangers' training ground. From there he watched Wallace conduct his session with a fully-fit squad. Wallace looked at him: 'Ach, you cannae blame me for trying.'

Aberdeen, by contrast, had no dedicated training facilities, so anyone wishing to spy on their preparations would have to trail them all round the city. The players would travel by minibus to Seaton Park, a nearby municipal facility open to the public, or to Gordon Barracks, a military training ground two miles from Pittodrie. Sometimes the car park opposite the stadium would do. If bad weather prevented them from using those locations Ferguson had no reservations about training on Aberdeen beach beside the ice-cold, wind-swept North Sea. 'The training on the sand is fine for general fitness and stamina,' he said. 'The problem is that the constant running about on it can make players a shade sluggish.' He might have cited the threat of hypothermia as another hazard. The temperature could dip to minus 12 degrees Celsius. 'The wind's hitting your face, freezing your knackers off, you never get used to the cold,' said Ferguson. But provided they were sufficiently wrapped-up the players quite enjoyed the beach. Weir said: 'Sometimes it was hard running on the sand but you could have a bit of fun with the waves. The sea felt Baltic but if you had injuries it could help minor aches and pains.' It was a training venue with unique peculiarities. On one day Black and Hewitt found a seagull covered in oil and took the bird back to Pittodrie so someone could call the RSPCA. Another time Black found a distressed seal pup.

Everything had to run like clockwork at a Ferguson training session. Usually the assistant manager would take a minibus to that day's host venue. The youth players would carry the goalposts and gear so that everything was ready when another minibus arrived with the first team. Ferguson immersed himself in all aspects of training when Pat Stanton was his assistant manager, and carried that on when Archie Knox took over in 1980. One day Knox said: 'Why am I here? I do nothing. You shouldn't be doing all the training sessions.' Ferguson disagreed, but Teddy Scott backed up Knox. From then on the manager took a step back, overseeing everything but letting the assistant take charge of the fine detail. Garner revealed: 'Fergie was demanding. I had to come in every day with a plan for training, a plan that went from ten to five past ten, then five past ten to half past ten, then right to twelve o'clock. Every morning. He would have a look at it and say, "Right, I think we should do a bit of this, then a bit of that as well."' With the wise input of Scott the drills were never repetitive or boring, and the players' fitness was permanently high.

The natural competitiveness of the players led to flash-points. Dangerous tackling and injuries were a constant risk. Steve Cowan, one of the squad's strikers, remembered: 'Alex McLeish did me in a practice match. I was out for three months with torn knee ligaments. He came right through me, did me, off I went, not a word said. Training was like the games: aggressive. Not just McLeish but Miller, Kennedy, Bell. Nobody took liberties with that Aberdeen team.' Even a small player like winger Joe Miller, just 5ft 6in and only sixteen in 1983, could be spiky. Little Miller had been brought up in the east end of Glasgow. One day he took on Pittodrie's undisputed heavyweight, who was eight inches taller than him. 'I was running riot in training, nutmegging Dougie Rougvie all the time. He wasn't happy. I destroyed him. He started booting me up and down. Fergie told him, "Hey, calm down, he's only sixteen," and Dougie goes, "He's big enough." I think his mind was elsewhere because he wasn't going to stay at Aberdeen. So later in the dressing room Dougie goes, "Want a lift up the road, wee man?" I get in the car and he says, "I've just got to go somewhere first." He drives out to Balmedie Beach, opens the door and says, "Get out." He goes, "Don't ever make a fool of me like that again." I couldn't believe it. I kept it to myself, never said anything to Fergie. I just waited my opportunity. Then I tried to break his legs in training. He was going nuts.

"Gaffer, he tried to two-feet me there." I said, "Well, if you're big enough . . ." He said, "If you ever do that again I'll knock you out." Dougie left not long after that. But that was the sort of attitude among the players. We were all hard.'

Training was intense because that was the way Ferguson demanded they approach every fixture. In games the players were told to set a fast tempo: take quick throw-ins, quick corners, quick goal kicks, get the ball down and get playing. Don't give the opposition time to draw breath. Knox said: 'The message was that if you're winning you don't slow the game down, you increase the tempo.' The players were told to run off the pitch at half-time to show opponents they still had plenty of energy. McGhee said: 'If you watch the old games you can see we used to run down the tunnel. Did you ever notice that? We ran off the pitch. It was done to intimidate the opposition. At Pittodrie when you head from the pitch to the tunnel there is a downhill slope on the concrete, past the boot room and the referee's room, across the corridor to the dressing rooms. The opposition's door was to the right and ours was straight ahead. Our door would be open. The other team would be walking down the tunnel and we would all run down. If any of them were walking down you'd fuck right into them and you'd be in the dressing room before they could gather themselves and react. Quite often we'd all come piling in, running in, and the door would get shut and all you could hear outside was, "Ya fucking bastards!" By that time our door was shut we were all in and there was chaos out in the corridor, the opposition shouting and bawling.'

The focus was relentless. In a game at Morton, Walker McCall suffered concussion and was carried off on a stretcher and taken to hospital. Ferguson sent a message to him that the team bus would collect him after the match. McCall waited. An hour passed, and then another. McCall said: 'We got hold of Fergie and I said, "What's going on, I thought you were coming to get me." He said, "I had other things on my mind . . . I totally forgot about you. I'll tell you what, go and get the train up the road." I said, "Boss, I got carried off on a stretcher, I've still got an Aberdeen kit on!"' Eventually McCall's brother-in-law drove him north, receiving £200 in an envelope from Ferguson for his trouble.

Knox was Ferguson's longest-serving and most successful Aberdeen assistant. He bought into all of the boss's methods with enthusiasm, but sometimes Ferguson's individualism could wrong-foot even this most trusted right-hand man. One Saturday the pair of them agreed that day's team and then walked across the corridor to the dressing room to tell the players. To Knox's bafflement Ferguson read out a team with three changes to the one they had discussed seconds earlier. When the players left he asked him what was going on. 'Fergie said, "Ach, I just thought it would be better going this way." He would do things like that. It was about knowledge and instinct. You can have all the knowledge in the world about how your team will play, but then a bit of instinct will come in, and you have to follow your instinct. You can't coach that. To be honest he never really listened to me on the bench.' Sometimes the pair of them would launch into arguments at half-time, with the players reduced to the role of spectators. Strachan said: 'They used to argue all the time. We used to think it was hilarious. Brilliant. We used to sit back and watch. "That'll never work." "No, that's rubbish."'

Ferguson was not above superstition. He approached Knox and asked if he wanted to buy 'a good coat for £12'. A friend of his was selling them. The pair of them duly bought a coat each and first wore them at the start of a Scottish Cup campaign. When they won, Ferguson insisted they continue wearing the coats for every tie. Knox said: 'So we get to the final. It's roasting and I'm out on the touchline with the bloody trench coat on. We had to wear them in every round! Alex could be funny with stuff like that.'

All of his assistant managers – Stanton, Knox and Garner – became accustomed to his sometimes idiosyncratic demands. He would spend hours on car journeys with his assistant, making the 300-mile round trip from Aberdeen to Glasgow to watch opponents, potential signings or youth coaching sessions. His players could tell when he turned up for training after a late night away. 'He used to come in with his eyes popping out of his head,' said McMaster. 'Nae sleep, thinking about games, going to games, coming back up the road, going to training.'

The same demands were made of his assistants: 'If there was a game on somewhere you had to be at it,' said Garner. 'He said to me, "I've given you a company car, get to a fucking game." If he came with me he'd make me drive and he'd sleep in the passenger seat.' Travelling gave Ferguson thinking time. Not all of it was devoted to football. On one drive south with Stanton, Ferguson suddenly ended a quiet spell by asking, "Do you think we're alone?" Stanton said: "I started getting a wee bit worried." I says, "How do you mean?" He says, "Do you think we're alone in the cosmos? Do you think there are other beings on other planets?" That was all he said. I'm thinking, "What's brought this on? Was he heidin' that ball too much back when he played?"' Ferguson let the subject drop and the journey continued. 'Later that night we come out of the game and we were walking towards the car when he said, "What do you think about that?" It hadn't been much of a game so I said, "Ach, it wasn't much to look at," and he goes, "No, no, no . . . Do you think we're on our own?" That's still what he was thinking about! Obviously the game hadn't impressed him!'

Whether on football or metaphysics, Ferguson's mind was restless and inquisitive. He was also quick to take advantage whenever the opportunity arose. When suspended from the touchline by the SFA he had to rely on technology to maintain control. He began communicating with his assistant manager via rudimentary walkie-talkies during games. After arriving to play Hibs one time, and having exchanged pleasantries with John Blackley and Tommy Craig, the opposition management team, he told Garner to go to the dugouts so they could test the handsets they were using that day. Garner took his position on the trackside and looked up at Ferguson in the stand. 'So I switch it on and immediately I can hear Blackley talking to Craig. Fergie saw me and quickly put his finger up to his lips, telling me not to make a sound. That's the way it stayed. There was some sort of crossed line and for the full game me and Fergie never said a word to each other. We could hear everything they were doing. So we're doing stuff like moving Eric Black from one wing to another and I'm hearing Blackley going, "Christ, they've moved Black again."' Aberdeen won comfortably. When the two management teams had a beer after the match Craig gushed in admiration about how Aberdeen had anticipated their every tactical move. Garner said: 'So I tell him, "That's 'cos we could hear you on the walkie-talkie." Blackley goes, "Ya bastards, I thought I could hear something on the line! I thought it was crossed lines with a taxi company."'

Ferguson was not always so lucky with walkie-talkies. In one game at Pittodrie he could not get the handset to work and got angrier and angrier as Garner shouted above the crowd, trying to get a message to him. 'Press the green button . . . the green button!' Ferguson started banging the handset so vigorously it slipped out of his hand and smacked the bald pate of the person sitting in front of him. It was the head of Aberdeen's most senior civic dignitary, Lord Provost Alex Collie. The accidental blow caused a cut which left Collie wiping away spots of blood with his handkerchief. Ferguson spent the game alternating between managing and apologising.

NINETEEN

NASTY, TOXIC, AND VIOLENT: WELCOME TO ABERDEEN-RANGERS

When Ferguson's interest in football was first kindled there was only one team that mattered. The walk from his boyhood home in Govan Road to Ibrox Park was under a mile and took twenty minutes. By the early 1950s Ferguson and his brother, Martin, were attending matches every second week, drawn the length of Broomloan Road to the vast stadium that rose up before their eyes. The crowds sometimes topped 80,000 and if that was not enough to impress them there were the dimensions of Ibrox itself: a mighty testament to the power and prestige of what was seen as the Protestant half of the Old Firm. There were unmistakable symbols of tradition and class, from the red-brick facade of the main stand, the uniformed commissionaire at the front door, and the marble staircase and wood-panelled corridors within. Ferguson was a proud product of his environment. He could never be anything but a Rangers supporter.

However, the two harrowing years he spent there as a player changed his relationship with the club forever. Ferguson made profound and lasting friendships while at Rangers, not least with John Greig. He was the club's top scorer in his first season, but fell out of favour in his second and by the start of his third campaign he had been banished to train alone and turn out for the third team against the likes of Glasgow Transport and Glasgow University. He was appalled by Rangers for two reasons: first, for sacking the successful and popular manager Scot Symon – they sent an accountant to deliver the news – and, secondly, for employing Willie Allison as a public relations officer. In *Managing My Life* he wrote of Allison as a 'despicable' religious bigot who quietly spread poison about Cathy Ferguson being a Catholic. On a pre-season tour in Denmark in 1968 Ferguson learned the papers back in Scotland had carried reports that he was finished at Rangers. The leak had the whiff of Allison about it. Demoralised, he got drunk and tried to confront the PR man, but Greig had the sense to restrain him and shepherd him away. Through the five years when their Aberdeen and Rangers teams kicked lumps out of each other, Ferguson's respect and loyalty towards Greig would never waver.

But Rangers as a club lost its mystique and magic for Ferguson. He said no other experience in his decades as a player and manager produced a 'scar' comparable to being humiliated at the club he supported as a boy. He was not motivated by revenge when he faced Rangers as a player for Falkirk or Ayr United, or as a manager with St Mirren or Aberdeen. But he saw himself as a victim of mistreatment, pettiness and bigotry, and was disgusted at how Symon was summarily dismissed; it left him with an entirely different attitude to the club. The hold Rangers once had on him was broken. His refusal to defer to Rangers made a profound impression on his players. Frank McDougall included a revealing story in his autobiography. When he played at Ibrox for the first time with Aberdeen, Ferguson told the team to go and stretch their legs on the pitch. McDougall was first out but when he got to the trackside he saw a stern-faced groundsman presiding over a sign which said, 'Keep off the grass'. McDougall duly turned, jogged back to the dressing room and told Ferguson that he had been told to warm up in the dimly-lit, shale training area under the main stand instead. Ferguson was enraged. He marched past McDougall up the tunnel to confront the groundsman:

'What's the fucking problem?'

'No one's allowed on the grass until kick-off, that's the rules.'

'Fuck your rules.'

According to McDougall the sign was booted up in the air and Ferguson stood guard beside the pitch as the rest of the Aberdeen players ran on to it and warmed up. The moment was an eye-opener for McDougall. No one at St Mirren, where he had come from, would have dared to defy Rangers like that.

Three decades on, the animosity that still exists between Aberdeen and Rangers is usually attributed to the deterioration in relations between the clubs during the Ferguson era. In fact, the Aberdeen-Rangers rivalry also taps into the decades of mutual wariness and distance which existed between their two cities. As Scotland's most successful, best-supported club, Rangers naturally provoked resentment among supporters of every other team. From as early as the 1950s most Aberdeen fans felt victories over Rangers were even sweeter than those over Celtic, and defeats more keenly felt. Until Ferguson came along no club, except Celtic, had offered a lasting challenge to Rangers. Aberdeen's aggressive, uncompromising rise transformed the balance between the clubs and on-field clashes stirred the latent hostility between the fans.

Aberdeen versus Rangers in the 1980s became the nastiest game on the Scottish calendar. The furore over the fracas between Rougvie and Johnstone in the 1979 League Cup final had caused enormous bitterness at Pittodrie. Every incident, fight or flashpoint intensified the rivalry. In a 1980 cup tie at Ibrox, Rangers winger, Willie Johnston, was sent off twelve minutes after coming off the bench for stamping on McMaster's chest. It was wrongly reported that McMaster required the kiss of life on the pitch, but the foul did leave him with marks from Johnston's studs on his skin. McMaster said: 'I was a human trampoline for Willie Johnston. I don't know what went through his mind. He was one of the hardest guys to play against, but all of a sudden this maniac jumped on my chest with his studs. If big Dougie Rougvie had got a hold of him he'd have killed him.'

When Ferguson stepped on to the team bus after the match he approached McMaster and said: 'Anything that happened out there, don't say anything.' The red card was the thirteenth of Johnston's career and Ferguson was loath to increase the pressure on Greig. Years later he would describe the stamp as 'disgusting' but at the time he kept his own counsel. Johnston gave his version of events in a 2009 autobiography, saying he was not proud of his actions but thought his victim was Willie Miller. 'Unfortunately I got the wrong player,' he said in misguided mitigation. 'Willie was a great player but he was a hard man and deserved some of his treatment back.'

No fixture was more demanding on referees than Aberdeen against Rangers. The red card rarely remained in their pocket. In addition to those shown to Rougvie and Johnston, there was a long list of others. In 1983 Rangers' John MacDonald went off for butting Bell at Pittodrie. Black and Ally Dawson were shown red cards a year later at Ibrox. Twelve months on and McKimmie was sent off for a sliding challenge on Dawson, who also went for retaliating by angrily grabbing McKimmie's shirt. That same year Rangers were reduced to nine men at Ibrox when Craig Paterson and Hugh Burns were dismissed in an especially poisonous encounter. Five months later two players who had swapped clubs – Jim Bett to Aberdeen and Bell, now at Rangers – trooped off at Pittodrie. The tally of bookings in these battles was eye-watering.

Even a character as composed and self-contained as Black succumbed to the heat of a Rangers game. His red card for grabbing Dawson by the throat was the only one he received in Scottish football. Black said: 'You ended up playing against teams so often that there was always a score to settle. You were constantly coming up against the same people and obviously there were memories from the previous meeting. I wasn't noted for my fighting qualities. One or two others were a bit better than me at that. I suffered one or two smacks in the face, elbows, punches, everything else. You just got on with it and tried to react and get your own back when you could. I don't remember what Fergie said that day at Ibrox, but he didn't like players being sent off.' Ferguson wanted aggression, confrontation and strength, but only so long as they did not result in anything which might weaken the team. Steve Cowan said: 'I remember one day against Rangers, up against Craig Paterson and John McClelland, and I burst both their noses. After it Fergie was going, "Well done, Stevie, brilliant, great performance." Not just for doing that but for being physical against them and not being intimidated.'

Ally McCoist emerged as an outstanding striker in the Rangers team during the 1983–84 season when Aberdeen were at their most formidable. He became a permanent presence at a time when the fixture was especially bruising and physical. Twice he suffered a broken nose inflicted by Miller. McCoist said: 'I remember one time smashing him back at half-time. I waited on him playing one up the line and I went over and did him. He got up screaming the odds and I said, "It's still 14–1 to you." They could handle it. They could all handle it. That Aberdeen side had a spirit that big Jock Wallace would have loved in his own team at Rangers.' In one respect the admiration was mutual. Ferguson tried to buy McCoist from Rangers. At St Mirren he had taken McCoist, then thirteen, to train with the club's apprentices once every week. When the apprentices finished McCoist would wait around eating chips, while Ferguson attended to some paperwork and then drove him back to his home in East Kilbride. Back then Ferguson decided not to sign him, fearing he was too small. But by the summer of 1984 McCoist had yet to win over the Rangers support and Ferguson tried to talk Jock Wallace into a move. McCoist said: 'Would I have gone to sign for Fergie? Of course. Absolutely. He had a chat with Jock Wallace about it. And that was as far as it went. Big Jock told me, but he didn't give much away. He growled, "I've had Ferguson on the phone for you." That was it! I didn't dare ask him any more about it.'

Broad parity in the wages paid to the players in the early 1980s meant trade between the leading Scottish clubs was minimal. Direct movement between Rangers and Celtic was unthinkable because of the animosity among the supporters, and to a lesser extent the same applied between Rangers and Aberdeen. Ferguson sold Dom Sullivan to Celtic but never signed anyone from them, nor from Rangers, in his time at Pittodrie. The move for McCoist was unsuccessful and he also admired the Rangers midfielder Bett. He eventually signed him in 1985, but only after Bett had left Rangers and spent two seasons in Belgium. Neale Cooper said: 'Fergie used to say to me, "Jim Bett hates playing against you, you torture him, he never gets away from you, he's no use." One day I pick up the paper and it's "Ferguson signs Jim Bett"! It was a wee game he played.'

In the summer that Bett arrived, Bell left to join Rangers. As usual the departure was on Ferguson's terms after he decided the midfielder's mobility had been impaired by injury. Bell said: 'I couldn't believe Rangers signed me. Jock Wallace said, "You've failed your medical, son, but do you want to play for Rangers?" I said, "Aye," and he goes, "Well, sign there." The first time I went back to Pittodrie I was sent off. The Aberdeen fans were shouting "reject". So I gave the king's salute to them. The police chief inspector was going to charge me but I was very apologetic.' Bell kicked Bett and then elbowed him when he retaliated. Both received red cards.

Bell's eagerness to join Rangers was down to the fact he had supported the club as a boy, as had McLeish, Leighton and, of course, Ferguson himself. Team-mates like McGhee, Cowan and Joe Miller had grown up supporting Celtic. Strachan had followed Hibs, McMaster Morton. The Aberdeen fans in the dressing room included Simpson, Cooper, Weir and Hewitt. Miller, despite being raised in the Rangers stronghold of Glasgow's Bridgeton, had not supported anyone. What Ferguson fostered was a collective so strong that past allegiances did not matter. No one asked or cared how Celtic or Rangers got on after a game unless the result directly impacted on Aberdeen. Bell said: 'I hated Celtic when I was growing up. I was a Rangers supporter so every time I played Celtic I didn't need any motivation. But at Aberdeen I ended up feeling the same way when we played Rangers. All that mattered was Aberdeen. You just wanted to beat everybody.'

The Scottish Premier Division, in which teams played each other four times a season, was introduced in 1975. Rangers took seven years and thirteen attempts to win at Pittodrie. Aberdeen made nineteen trips to Ibrox under Ferguson and lost only five. They finished above Rangers in seven consecutive seasons. Under Greig, and then Wallace, Rangers were weak and impotent. They regularly finished fourth and even fifth in the league. Mediocrity was hard for their supporters to swallow, especially when the teams above them included not only Celtic but also Aberdeen and Dundee United. In January 1985 Rangers went to Pittodrie and suffered their heaviest league defeat in nineteen years. McDougall scored a hat-trick in a 5–1 rout. The Rangers team was taken by assistant manager Alex Totten because Wallace had been diagnosed with a hernia and advised not to travel north. 'Lucky Jock,' said the *Sunday Mail*'s headline.

Eight months later Aberdeen administered another dose of punishment, this time at Ibrox. It deteriorated into the most toxic of all the games during Ferguson's tenure. All of Rangers' frustrations bubbled over on 28 September 1985. Within thirty-five minutes Hugh Burns and Craig Paterson had been sent off to reduce them to nine men. When McLeish and Stark scored to put Aberdeen 2–0 up before half-time the Rangers support was incandescent. Ferguson reacted to the unmistakable sense of menace pouring from the stands with what, for him, was a unique instruction to his players: take it easy. Stark said: 'At half-time it's the only time I can remember him taking that tone where he basically said, "Make sure the game gets finished, don't be going scoring five, six, seven, just make sure we're in control of the game and we come out with the three points and get away." You could sense a real nastiness in the air. Anything could have happened. He just wanted us out unscathed, three points in the bag.'

Shortly after half-time the referee had to stop the game and take the players up the tunnel for four minutes when Rangers fans spilled from the standing area on to pitchside. Almost fifty were arrested that day and the SFA later launched an inquiry into violence and coin throwing. Enough order was restored for the game to resume. 'Aberdeen played out the second half as if at a training exercise,' wrote Jim Reynolds in the *Glasgow Herald*. Hewitt added another goal to make it 3–0. 'I can say in all honesty that I have never been so pleased in my whole career to see a match end and get on the way back home,' Ferguson wrote in his next programme notes. 'That reaction has nothing to do with the scoreline. At no stage did I feel any concern that we would be held to a draw, much less get beaten. The fact was that I had a genuine fear for people's safety as the widely-publicised problems developed. It was a relief to get it all over and behind us.' With some justification, Aberdeen were furious when the SFA fined them £1,000 for their 'involvement' in the scenes. Their culpability extended no further than four bookings. Rangers were fined £2,000. 'We went out to win a game and within twenty minutes three players were booked, all of them from Rangers,' said Ferguson. 'What they are saying, in effect, is don't beat Rangers at Ibrox because you might cause trouble. This decision sets a terrible precedent.'

Watching Scottish football in the 1980s could be dangerous. After the riot between Celtic and Rangers fans at the 1980 Scottish Cup final, legislation was introduced banning the sale or consumption of alcohol at matches. That reduced drunkenness and put an end to the hail of bottles that rained across segregation fences and littered terraces with broken glass. But the grounds were still primitive, dark and unsafe, and attacks and ambushes in and around them were common. Spontaneous outbreaks of violence continued and there was a rapid increase in organised hooliganism. Aberdeen's rise coincided with a parallel development which the club was less keen to celebrate. From 1980 a swaggering, violent streak, previously unknown in the Aberdeen support, began to show itself. For the big games in Glasgow, Edinburgh or Dundee up to 500 youths with trademark side-shed haircuts and designer clothes would march from the train stations to the grounds looking for trouble with rival hooligans. At Pittodrie there could be around 1,000 of them, massed as close as they could get to the away fans. None of them wore Aberdeen colours, but the 'Aberdeen Soccer Casuals' established themselves as the first and biggest 'firm' in Scotland. Their expensive clothes reflected the city's affluence. For five or six years a large casual following was a permanent feature of Aberdeen games. Fighting was frequent, especially on trips to face Hibs, Motherwell and the Old Firm. The casuals were unpopular among mainstream supporters and condemnatory media coverage followed in their wake. But when Celtic and Rangers supporters came to the city, some Aberdeen fans were quietly grateful for the casuals, seeing them as a vigilante force who kept the visiting hordes in their place.

The club's attitude to the casuals was surprisingly vague. Violence was total anathema to the douce figures of the board room, who identified Aberdeen with old-fashioned decency and civility. Yet public condemnation from the club was infrequent and rarely fierce. Whatever damage the casuals did to Aberdeen's image, there was an inextricable connection between the football club and the city's youth culture. Several hundred young men coming to every home game provided valuable income, not to mention a noise and energy which enlivened Pittodrie's otherwise sleepy atmosphere.

Ferguson had often tried to encourage the supporters to be more vocal and expressive during games but he was also frustrated by the size of the attendances. He began to criticise the level of support openly soon after winning the league in 1980. When Harper's testimonial match against a select XI attracted only 14,000 three months later he pressed his point: 'We must all remember that these games are part of our efforts to reward loyalty and service of players in Scotland. It's so easy to lose them to the attraction of more lucrative contracts in the south.' Weeks later he returned to the theme: 'I just wonder how much more the club must achieve this season to win the confidence of more supporters. Apart from the Rangers and Celtic games our attendances have been extremely disappointing. If we cannot attract good, healthy crowds when the side stands out as the best in the country, what prospect is there for Pittodrie if Aberdeen should fall below such standards?' He said the team felt 'let down' when the ground was only half full. One attendance in particular was singled out in *Managing My Life*: the home crowd when IFK Gothenburg visited in the European Cup quarter-final first leg on 5 March 1986. 'My first disappointment with the occasion was the meagre attendance of 17,000 at Pittodrie on that March evening,' he wrote. 'It crossed my mind that perhaps the Aberdeen supporters were spoiled and took success for granted, and the suspicion planted seeds of restlessness in me.' In fact the club's own histories put the crowd at 22,000 and newspapers at the time reported that more than 20,000 were present, which would have made the ground look and feel almost full. When Ferguson was mildly critical of the crowd in his subsequent column for the programme it was for not doing enough to rouse the team in the first half. 'I feel at that time the supporters could have made a positive contribution by giving the players a lift just when they needed it,' he wrote. He did not mention any disappointment about how many turned up. But Aberdeen's inability to increase their support was always likely to gnaw at him. In each of his first four seasons the average league attendance at Pittodrie was lower than the season before. An average of 16,115 for league games in McNeill's season had dropped to 11,360 by 1982, despite the team delivering a championship and a Scottish Cup. Only in 1983, the Gothenburg year, and the following season, were there year-on-year increases, peaking at an average of 17,138. The figure for 1986 had dropped back to 14,326, lower than Rangers, Celtic and even Hearts. There was no obvious explanation, other than that the supporters had quickly grown complacent, taking annual success for granted without feeling the need to support it.

Ferguson's reaction to the IFK Gothenburg game confirmed that he had outgrown Aberdeen. 'I was finding that the afternoons at Pittodrie were becoming a bit of a drag,' he admitted in *Managing My Life*. 'The club was so well run that the challenge for me had diminished. I was feeling the need for the painful stimulation of again having to build a successful team.' During one of his daily chats with chairman Donald, in April 1986, he told him he was thinking about leaving at the end of the season. Donald calmly replied that there was only one job worth leaving for: Manchester United.

TWENTY

FERGIE GOES TO MEXICO

Games between Aberdeen and Celtic in the 1980s were not known for moments of reflective silence and calm. Even displays of respect were given grudgingly. What happened on the afternoon of 14 September, 1985, amounted to football tribalism being put to one side and a display of normal human decency breaking out. Almost 40,000 people filed into Parkhead that day and before a ball was kicked both sets of fans stood motionless, heads bowed, in an expression of shared mourning. Four nights earlier Jock Stein had collapsed at the end of Scotland's strained World Cup qualifier against Wales and within minutes he was pronounced dead. The man Scottish football knew as 'Big Jock' was gone at sixty-two.

There was no prospect of the minute's silence being interrupted by petty taunting. Aberdeen supporters had laid a wreath behind the Celtic goal and were generally as stunned by Stein's death as those at the club he had served for thirteen years. Several Aberdeen players who knew Stein from international duty had arrived in Glasgow earlier than usual to join Alex Ferguson at the funeral the day before.

Leighton, McLeish and Bett had all played in Wales and were there again ready to play at Parkhead, along with Miller, who was captain for both managers. The players grieved, but none was hit harder than Ferguson. His father had died in 1979 and now he had lost his managerial mentor.

Their careers first crossed in 1964 when Stein was manager of Dunfermline and tried to sign Ferguson from St Johnstone. The deal did go through but not until after Stein had left for Hibs. The first time they bumped into each other, and Stein said 'Hello, Alex,' it made such an impression on the younger man that he wrote about it in his autobiography thirty-five years later. He had not presumed that Stein would know who he was. They encountered each other again when Ferguson was playing for Rangers and Stein was in charge of Celtic. On Saturday nights both would occasionally frequent The Beechwood, a pub-restaurant near Hampden, and Ferguson often found himself blurting out in-house secrets, unable to stop himself spilling information to the wise Stein. 'I was utterly helpless. It just came out without my even realising it. That was the effect he had on people.' He joked that Stein knew everything that was going on at Rangers because he was the one who told him. 'You have that power as a manager. People want to tell you things.'

Ferguson's thirst for knowledge, his fascination with Stein's methods, as well as the sheer magnitude of the occasion, took him to Milan to watch Celtic's 1970 European Cup final against Feyenoord. It was a remarkable trip given that only six months earlier he had still been a Rangers player. The broadcaster Archie Macpherson saw him at Milan Malpensa Airport the day after Celtic had lost the game. 'In this mass of green and white, sitting there was this one bluenose, Alex Ferguson. He had gone all that way to see a European final. He was getting barracked by the Celtic support – good-natured, mostly – because he was recognisable. He was in amongst "the enemy". Most ex-Rangers players wouldn't have watched the game, even on television.'

As Ferguson moved into management and grew into a compelling figure in his own right, the pair were inevitably drawn together. He regarded Stein as a one-man university. When he was uncertain about whether to leave East Stirlingshire for St Mirren in 1974 he was sufficiently confident of his relationship with the older man to telephone for advice. Contact between them continued. Coincidentally, on 29 April 1978, Stein's final game in charge of Celtic was also Ferguson's last with St Mirren, not that anyone knew at the time. In hindsight it can be seen as a clash between sorcerer and apprentice with the apprentice winning 3–1. Within a month Stein had left Parkhead and had made a private call to Chris Anderson recommending Ferguson for the Aberdeen job suddenly vacated by Billy McNeill. The relationship deepened with the regular contact necessitated by Stein, as Scotland manager, having to notify Ferguson and seek his insight when selecting Aberdeen players. Stein's background was in Lanarkshire coalmining, Ferguson's in Govan shipbuilding. Culturally and politically they were cut from the same cloth and shared the same beliefs and interests. Stein had been invited into the official Aberdeen party for Gothenburg in 1983 and when Jim McLean stepped down as Scotland's assistant manager the following year Stein immediately offered the job to Ferguson. There was a 19-year age difference between them and Stein enjoyed being exposed to Ferguson's youthful energy and drive.

They were together for eight Scotland games over thirteen months. The first was a startling 6–1 rout of Yugoslavia in a friendly on 12 September 1984. There was a vintage 3–1 World Cup qualifying defeat of Spain and a 1–0 win over England in another friendly at Hampden. But the six-game campaign to reach the 1986 World Cup in Mexico had been marked by defeats in Spain and at home to Wales. Scotland had travelled for that awful night in Cardiff needing a point to be certain of at least a play-off place. Wales, led by world-class strikers Ian Rush and Mark Hughes, had only to repeat the beating they had given Scotland in Glasgow. Scotland had qualified for the World Cup finals in 1974, 1978 and 1982 and pressure was heaped on Stein to ensure they did so again. He was not helped by the fact that key players like Kenny Dalglish, Graeme Souness, Alan Hansen and Mo Johnston were all unavailable because of suspension or injury. Stein went into the Cardiff game conscious of press coverage questioning whether he was still the same manager of old. He was suffering from a heavy cold, but as usual ignored doctor's orders by not taking diuretic tablets on the day of a match. The pills were an important part of his treatment for a heart muscle defect detected several years earlier but they made him need to pee and he did not have time for that before and during a match. On the night before the game he had called Ferguson and coach Andy Roxburgh into his hotel room for a long blether. Uncharacteristically he talked about himself, going over his long career, rather than about the impending fixture. When the two younger men left him they looked at each other, asking: 'What was all that about?' Others who saw him in the hours before kick-off noticed him sweating and thought he looked grey.

Ninian Park felt tight, suffocating and claustrophobic. Scotland had 15,000 fans to Wales's 20,000 and there was scarcely room to breathe. The tension was cranked up when Wales took the lead through Hughes in the thirteenth minute. Scotland struggled throughout the first half and near the end Leighton uncharacteristically misjudged a cross and almost let in Hughes to score a second. At half-time the reason for the error became clear. When the players went into the dressing room Leighton immediately headed to a separate part of the shower room and called SFA physiotherapist Hugh Allan to follow him. Moments later Stein and then Ferguson came in, too. Leighton had been at fault with a number of crosses and shots because one of his contact lenses had been knocked out during the first half. Without it he was half blind. Not only did he not have any spares, neither Stein nor Ferguson had known that he needed lenses in the first place. Both of them were stunned and then furious. Ferguson felt embarrassed that he was unaware of such a crucial fact about one of his own players – and because it had come to light in front of Stein.

Throughout his long and distinguished career Leighton was an exemplary professional. He was also a deep character who gave little away. Only a handful of people knew he wore contact lenses. He had not told the physiotherapist at Aberdeen, nor even his own father. The reason? He was fearful that Ferguson would see it as a weakness and look for another goalkeeper. Leighton said: 'I was the first person in Aberdeen to get soft contact lenses. Fergie was always very negative about contact lenses. I was building myself up to tell him about them, but if I ever dropped anything into the conversation about lenses he would shoot them down. I came back from the 1982 World Cup in Spain, where [goalkeeper] George Wood had worn them. I decided that the day before pre-season training started I was going to tell him. I mentioned Wood wearing contact lenses and he goes, "How the fuck can he play in goal when he wears contacts? There's no way he can play." So I thought, "I'll tell him tomorrow." Tomorrow never came. He was so negative about them, and remember at that time lenses were still pretty experimental. Nowadays it doesn't make any difference if you wear contacts or not, but at that time there was a stigma about it. It could have been detrimental to my career in terms of what he thought. I apologised unreservedly about a million times to him after Cardiff. He shouldn't have found out the way he did. But he let me know about it.' With only one lens Leighton had no depth perception. The only option was to replace him with the goalkeeper on the bench, Alan Rough.

The players made their way back up the narrow tunnel and Stein retook his place in the cramped, busy dugout. Allan sat on one side of him, Ferguson the other. Scotland grew into the game and turned the pressure on the Welsh. Stein took off Strachan and sent on winger Davie Cooper. With ten minutes left, Scotland striker David Speedie tried to lift the ball over David Phillips and it struck the Welsh defender's arm. Wales vehemently disputed the Dutch referee's decision to award a penalty, but Cooper remained calm and buried the ball low in the corner. Scotland had the goal they needed to stay in the World Cup.

Throughout the second half Ferguson shot glances at Stein, worrying about his colour and apparent frailty. Photographers had crowded around the dugout and the encroachment of one in particular irritated Stein. With a couple of minutes left he mistook a free-kick decision for the final whistle and came off the bench. As he returned to his seat he stumbled and collapsed. Allan caught him and a moment later Ferguson leapt in to help keep him up. Paramedics and police officers took over and carried Stein up the tunnel. In the medical room he said a few words to those desperately treating him, reassuring them that he felt better, and then slipped into unconsciousness. Resuscitation attempts failed. He had suffered a cardiac arrest, though the formal cause of death was recorded as heart failure. Failing to take the diuretic pills had caused a build-up of fluid in his lungs.

Outside Ferguson thought on his feet. He ordered the jubilant Scottish players to stay out on the pitch at the final whistle. He made his way into the tunnel and bumped into Souness, who had missed the game through suspension.

Souness had found the tense final minutes unbearable and had gone inside the stand, unwittingly putting himself close to the drama unfolding around Stein. By the time Ferguson saw him, Souness was in tears. 'I think he's gone,' Souness told him. It was quickly confirmed. When the happy players flooded into the dressing room they saw Ferguson ashen-faced. He told them Stein had died and then took on the responsibility of phoning Stein's wife, Jean, to deliver the news. There was no answer, but on a subsequent attempt Stein's grown-up daughter Ray picked up the phone. She found out she had lost her dad from Ferguson. It was Souness who eventually emerged in front of the waiting football writers and said simply: 'He's gone.'

In his 1999 autobiography Ferguson wrote that the night after Cardiff he had to be back in Aberdeen for a game against Partick Thistle, and that during the car journey north he had pulled into a layby and cried. In fact he had blurred the memories of what happened after Stein's death and the loss of his father six years earlier. The Partick game had been on the night of his father's funeral in 1979. The slip is insignificant, except that it reveals something about the impact Stein's death had on him. It was like losing the very closest family member.

Scotland had thirty-six days until a friendly against East Germany, the only fixture before the World Cup play-off double-header against the as yet unknown winners of the Oceania section. 'I don't want people to think we are being callous, but the Scotland team needs leadership. It is our duty to find the man to give it,' said Ernie Walker, the SFA secretary. The short-term solution was obvious. Walker sounded out Ferguson, Dick Donald and Chris Anderson. A sense of duty compelled all three to agree that Ferguson should be in charge for the East Germany game. 'It would be a one-off basis and no one should assume anything else,' said Walker. 'It should be remembered that Alex Ferguson is the manager of a Premier Division club.'

Aberdeen were eight games into the 1985–86 season when he took the Scotland job. They had made an unbeaten start, were second in the league and had reached the semi-finals of the League Cup. That tournament has always been the little brother of the three major Scottish competitions, yet it remained the one trophy Ferguson had never won. After losing in the final to Rangers and Dundee United in his first two seasons, Aberdeen had twice gone out in quarter- or semi-finals to Dundee United and also had been beaten by Dundee and Celtic. In 1984 there had been the shock second-round defeat by the minnows of Airdrie. The League Cup had been modified in 1979: the competition was shortened and accelerated so that the final could take place as early as October. Ferguson attributed Aberdeen's lack of success to the fact that the rounds were played when seasons were in their infancy. 'We know from experience that we tend to build slowly and improve as we go along. You could say that we are a "second half of the season" side.' That was a claim he made about his teams throughout his career and which, he admitted on his retirement, was a psychological ploy to make opponents believe they remained vulnerable right to the end of a campaign.

Signing Bett in the summer of 1985 brought great passing and intelligence to the centre of Aberdeen's midfield. He had won both cups while at Rangers, which further persuaded Ferguson he was a winner who would quickly settle into the squad. 'The fact is that we have at Pittodrie a nucleus of players who have been bred to win,' he said. Weir had echoed that in an interview just before Ferguson became Scotland's caretaker manager. 'This is not just any club. The Dons are the best team in Scotland. Aberdeen are one of the best clubs in

Britain. What player could ask for more than we have achieved in recent years? Because of the standards we have set ourselves it looks like a failure when we draw the odd game.'

For once United were beaten home and away in the League Cup semi-final and Aberdeen eased through to face Hibs at Hampden. Hibs had done the hardest work, beating both Celtic and Rangers, but they had not won anything in thirteen years and few expected them to upset Aberdeen. The game was remembered as 'the twelve-minute final' because that was how long it took Aberdeen to build an unassailable two-goal lead. Superb play from Hewitt created headed goals for Black and Stark. When Black added another in the second half the Dons had a consummate 3–0 win. It had been a mismatch. Later Leighton learned that Hibs had been beaten before a ball was kicked. 'I remember speaking to Tommy Craig, the Hibs coach. He felt they lost the game in the Hampden tunnel. When the two teams were lined up to come out it was Willie, then it was me, then it was Alex. The focus the three of us had at the front! We had Vaseline across our brows, everything. The Hibs players were looking at us. Tommy said, "Our players were beaten before they started." We did have an aura about us.'

As Miller lifted the trophy the television coverage cut to a shot of Ferguson watching from the pitch. He was smiling but swallowing hard as though there was a lump in his throat. Some emotion was inevitable because Ferguson had finally completed his set of Scottish football's major honours. In his next programme notes, when Celtic visited Pittodrie on 2 November, he wrote: 'A lot of people were making the point that it was a magnificent day for me personally because the League Cup was the one trophy we had not won since I came to Pittodrie. I can honestly say that particular point did not enter my head. It's not just important to get to finals, it's important to keep winning them. As I said at the start of this season, we are not satisfied to win one honour.'

The only surprise at Hampden was that Frank McDougall failed to score. His rich form had continued into his second season and he helped himself to five goals in his first dozen games. Hibs were fortunate to be spared; six days later he was savage against the club he had supported as a boy. Celtic were taken apart 4–1 at Pittodrie and McDougall scored all four. The only mercy shown was courtesy of a broadcasters' strike which began two hours before the game, ensuring the punishment administered by McDougall was never captured on camera.

Aberdeen had bookended 1985 by beating Rangers 5–1 in January and now Celtic 4–1 in November. Those were perhaps the two most vibrant domestic games Pittodrie witnessed in the entire Ferguson era. As the season progressed Aberdeen's home remained a fortress but their away form suddenly collapsed. When they beat Rangers at Ibrox at the end of September, it was inconceivable that they would go almost five months before winning another away game in the Premier Division. But that was how long they had to wait before taking full points from a trip to Hibs. It was a poor run which sunk their chance of landing a third consecutive league title. 'I have to say that there have been occasions in away games when players have not been hungry enough for success and have not fought as hard as they should against adversity,' said Ferguson. 'They must have the desire to win trophies. They must hate the thought of defeat.'

Aberdeen's stuttering league form had coincided with Ferguson taking on the Scotland role. They slipped off the top of the league in December and never made it back. The demands on his time were immense and his attention was divided. He had to scout an East Germany game in Belgrade before his first friendly as Scotland manager, which finished 0–0 on 16

October. On the day before the match it was confirmed that he would stay in charge on the same part-time basis for the rest of the World Cup campaign. That meant he would remain in position at least until the end of the play-off and potentially through to the finals themselves the following summer. 'It's exactly what I wanted,' he said. 'There was never any chance of me walking out on Aberdeen and taking a full-time job as manager of Scotland. I'm too young for that. I know people have questioned my ambition. They have pointed out that I have turned down Rangers, Spurs and other clubs. Why should I leave Aberdeen to have any ambition? I have been at Aberdeen for seven-and-a-half years and although you never know what lies ahead in life, I would be happy to spend another seven-and-a-half years there.' Dick Donald, he stressed, realised he was not using Scotland 'to put myself forward for another job'. Still, he admitted, it would be a 'strain' to maintain Aberdeen's success while taking Scotland through a two-legged play-off against Australia, who had won the Oceania group, and then six months of preparation for the World Cup finals. Davie Cooper and Frank McAvennie, the latter given his Scotland debut by Ferguson, delivered a 2–0 win in the first leg. For the second leg in Melbourne Ferguson would have to abandon Aberdeen for several days and travel to the other side of the world.

While away with Scotland he delegated training and much of the day-to-day work at Pittodrie to Willie Garner, but inevitably his absences were noted and discussed. Miller said: 'I think there was a feeling within the city and within the club that it did distract him. It would have been very difficult for him not to take it on. It was almost one of these situations where he had to accept it, and the club had to accept it. It was a responsibility to just take on the job under those circumstances. Did it make a difference? We won a cup double that season, but there was a feeling within the club that it was a distraction.'

And it came just as Aberdeen were making their third assault on the European Cup. The campaign started against Akranes of Iceland on 18 September (eight days after Stein's death). The 7–2 aggregate win was comfortable but in the second round Servette, the champions of Switzerland, made Aberdeen sweat. The first leg in Geneva was placid. 'The players of Servette were in so much awe of Alex Ferguson's men that they failed to mount an effective challenge,' wrote the *Glasgow Herald*. But the Swiss were sharp and forceful at Pittodrie. McDougall scored early, but had Servette been able to take their chances they would have recovered and turned the tie around. 'Their performance was the best by any side at Pittodrie in European competition,' said Ferguson. It was quite a claim. If he had not been involved, he said, he would have been applauding them. Still, the tight 1–0 aggregate win carried Aberdeen through to the quarter-finals. Ferguson made it known he was eager to avoid Juventus in the draw, though the last eight also included Barcelona and Bayern Munich. He was hoping for a team who would be sluggish after their winter break at the time of the ties in March. That meant either the Finnish champions Kuusysi Lahti or IFK Gothenburg of Sweden. He was granted his wish. Aberdeen were handed the draw that sent them back to their beloved Ullevi Stadium.

The first leg at Pittodrie was preceded by a minute's silence for Olof Palme, the Swedish prime minister who had been assassinated on a Stockholm street five days earlier. IFK Gothenburg were a team of Scandinavian giants and Ferguson's wish to be drawn against them was misguided. Not since Bayern Munich three years earlier had a European team scored twice at Pittodrie, but IFK Gothenburg secured a 2–2 draw and deserved more. Leighton suffered another match-night drama. He had gone through his pre-match warm-up before accepting that an eye infection would prevent him playing. His deputy, Bryan Gunn, kept Aberdeen alive with three crucial saves in the second half. But the towering striker Johnny Ekström caused all sorts of problems to an Aberdeen team who looked desperately uncomfortable playing with an unfamiliar three-at-the-back formation. Ferguson was typically bombastic about how the tie stood. In some ways the score worked in Aberdeen's favour, he told the newspapers. The Swedish crowd would think they were in the semi-final and would pressurise their team to finish off Aberdeen in the second leg, he said. 'We will win the second leg over there. I am convinced of that.' He was wrong. They crashed out of the European Cup after a frustrating goalless draw.

Aberdeen had failed in the Ullevi, of all places. Ferguson drew an analogy which showed he was acutely aware of how difficult it would be to emulate 1983 and repeatedly compete with the European elite. When Juventus sold the outstanding Zbigniew Boniek to Roma they had replaced him with Michael Laudrup, said Ferguson. 'When we lost Gordon Strachan we were not in a position to replace him with a player of similar calibre. There will be no rash or hasty moves because Aberdeen failed to reach their European expectations. Losing out in Europe could have the opposite effect and bind the club tighter for our Scottish assault.'

Winning the league was too much to ask. They had only eight league games left when they lost in Sweden and eventually trailed home fourth, behind champions Celtic, Hearts and Dundee United. The season in which the Scotland job pulled on Ferguson's time and energy was also the one in which Aberdeen posted their lowest league finish since 1979. The chance to fulfil the manager's 'two trophies a season' demand rested on the Scottish Cup. An effortless semi-final defeat of Hibs put them into a cup final against the team who had been the story of the Scottish season.

Few paid much attention when Hearts lost five of their first eight league games in the autumn of 1985. They had been promoted to the top flight only two years before and despite a proud history and a massive support they had not been a force in Scottish football for a quarter of a century. Then something extraordinary happened. After losing at Clydebank on 28 September they stayed unbeaten in the league and the Scottish Cup for thirty-one games, a mesmerising run which took them to the brink of a double. In January they were the first visiting team to win at Pittodrie for more than a year. Immediately after that 1–0 defeat, Ferguson was magnanimous and fulsome in his praise of Hearts, but in his next set of programme notes he sounded a different message. 'They are not a great side and a true Aberdeen performance would beat them. The fact is that we have been falling below the standards we set for ourselves and the standards we expect. It is a problem which I have to look at very carefully. Truth is, I may have to build a new Aberdeen.'

What he did not realise was that he was about to be hit by the unwelcome departure of a fourth senior member of his Gothenburg team. Eric Black was twenty-two years old and had been connected to Aberdeen and Ferguson since 1978. He had won two league titles, three Scottish Cups, the League Cup, the European Cup Winners' Cup and the Super Cup. A youthful face and wholesome demeanour gave an impression of innocence, but on the pitch Black was as nerveless as an assassin. Every time he started a cup final he scored, including against Real Madrid. Four cup final starts, five goals. He had pace and was an excellent sniffer of penalty-box chances, but above all he possessed fantastic heading ability. He timed his jumps so well he seemed to hang in the air in the moment before a cross reached him.

Black had never given Ferguson any trouble. He married young and was one of the most popular players around

Pittodrie. But in the summer of 1986 he was due to come out of contract and had made up his mind to leave and seek a higher wage elsewhere. When he told Ferguson he intended to employ an agent he was told not to, but did so anyway. Talks were held with clubs in Germany and France and Black signed a contract committing himself to Metz. He informed Ferguson nine days before the Scottish Cup final. The news was kept in-house for five days until Ferguson told reporters. Aberdeen would not deal with agents, he said. It was time for the club to take a stand and show their displeasure. 'We are big enough to do that by not playing Eric Black against Hearts on Saturday. He is finished with this club.' He added a cold dig at Black's choice of destination. Metz had knocked Terry Venables' Barcelona out of the 1985 Cup Winners' Cup with a breathtaking 4–1 win in the Camp Nou, but the little club from north-east France had an otherwise unremarkable history. 'He has gone to an insignificant club in Europe,' said Ferguson. 'His agent has done him no favours at all. It's a travesty that a player like Black is going to a club like Metz.'

Ferguson had strong grounds to be irritated by Black's choice. If he had been sold to an English club Aberdeen might have received more than £500,000. But European clubs benefited from an agreement to pay a fee equivalent to ten times a player's salary, which would mean a figure closer to £300,000. Garner still vividly remembers Ferguson's insistence that Black had to be dropped. 'Fergie says to me, "Ask Black if he's still got his agent. If he has, tell him he's not playing in the cup final." I asked if he was joking. "Am I fuck. If he's still got his agent he's no' playing. I don't give a shit about his record in cup finals." Eric told me wasn't getting rid of the agent. And that was it, Fergie didn't play him. Brave.'

The episode effectively ended the relationship between Ferguson and Black. Years later, in *Managing My Life*, Ferguson wrote of his anger about 'cloak and dagger' behaviour, Black having 'plotted in secret' and even kept his intentions hidden from his team-mates. Black, however, has always been comfortable with his decision to leave and has no criticism of Ferguson. 'I don't regret it. I thought it was the right thing for me personally. Obviously it wasn't the right thing in the manager's mind, for him or for Aberdeen, but I had made my mind up to go. The opportunity was there. It was financial.' Chairman Donald had told him there had been offers from Tottenham, Everton and Aston Villa, but by then he was committed to the move to France. 'I didn't wake up having dreamt of going to Metz. I'd signed a five-year deal to go to Monaco, but the deal was dependent on them getting Arsène Wenger as coach and the whole thing changed because Wenger couldn't get out of his contract at Nancy. But I liked the Metz coach.' Had he thought he might be dropped for the final? 'I hadn't considered that. I didn't enjoy it. I never went near Hampden, I watched the game on television in Aberdeen. It was unfortunate it ended that way, but I don't blame Alex Ferguson for reacting the way he did, he was quite right. I feel I was quite right to do what I did as well. It wasn't personal. Some of the boys knew what I was intending to do. They knew and he didn't. I understand why he wouldn't be happy about that, but for the move to happen that's the way it had to go.'

Sacrificing Black was a gamble. He was a proven big-game player and the team's second-top goalscorer that season. Such rigid decisiveness was typical of Ferguson, though, and he did not worry that his team had been weakened. He looked around his dressing room and saw players who had won leagues, cups, European trophies, and been over the course time and time again. Hearts were a different story. Other than the former Rangers men, Sandy Jardine and Sandy Clark, their squad had won nothing. 'In the early days Aberdeen didn't see us as a threat,' said Hearts' prolific goalscorer John Robertson. 'When we came into the Premier League we were just another team of whipping boys and we got battered by them. Not only were they an intimidating team, they had a very intimidating manager.' There was an unspoken feeling at Pittodrie that the cup final had been won a week in advance. For weeks Hearts had looked and played like champions-elect. Their momentum seemed unstoppable and huge crowds followed them home and away as they closed in on winning the league for the first time in twenty-six years. On the last day of the season they had only to avoid defeat against Dundee and they would be champions.

Their fans packed into Dens Park to watch history unfold. A gastrointestinal bug had gone through the Hearts players, though, and late in the game they began to tire and struggle. With just seven minutes left Dundee scored. Celtic were beating St Mirren 5–0, enough to snatch the title on goal difference. Hearts were broken. They conceded a catastrophic second goal. At full time their shattered players limped back into the dressing room and sat in stunned silence. On the bus back to Edinburgh several of them were in tears.

On the same afternoon Aberdeen won 6–0 at Clydebank. Leighton said: 'As soon as we heard Hearts had lost at Dundee we were saying, "We're a shoo-in for the cup final." We had eight or nine international players. We had players who'd played in Scotland-England games, World Cup games, cup finals, games to decide league titles. Hearts didn't have any of that. They were a one-season wonder at that time. Probably the last team they would have wanted to play in the final after losing the league was Aberdeen.'

The rebuilding of Hearts began when they reported for training on the Monday morning. Manager Alex MacDonald and his assistant, Jardine, were in the players' faces. Loud, upbeat, encouraging. 'Training was sharp, we were ready to go, everything was very, very positive,' said Robertson. By the morning of the final the Hearts management had done a decent job of lifting the pall which had descended at Dens Park. What they had not considered was that Ferguson would anticipate their psychological gambit and deliberately set out to destroy it. Tommy McQueen said: 'He got all these red roses for the buttonholes. He'd say, "You have to show the other side that this is what we do, we're always in cup finals, this is not novel to you." We had the suits with the red roses. I think Hearts came in their tracksuits.'

The Aberdeen bus arrived at Hampden earlier than usual, before Hearts. Ferguson told some of the players to mill around in the stadium reception area, as if waiting to distribute their complimentary tickets to friends and family. When the Hearts players arrived, they were to make a point of approaching them, shaking their hands, telling them how unlucky they had been not to win the title, how Aberdeen had been rooting for them, how it was a terrible, awful way to end their season after all that hard work. Robertson said: 'It was about getting it right back in our heads that we'd lost the league. I only found out about it much, much later. Fergie had guys waiting to make sure the message was subtly put across. As soon we were on the pitch the rest of the squad came over to us with more of the same. "Oh boys, you were unfortunate." That was part of his psychology. "Get it back into their heads that they've just lost the league title and see if it puts them on a downer."' Garner saw it all from the Aberdeen dugout: 'You could see the Hearts boys going, "Last week, last week . . . I thought I'd just got that out of my head." It just absolutely did them. You could see the confidence draining out of them.'

Hewitt drilled a low shot into the corner of the Hearts net after only five minutes. At the start of the second half, Weir attacked the line, McDougall dummied his cross and Hewitt scored again. Hearts had folded: their captain, Walter Kidd, had been tormented by Weir and was sent off for throwing the ball at Cooper and then McDougall after conceding a free kick. Stark scored again for 3–0 from another Weir cross. 'That Hearts team should have won at Dundee,' said Weir. 'To go to Dens Park on the last day to be champions of Scotland: if that had been Aberdeen we wouldn't have lost. We'd have got the job done. We gave Hearts a doing. I felt sorry for them.'

By 1986 Aberdeen had won so much silverware that Miller had developed his own distinctive way of lifting a trophy. Most captains raised them straight above their heads with a hand on each ear of a cup. But Miller gripped a cup by the stem in his right hand and held out both arms like a Messiah before the faithful. They had won both domestic cups and gone out of the European Cup quarter-finals on away goals. They played eighteen cup ties in 1985–86 without defeat. Ferguson was entitled to his view that they would have won the domestic treble had it not been for injuries to Simpson, Weir, McDougall, Black, Hewitt and Bett at key points in the campaign. The usual formalities were observed: an open-top bus along Aberdeen's Union Street, the cup shown off to the crowds from the balcony of the Town House, and a civic reception. But Ferguson's mind was already on other matters. The bus parade was on Sunday; on Wednesday he was due to board a plane to Mexico with the Scotland squad. Having comfortably seen off Australia in Melbourne they were heading for the World Cup finals.

Managing his country asked different questions of Ferguson and he had the intelligence to produce fresh answers. He had to be more measured with Scotland's players than he was with those under his control at Aberdeen. He recognised that players of international standard operated at a higher level and would not respond to being shouted at and bullied. 'I think he was mellower,' said Strachan. 'You can't make the same demands of international players and "Sir Lex" was clever enough to realise that.'

Players who had heard of the terrifying, tyrannical Aberdeen manager could not reconcile his fearsome reputation with the warm, sociable figure they met at Scotland gatherings. 'What probably surprised me was that there wasn't any ranting and raving from Fergie,' said Dundee United full-back Maurice Malpas. 'We knew Fergie or Archie would chase Aberdeen players down the track. Or he'd have someone by the throat as you were going down the tunnel. But there was nothing like that. I was pally with Jim Leighton and Willie Miller. We had our own wee clique at night time or at the dinner table. They'd tell stories about Fergie and the United boys would tell our stories about wee Jim McLean. The chat would be, "Remember that time you got beat . . . what did he say after that?" "Oh, he went bloody mental." But the Aberdeen lads would tell us, "This isn't Fergie, by the way." This wasn't Fergie the Aberdeen manager. This was Fergie the international manager. They said he was like two different managers.'

Ferguson used his seven games before Mexico to build a squad and a backroom team. Walter Smith was his assistant, Knox and Craig Brown acted as coaches, and his wise old ally at Aberdeen, Teddy Scott, was drafted in to help with the training. He gave debuts to Frank McAvennie, Ally McCoist, Andy Goram, Pat Nevin and Bobby Connor. The results were solid. There was a 1–0 victory over Israel in Tel Aviv, a 3–0 home win against Romania and a 0–0 draw with the Netherlands in Eindhoven. The only other friendly brought a 2–1 defeat by England at Wembley. Losing to the English irritated Ferguson. He had brought the Chelsea winger Nevin on as a substitute. 'I did okay, I did fine, but there was one moment that sticks out,' Nevin remembered. 'I dummied a defender twice and went by him, but he caught me in the box. I didn't go down. I stayed on my feet. We were 2–1 down at the time. After the game Fergie was going around the players and he said to me, "Did you get touched in the box?" I said, "Yeah, he caught me but I stayed on my feet . . ." Silence. He didn't say a word. He just looked at me. It's funny how some people don't even need to say anything to make you wonder, "Did I do the right thing there?" There's no actual proof to say he thought I should have gone down. But I never got to that World Cup . . .'

The Netherlands game was the last international before the finals in Mexico. A story from the journey home reveals how close to the surface Ferguson the Aberdeen manager remained. With the decisive final weekend of the league season still to be played, he pulled aside the Hearts players Robertson and Gary Mackay and wished them the best of luck in the run-in against Celtic. Robertson recalled: 'He said to us, "You've had a great season, you've got a great chance of winning the league." And then he said, "You realise you can't win the cup?" We didn't understand what he was on about. Why couldn't we? He said, "Aberdeen are definitely going to win the cup. It happens every year." He was trying to put it in our heads that his team were going to win at Hampden no matter what, and we couldn't beat them. The Scotland game was over and he was already thinking two games ahead. I told our manager Alex MacDonald what he said. He told me, "It's Ferguson, don't worry about it, son."'

Three days before leading Aberdeen out for the Scottish Cup final, Ferguson had to make a long round of telephone calls to those he was taking, and not taking, to the World Cup. Surprisingly there were five players from Dundee United in the squad compared to Aberdeen's four. But the big story was the exclusion of Alan Hansen. He was thirty, had just captained Liverpool through another league-winning season and would complete the double by lifting the FA Cup the day after the Scotland squad was named. To English audiences unfamiliar with the excellence of Miller and McLeish the fact that Hansen was not a regular for Scotland was baffling. For him to be omitted from the squad entirely seemed incredible. But Ferguson trusted his two Aberdeen men and felt the four other defenders he selected were more versatile than Hansen. To anyone who had paid attention it was no shock. Miller had started all seven games under Ferguson and McLeish had started five. 'He is an absolutely magnificent bloke and when I was talking to him I felt as low as a snake,' said Ferguson about Hansen. He claimed Hansen had understood and had said he would be delighted to be kept on the standby list and called up as a replacement if required. 'That speaks volumes for the kind of breeding he has had with his club.'

What Ferguson really thought about Liverpool's 'breeding' went unsaid. A year earlier he and Stein had been angered when Hansen, Dalglish and Stevie Nicol refused to co-operate when asked how Scotland should best nullify their Liverpool team-mate Ian Rush when Wales played at Hampden. Hansen had also withdrawn from a series of squads, telling the management team he was injured before returning for treatment at Liverpool.

Hansen's big pal was Dalglish. On the Monday, four days after the squad had been revealed, and only forty-eight hours before they flew across the Atlantic, Dalglish dropped a depth charge. 'Dalglish pulls out of World Cup,' reported the *Glasgow Herald.* The story was too big for the sports section and went straight to the top of the front page. Dalglish had received a specialist's report on a knee injury which he had subsequently aggravated during Liverpool's FA Cup final defeat of Everton on the Saturday when he played the entire ninety minutes. Dalglish claimed the X-ray showed his ligament had lifted away from the knee cap and there was no alternative but complete rest. 'It is a terrible disappointment that he has had to be withdrawn,' said Ferguson at the time. 'It came out of the blue. He was so vital to our plans. We can only feel sympathy for Kenny.'

In *Managing My Life* Ferguson wrote that when he told Dalglish about Hansen's omission from the squad Dalglish had replied: 'You can't leave him out,' but had ultimately accepted reluctantly that it was the manager's decision. Ferguson offered no opinion on speculation that Dalglish had pulled out of the World Cup because his friend had not been picked. In his autobiography Dalglish insisted that those who voiced such a view were libelling him and impugning the integrity of the surgeon who had declared him unfit.

Those who were around him at the time were impressed by the measured way Ferguson managed the squad. He had picked thirteen home-based players, seven so-called 'Anglos' (those from English clubs) and two who were playing in Europe. He had inherited an invisible but distinct 'them and us' split between the Scottish League players and the Anglos which had been a feature of Scotland gatherings for years and which even Stein had been unable to erase. Those who still played in Scotland tended to hang around together within the squad, and some felt the Anglos looked down on them and regarded their English club games as more important than the internationals. Nevin admitted: 'There was a horrible, horrible atmosphere in that squad. From my vantage point it looked like the Anglos against "the Scots" and I certainly didn't feel like one of the Anglos. They wouldn't have been nasty to each other's faces but I still didn't like it. I felt it was our country, everyone should be together. But there seemed to be a vague aloofness from the Anglos and I despised that. Alex seemed to know that. He seemed to understand that.'

Ferguson was typically thorough. He travelled to Suffolk to pick Sir Alf Ramsey's brain about how to acclimatise to the heat and altitude of Mexico, Ramsey having taken England there for the 1970 World Cup. Because Scotland had been the last country to qualify for the tournament, the best training bases had already been snapped up. From Glasgow via London, Texas and Albuquerque, he took the squad to Santa Fe, arriving on 14 May, 1986, for fifteen days of altitude training at 7,000ft above sea level. The squad's hotel had a lounge with a white grand piano and Ferguson discovered it had a mechanism which meant it could play automatically. He devised a practical joke with the hotel manager whereby it would appear as if Ferguson was playing the notes. With his backroom staff gathered he offered to play a tune before appearing to do so with flamboyant flourishes. His audience watched the deception in disbelief as he battled to suppress his laughter.

From Santa Fe they flew to Los Angeles for three days and two warm-up games at sea level before returning to Mexico. In fact, the World Cup kicked off without Scotland: they were still in LA when the opening ceremony and first game took place. Their absence produced some mild grumbling but Ferguson was unperturbed: 'The least of my worries is what other countries think of us.' What did prey on his mind was the awful draw the team had been dealt. Group E at the 1986 World Cup finals helped popularise the phrase 'the Group of Death'. Scotland were up against Euro 84 semi-finalists Denmark, Franz Beckenbauer's powerful and improving West Germany, and reigning South American champions Uruguay. 'The toughest imaginable group,' according to Ferguson.

Denmark had never qualified for a World Cup before, but they were an excellent side. When the countries met in Neza on 4 June, Richard Gough almost put Scotland ahead before Denmark took control in the second half. After almost an hour Preben Elkjaer attacked Miller and got a lucky break of the ball, capitalising to rifle a shot across Leighton for the only goal of the game. With eleven minutes left, Klaus Berggreen made a horrible challenge on Charlie Nicholas. 'It's the worst tackle I've ever suffered in my life,' said a distraught Nicholas. With his ankle ligaments damaged, his World Cup was effectively over, though he did manage a few more minutes off the bench in the final group game.

Another ankle injury meant Scotland's other striker, Paul Sturrock, also missed the second fixture, against West Germany. So did McLeish, who had fallen sick with a virus. Ferguson had three days to conjure up a team. The temperature during the opening game in Neza was nothing compared to what awaited 140 miles north in Querétaro. The match against Germany kicked off at lunchtime and was played in 90-degree heat. The 1,000-strong Scottish support reddened on the exposed terraces and when it was over some of the Scottish players had lost 8lb in weight. The opening goal was glorious and it was Scotland's. Strachan whipped a shot across the goalmouth into the far corner before producing an iconic celebration that saw him plant his outstretched leg on an advertising board because he was too wee to jump over it. The lead lasted from the eighteenth minute until the twenty-second. Scotland were opened up and Rudi Völler equalised with a tap-in. Early in the second half they suffered their second unlucky break of the tournament when the ball spun away from David Narey to Klaus Allofs, who scored the winner.

Scotland had performed valiantly in a memorable, open game, but they were staring at elimination. They needed to beat Uruguay in the final match and pray that two points would be enough to sneak one of the four places available to the countries who finished third in their group. Uruguay had drawn with West Germany but been smashed 6–1 by Denmark. All they needed to reach the last sixteen was a draw against Scotland. On 13 June Ferguson made the most controversial and debated selection of his managerial career thus far. 'I only slept for an hour last night,' he told the Scottish press pack on the eve of the game. 'I was tossing and turning all night, going over all the possibilities. Without meaning any disrespect to my own club, Aberdeen, this is the most important match I have been involved in throughout my career. I simply must pick the right team.' The consensus was, and has always remained, that he didn't. No one cared about Arthur Albiston replacing Malpas at left-back or Narey retaining his place despite McLeish being available again. Attention and criticism was focused entirely on the decision to leave out the team's captain and undisputed leader, Souness, in favour of the young Celtic midfielder Paul McStay. Souness was thirty-three and had fifty-four caps. McStay was twenty-one, had fourteen, and had not been selected by his country for the previous four-and-a-half months. Ferguson believed Souness was struggling with the heat and had faded in the latter stages of the first two games. But conspiracy theorists had a field day with the decision. Souness had just become manager of Rangers. Was Ferguson deliberately trying to embarrass him? Was this an early attempt to dominate a new rival? Could it even be that he was settling a score that dated back to Liverpool's humiliation of Aberdeen in 1980?

Such fantasies are testament to the grip Ferguson's public persona exerted on Scottish football at the time, not to mention the intense animosity felt towards him at Ibrox. For his admirers and his detractors alike, he was an arch-manipulator with the Midas touch. If Ferguson made a 'mistake' there was sure to be more to it than plain fallibility. But the truth was just that: he made the wrong call. And Scotland did not get the win they needed.

Uruguay delivered an ugly, brutal, cynical performance which became infamous for José Batista scything down Strachan after forty-nine seconds and receiving an immediate red card from French referee Joël Quiniou. There were still eighty-nine minutes left for Scotland to score. The closest they came was when an open goal beckoned for Steve Nicol. He struck the softest of finishes and allowed the goalkeeper to claw it off the line. McStay did not impose himself on the game in the way that Souness might have done, especially against ten men. Souness remained diplomatic: 'I wasn't happy at missing the game against Uruguay, but I know that there are times when I will have to make similar decisions now that I am on the other side of the fence. A manager can't keep everyone happy.' He accepted that his international career was over.

Leighton said: 'Graeme would have been perfect for the Uruguay game. He could have kicked the shit out of everybody. That would have been right up his street. We all felt at the time that it was a big mistake, but it's easy to say in hindsight.' Uruguay had the draw and the point they needed. They were through but their performance had been a disgrace. They repeatedly kicked Strachan and Graeme Sharp. They play-acted, they wasted time, they pressurised and jostled the referee, they even spat at Scotland players. In a chaotic press conference after the event Ernie Walker, the SFA secretary, was asked what he thought of the match. 'What match? There was no match played here this afternoon. What you saw out there was the scum of world football.' (The remark is often misquoted as 'the scum of the earth'.)

Ferguson's comments that day have not attained the same notoriety but they were equally scathing. 'As a nation they seem to have no respect for anyone,' he said. 'That was a debacle out there. I know we are out of the World Cup, but honestly I am glad to be going home because this is no way to play football.' Ferguson had heard Uruguay manager Omar Borrás call the red card 'murder by the referee'. He responded: 'I have had to sit here and listen to Borrás lying and cheating. My players are very upset and I will not criticise any one of them. I cannot say "good luck" to Uruguay. They do not deserve it.' Uruguay were fined £8,000 for misconduct and warned by Fifa that they could be expelled from the tournament if there was any repeat. Borrás was censured and banned from the touchline. The punishment was meaningless for a country caught up in the excitement of going through to the last sixteen. Scotland took unapologetic delight in their defeat by Diego Maradona's Argentina in their next game.

Scotland's World Cup was over and so was Ferguson's spell as an international manager. The SFA had agreed that he would remain in charge until the end of the tournament and then relinquish the role to devote himself to Aberdeen again. It had been by far the most demanding and intense nine months of his managerial life. By the end players like Nicholas, who had once 'hated' him for Aberdeen's tactics against Celtic, saw an entirely different character. 'He was knowledgeable, approachable and very friendly. I thought, "I could start liking this guy," and very soon I did. I thought he was sensational. I felt blessed. Those six weeks I had with him really did open my mind about football.' Ferguson also found the challenges constantly stimulating. He joked that until sitting with SFA officials as the Scotland manager he had never been in a room with them without being fined or suspended.

The team flew home via Texas where a mix-up at the airport meant Scotland were put in economy seats rather than first-class. All complaints to the airline fell on deaf ears. The travelling party had three Fergusons: Alex the manager, Alan ('Fingers') the marketing advisor who had been with Aberdeen in Gothenburg, and Eric the physiotherapist from Dundee. Fingers recounted: 'The airline guy says, "We've been able to get one seat in first-class and we're going to have a draw to see who gets it." So he does it. "It begins with an F . . . it's Ferguson." Fergie goes, "Yes," and I go, "Hey, wait a minute, there are three Fergusons." We look at the guy again. "Initial? Initial?" He goes, "A." We go, "Name? Name?" "Alan!" All the players are laughing. You could see Fergie wasn't happy. I gave it to him. I said, "I'll give you this ticket for one reason only. You took our country to the World Cup."'

TWENTY-ONE

SOUNESS

Chris Anderson first noticed the symptoms towards the end of 1984. A couple of months after a routine hernia operation he began to suffer stiffness in his right leg and right hand. When it gradually became worse he visited his doctor for a check-up. Anderson was teetotal and a non-smoker, he exercised regularly and joked with some degree of truth that, at sixty, he might be the fittest man for his age in the whole of Aberdeen. He took early retirement from his day job to make time for travelling with his wife and to help the Dons stay on top. The doctor told him he had Motor Neurone Disease. That horrible illness, which gradually imprisons its victims within the atrophied muscles of their own bodies, took its toll swiftly. By the time Anderson went to Switzerland to represent Aberdeen at the draw for the first round of the European Cup in July, 1985, his condition had become apparent and he made the news public the following month. By October, when Aberdeen beat Hibs in the League Cup final, he was savouring what remained of his life. 'I found myself looking round the great stadium and knowing that it would be the last time I would see it,' he said in his final interview. 'Afterwards I went to congratulate the players and found I could face them all . . . with one exception. Somehow I choked up when I came face to face with Eric Black. And so did he. He epitomised for me all that was good in football. He seemed to stand for all that Aberdeen had done in recent years.'

When Aberdeen returned to Hampden to face Hearts in the Scottish Cup final, Anderson was not with them. By then desperately ill, he watched the game on television, having tapped out his prediction of the score: Aberdeen 3, Hearts 0. On the Monday after the final Ferguson and his wife, Cathy, took the cup to his home. 'It was heartbreaking to see how he had been ravaged by that dreadful wasting disease,' said Ferguson. 'I never saw Chris alive again after that visit.' Fifteen days later, after Ferguson had flown out for the World Cup, he was told that Anderson had passed away. Before his illness the expectation had been that he would eventually succeed Dick Donald as chairman. His death cast a sombre mood over the club. Leighton wore a black armband for one of Scotland's warm-up games in Los Angeles. All the Aberdeen men felt an acute sense of loss.

Anderson's death coincided with another ripple of turbulence at the club. Black had slipped away to Metz and the day before Ferguson set off for Mexico a fifth member of the Gothenburg team, Neale Cooper, confirmed that he wanted to leave under freedom of contract. He blamed Scottish referees. 'I feel I am being victimised. I was booked nine times this season, only three of which have been justified. The manager agrees with that. It is impossible for me to stay on.' Ferguson thought Cooper was going to Sheffield Wednesday but the player changed his mind and joined Aston Villa instead. 'I had a chance to go to Celtic and I met people from Parkhead. It was all hush-hush. Their chairman was there, Davie Hay was the manager. Fergie knew about it. But the deal wasn't worth it. I'd get the same money with Aberdeen without the hassle. Aberdeen was my team even though I later went to Rangers. Aberdeen is still my team. All my life.' Cooper's departure was no surprise; his contract had expired and he had declined to sign a new one. What Aberdeen had not anticipated was the impact the World Cup would have on their season.

Leighton and Miller played in all three games in Mexico, McLeish played in one, and though Bett was an unused member of the squad he was also there for the duration. By the time they returned, halfway through June, they had been away for more than five weeks. Pre-season training started within a month and Aberdeen were due to play their first friendly, in a suburb of Gothenburg, on 22 July. Travel broadens the mind and World Cups inflate footballers. They are playing at the very pinnacle of the game, their actions and words transmitted around the planet and devoured by hundreds of millions of people. Despite the early elimination, the experience of Mexico was one of the highlights of the Aberdeen players' careers. But the comedown was brutal. Leighton went from the pulsating adrenalin rush of facing Uruguay in Neza to a friendly against Stuttgart in front of only 7,000 at Pittodrie.

The goalkeeper said: 'When we came back from Mexico I wanted to leave. I felt I had done everything at Aberdeen. I'd seen Gordon [Strachan] go to Man United, Mark [McGhee] had gone to Hamburg, Eric [Black] had gone to Metz. I had won everything I could win. There was nothing else that I could do. I'd had the taste of playing in Mexico, I learned a lot about myself by playing there, and after that it took me three or four months to get back into enjoying football again. I'd played at a level that was the highest anyone can play at. To come back to pre-season a couple of weeks later was impossible. I wanted to leave but Fergie wouldn't have let me go.'

The mood at Pittodrie was further darkened by the realisation that Frank McDougall was in serious trouble with a back injury. He had first suffered with it around the time of the Scottish Cup final and over the summer it became worse. An appearance as a late substitute in the second game of the season, at home to Hibs, turned out to be the last match of his career. Months of treatment and examinations culminated with a doctor telling him he would never play again. The news was delivered on his twenty-ninth birthday. McDougall delivered the best pound-for-pound return of all Ferguson's signings, with forty-four goals in seventy-five games. The previous season his partnership with Black had yielded thirty-five goals. Suddenly the team had neither of them. It soon showed. After ten league games Aberdeen had won only four times and were sixth in the Premier Division. They went out of the League Cup to Celtic in September and out of the European Cup Winners' Cup in October, losing 4–2 on aggregate to the Swiss team, Sion. The evidence of decline was impossible to miss: four years earlier they had beaten Sion 11–1 en route to Gothenburg.

These defeats came as major shocks to the club, not least because Ferguson had returned from Mexico intent on shaking things up. Before going away he had told his assistant, Garner, to draw up a schedule for pre-season training and to persuade Hewitt to sign a new contract (which he did). As soon as Ferguson was back he asked Garner to come and see him at the stadium. Garner remembered: 'He said, "Bring your pre-season plan and we'll have a meeting in the morning." So I come in and he suddenly goes, "I've got something to tell you, it's the hardest thing I've ever had to do in my life." I thought, "Oh, where are we going with this?" He said he was taking Archie Knox back as co-manager and there wasn't a position for me. I said, "Seriously?" There was no discussion. I wasn't on a contract so I was out the door. I had to sign on for unemployment money the following morning. That was hard to take. I thought we were doing well, the club was moving in the right direction, but he just wanted Archie back. Today I can look back on the whole period with real pride. Three years with a guy like that, it's a life experience.' Ferguson felt Garner was too young and easy-going to continue as his assistant and that his closeness to some of the older players, his old team-mates, made it difficult to assert his authority. Garner disagreed but the boss's decision was final.

Knox had been part of the Scotland backroom team in Mexico. He had still been the manager of Dundee while he was on World Cup duty, as he had been for the two-and-a-half years since Ferguson had given him his blessing to leave and become a boss in his own right. Six days after the Uruguay game the pair of them stood side-by-side in the Pittodrie boardroom. They were presented as 'co-managers', not that anyone was fooled by that. 'This is a relationship we know works,' said Ferguson.

Aberdeen's main summer signing was the Dundee midfielder Bobby Connor, to whom Ferguson had given a Scotland debut in April. Between the Sion games he paid another Swiss club, Neuchatel Xamax, £215,000 for the former Dundee United striker Davie Dodds. Back in May Ferguson had sat with the Scottish press pack in Los Angeles and catalogued the key players he had lost over the previous six years: the five he name-checked were Archibald, Strachan, McGhee, Black and Cooper. 'I have something like a million pounds available for new men coming to Pittodrie,' he said. In the summer of 1986 £1 million sounded like a lot of money in football. A couple of months earlier it would have sounded like headline news. But by the time he briefed them in LA, Ferguson, who had been such a gift to the press over the last eight years, had a rival for their attention. All of a sudden the story was not the Aberdeen manager and his budget. It was Rangers, the charismatic young leader they had just appointed, and what already looked like an open-chequebook policy to go out and hunt down any player they wanted. The 1985–86 season had been particularly wretched for Rangers even by the standards of their dismal early 1980s. For the only time in their history they lost more league games than they won. They struggled to finish even fifth in the table, went out of Europe and the Scottish Cup in the first rounds and lost to Hibs in the League Cup. Their crowds were dwindling. Years of mediocrity had pushed them towards irrelevance.

On Tuesday, 8 April deliverance arrived. 'Souness is to take over at Ibrox' said the *Glasgow Herald* on its front page. Rangers had sacked Jock Wallace and flown in Souness from his Italian club, Sampdoria, to take over as player-manager. It was impossible to miss the significance. Souness was box office. Handsome, tanned and fit, he looked ready for anything. He bought instant international profile and prestige, and most realised he would not have agreed to move if Rangers intended to limp along at the same level of investment they had allowed John Greig and Wallace. This was an unmistakable declaration of intent. The writers were briefed that Rangers would be pursuing bigger and more expensive targets than Scottish football had seen. Rangers were at last waking up to their potential to make millions from bigger crowds, sponsorship, corporate hospitality, advertising and merchandise. Souness was to be the figurehead for a new era. 'One has the feeling that things are about to take off at Ibrox again after the lean years,' wrote Jim Reynolds in the *Glasgow Herald*.

When he was presented to the media Souness went through the obligatory question-and-answer session about whether he had been given the freedom to sign Catholics. 'How could I possibly be in this job if I had been told I could not sign a Catholic? I am married to one. Do you think I could go home in the evening if I was under such a restriction?' This was significant, but the biggest story was about money. 'I would like to think that in my time at the club players with the class of Michel Platini and the likes would be happy to come here. Rangers are as big as Manchester United, certainly bigger than Liverpool or Everton, Arsenal or Tottenham. At the moment, all I can promise the fans is that I will bring quality players to the club.'

The line was a familiar one but from Souness it sounded different. The Scottish transfer record stood at £450,000, when Celtic signed Mo Johnston from Watford two years earlier. Within two months Souness had smashed that to land goalkeeper Chris Woods from Norwich City. Another two months later he broke it again to bring Terry Butcher from Ipswich. There was an unsuccessful £500,000 bid to take Richard Gough from Dundee United, too. Not only were the signings expensive, they brought a calibre of player who would previously have considered it unthinkable to move to Ibrox over one of the big English clubs. Woods was twenty-six and a regular in the England squad. At twenty-seven, Butcher was an even bigger international name and at the peak of his career. When Rangers began their season at Hibs, four players – Souness himself, Woods, Butcher and striker Colin West, signed from Watford for £180,000 – had been added to the previous season's unimpressive squad. Hibs beat them and Souness was sent off for a crude tackle. The setback was only temporary. They beat Celtic in the season's first Old Firm game and after eight league matches had reached ten points, the same as Aberdeen.

Souness knew the New Firm remained a major obstacle to Rangers' ambitions. Butcher said: 'When he signed us he outlined the fact he didn't like any other team in Scotland.

Particularly Aberdeen, particularly Celtic, particularly Dundee United.' On 27 September Ibrox hosted what turned out to be the only meeting between Ferguson's Aberdeen and Souness's Rangers. The dynamic between the two men at the World Cup had been complicated and unique. Ferguson was Souness's manager and had exercised his right to drop him, even though Souness was his captain. At the same time they were rivals, simultaneously plotting signings and how to beat each other in the coming months. They even shared a right-hand man. Walter Smith was Ferguson's assistant for Scotland and Souness's for Rangers.

For almost three-and-a-half years Aberdeen had not lost a game at Ibrox. But a new Rangers was stirring and that September clash became symbolic. 'Britain's most attractive-looking fixture of the day,' wrote the *Glasgow Herald*. The crowd was the biggest in Britain that day, too. The stadium was packed with just over 40,000 fans, all but 3,000 of them roaring on Rangers. The first half was cagey. Rangers tried to make the running but Aberdeen were calm and resolute. It was tight, and the breakthrough did not come until five minutes into the second half. Souness drove a low shot which hit the post and rebounded into the net off Leighton's head. Ibrox was euphoric. Aberdeen still posed a threat but the momentum was against them. 'Now in outstanding form, Rangers poured down on Aberdeen,' wrote Alan Davidson in the *Evening Times*. Nine minutes from time Ally McCoist scored a second from a swift counter-attack. He looked offside when he collected a pass from Robert Fleck and tapped the ball into the net, but referee Jim Duncan let the goal stand. Aberdeen crowded the linesman at the halfway line. Leighton, McLeish, Miller, Weir, Bett and Connor were all in the official's face. Even Knox joined in until he was led back to the dugout by a policeman. McCoist had been playing against Aberdeen since 1983 and never previously scored against them: 'I remember Leighton chasing the linesman halfway down the park that day screaming that the goal was offside. Willie with his face tripping him, Alex no' happy. I'm thinking, "Fucking hell, you can't grudge me a goal at last, you miserable bastards."'

Another flashpoint came in the directors' box when Aberdeen director Ian Donald was butted. He had asked a nearby Rangers supporter to sit down after the second goal. Donald played down the incident and chose not report it to police. The game finished 2–0.

Celtic may have been the reigning champions at the time but Aberdeen had been the dominant team of the previous five years. Now, suddenly, Rangers threatened to undo them. Butcher can still remember the edge to the atmosphere that day: 'Aberdeen was the big game. It was the whole hostility of Aberdeen against Rangers. You thought to yourself, "What the hell have I walked into here? Jesus Christ." I was used to some rivalries down south but never as intense as that. There was a nastiness about the Aberdeen fixture, from history, and it seemed to get even nastier. To beat Aberdeen showed how far Souness had taken Rangers straight away. I can still feel a tingle now. When we played Aberdeen it was a war, a bloody war.'

The significance of the win was immediately obvious to McCoist: 'That day at Ibrox was a massive, massive result because Souness really wanted to win that one. We were just starting to take over. It was obvious Aberdeen weren't going to go down without a fight because that had been instilled in them by Fergie. It was like we were the new kids coming on to their block and Aberdeen were probably a little bit like a boxer who had had one fight too many.'

The game was covered on STV by the experienced broadcaster Jock Brown and his journalistic instincts kicked in. 'There was still the story about supposed bad blood between Fergie and Souness over the World Cup. So at the end of the game the producer says to me, "What interviews should we try for?" and I said, "There's only one interview to go for: the two of them together." He says to me, "Oh, you'll never get that, it'll never happen." I told him, "Well, I'll never know unless I ask."' Brown approached the dressing rooms, having devised a mind game of his own. He told Ferguson that Souness had already agreed to the interview – and then fed Souness the same line about Ferguson. 'It worked. I got them both in front of a camera and the opening question was, "Well, the whole world will be astonished to see the pair of you standing side by side here after the World Cup, what are relations like between you?" I used to get told that when you interview like that you would get two minutes, maybe two-and-a-half, and then there'd be a guy in your ear saying, "Right, wrap it up." That day we went for seven minutes. And they showed every word.'

The two managers stood on the Ibrox pitch in front of Brown. Ferguson was in a suit and red tie, Souness in an open-neck shirt and a Rangers club blazer. The body language was fascinating: when one of them was talking to Brown, the other would look away into the distance. Otherwise they seemed relaxed. When they discussed the offside controversy Ferguson even gave Souness a playful nudge. Souness was first to take the question about whether there was bad blood between them because of Ferguson's decision at the World Cup. 'That's a nonsense. Alex came to me and spoke about it at the time. I disagreed and wasn't happy about not playing in the last game, but he was the manager and I had to accept that. We got on great before that and we get on great now. It makes good reading for people to write about vendettas and us not getting on. It's a nonsense.' Then Ferguson took his turn: 'You do get fed up reading, "This is going to be Graeme Souness's revenge match." It is nonsense. Graeme will now appreciate, even more so, that when you make decisions you hurt yourself too. People forget that. Life is too short for the likes of Graeme and me to be thinking and talking about revenge.'

When Ferguson looked at Souness he no longer saw the captain he had dropped in Neza; he saw the threat posed by a 33-year-old player-manager with the resources to assemble the most formidable domestic force Scotland had seen for a generation. Since 1978 Ferguson had taken on the remnants of Rangers' treble winners, championship-winning Celtic sides led by Billy McNeill and Davie Hay, vibrant Dundee United teams under the inspirational leadership of Jim McLean, and the powerful unit who had helped Hearts become a major challenger. But none of them had possessed Souness's spending power in the transfer market.

Leighton could sense the awakening of a sleeping giant at Ibrox: 'Aberdeen and Dundee United changed the face of Scottish football because we weren't scared of going to Glasgow and winning. As soon as Souness went to Rangers the whole thing changed again because they were throwing money at it. We weren't the same force after that and United weren't the same force. It was about them having an aura again. Souness changed the face of Scottish football.'

Rangers had already beaten Celtic, the league champions, but defeating Aberdeen that day was seen as the evidence that they were back. 'Ibrox men pass their biggest test', said the *Evening Times* headline. 'It took a side of all the class and experience of Aberdeen to prove that Rangers have turned the corner and moved on to a route leading to true prosperity,' wrote Alan Davidson. Ferguson was gracious in defeat but keen to emphasise Aberdeen's poor luck. It had taken 'a shot in a million' and a 'very controversial' late goal to beat them, he said, and Jim Bett had been outstanding in midfield. He had also watched the Rangers players' reaction at full-time: hugging each other, clenched fists pumping the air, arms aloft to their jubilant supporters. Ferguson spun this as a compliment to his own team's mighty reputation.

A few days after Ibrox he tried to reassure the Aberdeen support: 'One lesson for the players was the reaction in Glasgow because they had beaten us. The desire to put one over on Aberdeen has to be sampled to understand. Rangers' reaction to their win was simply a reminder of how much we have achieved and how eager they now are to do the same. We have had plenty of resounding successes in Glasgow and there will be more.' On official duty as the manager of Aberdeen, Ferguson never set foot in Glasgow again. Within six weeks he was gone.

TWENTY-TWO

A DEATH IN THE FAMILY

Tragedy struck at just after 11.30am on 6 November 1986. The Chinook helicopter was carrying forty-four passengers and three crew members on a routine 135-mile journey from the Brent oilfield to Sumburgh Airport in Shetland. There were strong winds and wintry showers off the southern tip of the island but visibility was good. A couple of miles from land a sudden transmission failure desynchronised the rotors and the blades collided. The effect was catastrophic. The Chinook dropped from the sky into the sea and immediately began to sink; radio contact cut out instantly. In that single helicopter crash more lives were lost than in the previous twenty years of flights to and from the oilfields combined. Only two men survived. It was the world's worst civil helicopter disaster and it had happened in the north-east. At the offices of the Aberdeen papers, the *Press & Journal* and the *Evening Express*, it was all hands to the pumps. Pages were cleared to make room for the coverage.

Among the few exempt from the hubbub were the football writers. They were soon into a heavy shift of their own, though, as a major sports story was also breaking in

Aberdeen that Thursday morning. Just over 350 miles to the south, Manchester United manager Ron Atkinson had been called in by chairman Martin Edwards and sacked. 'Big Ron', with his sunglasses, cigars and swagger, had brought flamboyance and a champagne style to Old Trafford. Since taking over in 1981 he had finished third, third, fourth, fourth and fourth again in the First Division while winning the FA Cup twice. Major investments had been made: Bryan Robson, Remi Moses, Gordon Strachan and Jesper Olsen were big-money signings; and the club had brought through Mark Hughes, Norman Whiteside and Paul McGrath. United had talent but often they were deeply mediocre. The one constant was their place in the shadow of England's pre-eminent club, Liverpool. Nearly twenty years had passed since their last league championship, in 1967, and Big Ron, though consistent, had brought them no closer to another. In the opening months of 1986–87 their league form was pitiful. They won only three of their first thirteen games and were rooted in nineteenth position, one above relegation. The crowd against Coventry City on 1 November, in what proved to be Atkinson's last home game, was 36,946, way short of the ground's capacity. Going out of the Littlewoods Cup at Southampton the following Tuesday night took the manager to the point of no return.

As the news media gathered information on the stricken helicopter and its victims, the sports reporters reacted to Atkinson's sacking. The likely consequences were obvious. FERGUSON THE FRONT RUNNER ran a secondary story on the back page of the *Evening Express*'s later Thursday editions, with the main story, perhaps surprisingly, being the sacking itself. The paper reported that there had been no approach to Aberdeen. There was even a quote from the man himself: 'Manchester United have not been in touch with me and they have not asked our directors for permission to speak to me.' That quote would have been supplied sometime late on Thursday morning. However, as Ferguson confirmed in his 1999 autobiography, he had spent the Wednesday evening with United's entire board of directors. Aberdeen were yet to realise it, but the deal had been done there and then: they had lost their manager. In Friday's *Evening Express*, just twenty-four hours later, there was a picture of Ferguson in United gear taking his first training session in Manchester.

Manchester United and Ferguson had periodically crossed paths during his years at Aberdeen. In the autumn of 1981 United travelled north to participate in a four-team tournament at Pittodrie. Two years later Aberdeen were at Old Trafford to play a testimonial for Martin Buchan, who had moved to United back in 1972. The following year Ferguson tried unsuccessfully to sign Arthur Graham on loan from United when Weir was injured. At the end of 1984 he showed up for two European games at Old Trafford: United against Dundee United and Celtic versus Rapid Vienna, the latter played at a neutral venue because of Uefa precautions against crowd trouble. In turn, United were seduced by Ferguson's energy and charisma, and watched with mounting interest as he clocked up trophy after trophy, growing into a figure of real substance. His football was aggressive, bold and exciting; it was how United saw themselves.

The connection between Ferguson, United chairman Martin Edwards and director Bobby Charlton evolved during the transfer of Strachan to Old Trafford in 1984. Ferguson had been infuriated by Strachan's decision to join Cologne and was determined to invalidate the agreement and manoeuvre Strachan to United instead. His handling of the negotiations impressed United. And when the deal was completed Ferguson took the surprising step of accompanying Strachan to the signing in Manchester. 'Think about it, he came to the signing with me,' Strachan said. 'Meeting Martin Edwards and all the rest of it. I always remember Martin asking a couple of questions about him in my first season there [1984–85]. "What does Alex do with this? What does he do with that?" I didn't think I was doing anything wrong by answering.' Ferguson also attended the 1985 FA Cup final when United beat Everton and was at the evening reception as Strachan's guest. Over the course of the weekend they discussed the idea of him leaving Aberdeen to manage a bigger club. Strachan recalled: 'He said, "I'm only leaving for Barcelona or Man United." I thought to myself, "I hope it's fucking Barcelona!"'

Rumours that Ferguson was being lined up by United had rippled through British football for months. Atkinson believed Ferguson had been given the nod long before his arrival in November. In *Big Ron*, his 1999 autobiography, Atkinson claimed that Ferguson had been offered the position by Bobby Charlton at the 1986 World Cup finals in Mexico. The United legend was at the tournament commentating for television and spoke with Ferguson at pitchside before Scotland's game against Uruguay in Neza. Charlton's version is that he simply asked Ferguson to let him know if he ever fancied managing in England. Atkinson also recalled bumping into Ferguson in Glasgow having travelled north to watch Celtic play Dynamo Kiev in a European Cup tie on 22 October. Previously the pair had been friendly but on this occasion Atkinson claimed Ferguson seemed distant and uncomfortable, unwilling to engage with him. Fifteen days later Ferguson replaced him at Old Trafford.

Ferguson has always dismissed such speculation as groundless but he could not deny that the rumours were widespread, as he acknowledged in *Managing My Life*. When Don Howe stepped down as Arsenal manager in March 1986, their board approached Ferguson and he went to meet them. The talks were not especially enthusiastic. 'They had this idea that I was all set on joining Manchester United,' he wrote. 'It was genuinely the first I'd heard of it.' In 2011 Ferguson revealed that he had been offered the Arsenal job and had asked Walter Smith to join him as his assistant. Smith, however, was about to join Rangers.

For his part, Smith remembered Ferguson being approached by the North London club in April while they were in London for the England versus Scotland game at Wembley. 'He was starting to get the approaches to go to England prior to going to the World Cup finals. You always got the impression that it was only a matter of time; that he felt he had done what he could at Aberdeen and he was prepared to move on. The progression to English football was a natural thing.' As it turned out Ferguson was unconvinced by Arsenal and the job went instead to George Graham.

One of Aberdeen's greatest triumphs in the 1980s was keeping hold of Ferguson for as long as they did. Overturning Scottish football's established order made him an intriguing figure to club chairmen in England and beyond. And that remarkable defeat of Real Madrid in Gothenburg had been like a flare going up to alert the football world to a new managerial talent. It was inevitable that Aberdeen's tyro of a manager would attract interest from further afield. Indeed, while he was in Australia with Scotland the previous December, he had been approached by someone claiming to represent Inter Milan. But he offered no encouragement.

In the course of the 1985–86 season there was also interest from Barcelona. Michael Crick's 2002 book, *The Boss*, detailed the informal talks Barcelona president Josep Núñez and three directors held with Ferguson, Howard Kendall and Bobby Robson in London's Connaught Hotel. The Barcelona manager at the time, Terry Venables, was considering stepping down and Ferguson later said it was Venables himself who approached him. The discussions were amicable but did not result in a job offer. Closer to home, Aston Villa also wanted him when Graham Turner was sacked in September 1986, but again he showed little interest. By coincidence the job went to his old sparring partner Billy McNeill.

Manchester United, however, was an irresistible proposition. Ferguson saw the club as the vehicle to realise all his managerial ambitions, including winning the European Cup. It did not matter that United had fallen on comparatively hard times: the size of the club, its history, its fanbase, its association with stylish play, its spending power and its untapped potential seduced him absolutely. For over a decade the official line from Manchester United and Ferguson remained that everything had been done by the book, with no approach made to him or to Aberdeen until after Atkinson had been sacked. In fact, as he wrote in *Managing My Life*, Ferguson took a call from United around 2pm on Wednesday, 5 November, the day before Atkinson found out he was being dismissed. United director Mike Edelson called the Pittodrie switchboard pretending to be Gordon Strachan's accountant. When he was put through to Ferguson, the phone was immediately handed over to Martin Edwards. They arranged to meet along with the other members of the United board at 7pm at a service station at Hamilton.

Before leaving he told his wife, Cathy, and Archie Knox. His co-manager was taking a training session with Aberdeen's reserves and younger players when Ferguson's car pulled up. Knox feared the worst: 'My mother hadn't been well and I thought, "Oh oh, here's bad news." He came along, toots the horn to me and I go across. He goes, "We're going to Man United." I go, "Are we?" He says, "You'll be offered the job here so what do you want to do?" I goes, "I'll be coming with you." That was it. No discussions. No agents. No talk of what we were getting paid. And he didn't say, "I'm going to Manchester United", it was "We".'

Ferguson and the United board of Edwards, Charlton, Edelson and Maurice Watkins, convened at Hamilton then drove in two cars to Ferguson's sister-in-law's house in Bishopbriggs, near Glasgow, where the deal was agreed. Ferguson wrote that he thought the wage on offer was 'disappointing': it was lower than his combined 1986 salary and bonuses at Pittodrie, but he did not allow that to get in the way. The following morning Atkinson was dismissed and Edwards and Watkins flew to Aberdeen to speak with Dick and Ian Donald. The old chairman made a last effort to talk Ferguson into staying, even telling him he could have the club. Ferguson was moved by the sentiment but felt both of them knew it was a token gesture borne out of desperation. In August Ferguson had joined the two Donalds on the board as Chris Anderson's replacement. 'The Dons are my life now,' he wrote in his programme column, but in the end his ambitions overrode his allegiances. The United job was irresistible. That evening he made a round of telephone calls to the players who had been with him the longest. 'I asked him if it was to say cheerio,' said McLeish. It was.

For the only time in their eight-and-a-half years together there was open tension between Dick Donald and Ferguson. Donald knew it was impossible to keep him but he resented the way the departure had been handled. He spoke bitterly to the *Evening Express*, accusing Ferguson of having broken a contract, and United of having behaved improperly and discourteously. 'We had no idea this was about to happen and Mr Edwards never approached me for permission to talk to our manager,' said Donald. 'The first I knew was when I heard he would be flying into Aberdeen to meet Alex. We don't know when he spoke to the manager or whether this was cut and dried before yesterday. We tried to hold Alex to his contract, but I don't know if he took it too seriously. This contract business is just a waste of time. A contract doesn't bind anyone.' Under the terms of his deal Aberdeen received the £60,000 compensation they were entitled to from United. But as Donald said: 'How can you evaluate the loss of his services?'

There was no anger among the players, only numbness. The likelihood of Ferguson moving on had been obvious to all of them, in some cases for years, yet the sudden reality of it was stunning. Even now most can recall their sense of shock. McMaster said: 'Suddenly there was a big, giant hole in your life.' McKimmie stated simply: 'It was like a death in the family.' The young full-back David Robertson found out when he was giving his dad a lift back from the golf course. With typical Aberdonian reserve Robertson senior turned to his boy and said: 'Well, that's Fergie away, then.' Having only just turned eighteen Robertson had never known a manager other than Ferguson. 'It was like someone taking a chunk out of you. It was devastating. There was an eerie silence in the dressing room the next time we were in. Dead quiet. No one knew what to expect next. It was as if everybody felt lost: the players, the staff, the cleaners, the kitchen staff.' If anyone was glad to see the back of Ferguson they have never said so. Leighton said: 'We thought it was inevitable. We were surprised that he was still with us for that length of time because he'd done so well. As soon as we heard that Ron Atkinson had got the sack some of us were in training, going, "Well, that's him away." We all knew he'd be going.'

Ferguson left Aberdeen in fifth place in the Premier Division. His final game was a friendly in the Highlands to mark Inverness Caledonian's centenary on Monday, 3 November, but the last league game was a 2–0 win at Dundee two days earlier. Leighton and Miller played in that last competitive game, just as they had in Ferguson's first, back in 1978. 'I regarded that as our best display of the season,' said Ferguson after the match. 'And a sign that the old, essential Aberdeen qualities are still there.' Others were less enthusiastic about where the team was heading. In a letter in the *Green Final* sports paper the same evening, R. Smith of Deeview Road, wrote: 'Aberdeen's season is all over. They are not good enough at the moment to finish better than fourth in the league. Ferguson seems to have lost his way, maintaining too much faith in his regulars.'

The real issue was not that Ferguson was losing his way but that his time with Aberdeen had run its course. Successes at home and especially in Europe had elevated the club but the glass ceiling remained low, especially as football began to focus on those clubs with the greatest financial power. The potential for investment and growth at Aberdeen was limited. Its status as the oil capital of Europe offered the tantalising prospect of the club securing lucrative sponsorship deals from the offshore industry, but none materialised. The market leaders were BP but no matter how hard the club lobbied, the oil company fought shy of their advances. BP's policy was to support football in a broad sense: they took executive boxes and backed the game in schools, but they did not invest in individual clubs. The bitter irony was that Hamburg, Aberdeen's great rivals from 1981 and 1983, were sponsored by BP throughout the 1980s. The company explained that its European arm followed a different policy. So the long-cherished plan to raise Pittodrie's capacity to 30,000 was never realised. Even Chris Anderson's ambition to install electronic scoreboards in the stadium never came to fruition until the summer of 2023.

Replacing players of the calibre of Archibald, Strachan, McGhee, Black, Cooper and McDougall became more challenging as the top of the transfer market moved further and further beyond Aberdeen's reach. Ferguson simply could not afford players like Terry Butcher and Chris Woods, whose arrival at Ibrox had shown the magnitude of Rangers' revolution under Souness. Aberdeen had gone from beating Bayern Munich and Real Madrid to being knocked out of Europe by Dynamo Berlin and Sion. If Ferguson was to realise his own soaring ambitions, he would have to move to a club with deeper pockets.

Club secretary Taggart worked with Ferguson on a day-to-day basis and observed the subtle shift in his mood: 'The season before he left I don't think he was as interested as he'd been. It's not that Aberdeen became an encumbrance to him but he wanted to do something more. You couldn't blame him, for God's sake. He'd wrung every bloody success he could out of a limited resource. The team was starting to age and he was losing players. He had outgrown Aberdeen. He got to the stage where he needed and wanted something else. When it happened, the timing was right.' The broadcaster Archie Macpherson knew Ferguson well enough to pick up on it, too: 'He had to cut himself free from a league that looked as if it was going to be compressed. It looked like Rangers and Celtic would simply sweep up. He wanted out of that and that's why he had to get to a big club.'

Aberdeen were left to pick up the pieces. After losing Ferguson the club were stunned to discover that Knox was going with him. The board had blithely assumed that the co-manager would take over whenever the vacancy arose. Ferguson clearly knew the club's succession plan when he told Knox he would be offered the job after receiving Edwards' call. Knox turned Donald down but agreed to stay on as caretaker manager until a permanent successor could be found. Like Old Trafford, the tunnel at Pittodrie was unusually positioned at the corner of the pitch and required managers to walk half the length of the track to reach the dugouts. When Knox emerged before the home game against St Mirren two days after Ferguson's departure, he was booed and verbally abused by the normally conservative regulars in the Main Stand. 'Caretaker manager Archie Knox received an astonishingly hostile reception at Pittodrie,' wrote the *Green Final*. The game finished 0–0 and the two biggest cheers of the day were for the public address announcer telling the crowd that Manchester United were losing 1–0 to Oxford at half-time and 2–0 at the final whistle. Ferguson was unimpressed by the treatment of Knox and retaliated by announcing that he would only allow Aberdeen to keep him for a month at the most. 'There is no way he will be staying there to be abused.' For Knox it was water off a duck's back. 'Ach, I remember they were rustling their sweetie papers, shouting "traitor". I expected it. It was a support that was hurt and so was old Dick. He was pleading with me to stay and keep it going. But it was never going to be the same.' Knox ended up staying for three games.

Who could replace Ferguson, though? His own recommendation was the Hearts player-assistant manager Sandy Jardine, a former team-mate from Rangers in the 1960s. But Hearts reacted to press speculation about his candidacy by giving Jardine a three-and-a-half-year contract. In 2013, another former Rangers man, Tommy McLean, revealed in his autobiography that Donald had telephoned him about the job. McLean was Motherwell manager at the time, but met Donald in Perth. Having discussed terms, he turned the offer down for family reasons. Twelve days after Ferguson resigned his successor was revealed. Ian Porterfield had not had a job since being sacked by Sheffield United eight months earlier. He was forty and a Fifer, but unfamiliar to supporters in Scotland except for those who remembered him scoring Sunderland's winner in the 1973 FA Cup final against Leeds. As a manager he had done well at Rotherham and initially in Sheffield, but he was no Alex Ferguson. 'He has got all the qualities we were looking for,' director Ian

Donald told the press. 'Ian has a different approach and after the success we have had we felt a new broom might be the best option.'

Porterfield was quietly delighted. 'Alex is a super manager and he's done a wonderful job. But I am my own man and I am ready to follow his achievements. I would place this club among the top eight in Great Britain. This club is built on the same lines as Liverpool.' Porterfield was a good man, easy-going and likeable. Aberdeen finished fourth under him, one place higher than Ferguson had left them, and fourth again in 1987–88, his first full season. He signed Charlie Nicholas from Arsenal having initially telephoned George Graham to inquire about a teenager called Paul Merson. He also tried to sign a young Matthew Le Tissier during his first season at Southampton. Some Aberdeen supporters put on a brave face. One wrote to the *Green Final*: 'The more sober personality of Ian can do the Dons a lot of good. After eight years of the overpowering cult of Alex Ferguson things may change a lot at Pittodrie and not necessarily for the worse.' A spokesman for the Association of Aberdeen Supporters' Clubs said: 'We must remember that it is the players on the park who actually earn the results. After all, how many goals did Alex Ferguson score for Aberdeen? How many world-class saves did Archie Knox make?'

Few took the change harder than the players who had been with Ferguson the longest. They were used to work, intensity, focus and fearsome tirades when standards slipped. Porterfield's approach was easy-osey and gentle. He was the Anti-Fergie. Simpson said: 'The standards weren't the same. Fergie was one extreme and Porterfield was the other. It was a helluva clash of styles. There were a lot of draws under Porterfield. He would go, "Well, that's a point more than we had at three o'clock". Fergie would have gone mental.'

Replacing Ferguson was impossible. After eighteen months Porterfield resigned for personal reasons. If there had been early signs of Aberdeen's decline in Ferguson's final months, the process quickened under Porterfield and gradually snowballed under nearly all of his successors at Pittodrie, Gothenburg heroes Miller and McGhee among them. At the end of 2013, exactly thirty years after their triumph in the Super Cup allowed Aberdeen to claim they were the best team in Europe, Uefa ranked them 290th.

The north-east mourned Ferguson, of course, but for a club like Aberdeen the truly irreplaceable loss was not the man, it was the era. All the factors which elevated them in the late 1970s and early 1980s lost their value as football evolved into a new age shaped by rampant commercialism, massive broadcasting deals and players' freedom of contract. In the summer of 1986 English football signed a television deal for the rights to live coverage of its best games: the agreement was worth £6.2 million. A decade later the same rights were sold for £670 million. In every major football nation serious money began to flow towards a select group of bigger clubs while the rest were marginalised. Aberdeen had been able to pay competitive transfer fees and wages, and to keep outstanding players and an extraordinary manager for more than eight years. By the mid-1990s they were hopelessly outmuscled, too small to survive as a competitive force and excluded from the emerging elite, just as their old sparring partners Ipswich, Hamburg and for a spell even Liverpool were to varying degrees. Now the game's true giants, clubs with long pedigrees and international brands like Bayern Munich and Real Madrid, prospered. And so did Manchester United under Ferguson.

In Scotland, in 1986, the shape of things to come was already apparent. Souness's arrival began a near-decade-long Rangers monopoly over the Scottish game, fuelled by massive season ticket sales and commercial and sponsorship income. Eventually Celtic hauled themselves level and once again Scotland's list of league champions resumed the dull rhythm – Rangers-Celtic-Rangers-Celtic-Rangers-Celtic – it had maintained until Aberdeen broke the sequence in 1980. Ferguson's league win in 1985 remains the last by any non-Old Firm club. In the 1990s the directors at Pittodrie saddled the club with major debts to replace the old Beach End with a new stand and gambled on some comparatively expensive signings, without an improvement in the Dons' fortunes. Lower and lower league finishes were posted until eventually they hit bottom in 2000. In any other season that would have meant the club's first-ever relegation, but issues around league reconstruction spared them.

Dick Donald died in 2003 and the incomparable Teddy Scott passed away in 2012. When Aberdeen collapsed to a horrific 9–0 defeat against Celtic at Parkhead in 2010 the score was so poignant it made headlines across the international media. The *New York Times* carried a column about the result under the headline FOR SCOTTISH CLUB, A CRUEL DECLINE; the names of Gothenburg, Real Madrid and Ferguson were mentioned in the first five paragraphs.

When Ferguson moved to United he vowed not to poach any of his old players, only to be irritated when Joe Miller was sold to Celtic without Aberdeen giving him first refusal. From then on he regarded Pittodrie as fair game and tried to sign McLeish before taking Leighton to Old Trafford in 1988. The relationship between those two fractured beyond repair when Ferguson dropped Leighton for the FA Cup final replay against Crystal Palace in 1990. Strachan and McGhee later fell out of favour with Ferguson after moving into management, but not to the same extent. Leighton said: 'I'm happy to speak about Fergie. He won't mention me. We've done Gothenburg twenty-fifth anniversary events, thirtieth anniversaries, he's either there or he's not, he does interviews or DVDs or whatever, and there's only certain of the boys who get mentioned. Some of the boys have said to me, "Did you actually play in that team?" He'll say, "Alex and Willie were brilliant at the back, the defence was magnificent." And then he'll mention midfield and Gordon won't get a mention. And up front Eric and Mark won't get a mention. It's a team with holes in it! But everybody played their part along the way: Ally MacLeod, Billy McNeill and then Fergie took it to a different level. We wouldn't have done it without someone like him leading the team.' Despite Leighton's impression of a team resembling a sieve, in fact Ferguson's relationship with Strachan in particular was fully repaired. Only Joe Harper and Leighton are really estranged from him.

Aberdeen's decline pained Ferguson from afar. He took Manchester United to Pittodrie for friendlies and testimonials in 1991, 1999, 2008 and 2012 and contributed to numerous official club books and DVDs. Aberdeen's retreat into mediocrity only heightened the nostalgia for the peaks they reached under Ferguson and he was a willing participant. When he promoted his 2013 autobiography the tickets for an event in Aberdeen under the billing 'In Conversation with Sir Alex Ferguson' sold out within thirty minutes. He was guest of honour when the club opened its Cormack Park training facility in 2019, finally severing the connection with public parks and a young sergeant-major tormenting his squad on a freezing Aberdeen beach. In the highly personal 2021 documentary *Never Give In*, directed by his son Jason, Ferguson smiled broadly as he was invited to sing 'The European Song' and very briefly went along with it: 'We're the Dons from Aberdeen, and we're gonna do it for you . . . that's all you're getting . . .'

By then Ferguson was back at Pittodrie on a permanent basis. The north-east is undemonstrative towards its heroes but after decades with nothing – no statue or stand named after him despite both already existing at Manchester United – Aberdeen commissioned a sculptor. A bronze statue was created of a young Fergie, attractive and maybe needing a haircut, with his arms raised and outstretched to forever celebrate the first title win at Easter Road in 1980. Football statues vary wildly when it comes to accuracy but fans agreed this one captured him. The sides of the octagonal plinth listed his honours and carried a quote: 'Winning that first title gave us the taste for success – the club, the players, the supporters, all of us. The more trophies you win, the hungrier you become for the next one. The pursuit of success became central to my life.' Ferguson attended and was fussed over at a ceremonial unveiling and since 2022 the statute has stood outside what used to be the Beach End. Facing out to the North Sea. Facing Gothenburg.

When interviewed for Aberdeen's official centenary book, he looked back warmly on his years in the north-east. 'There is no doubt that Aberdeen made me as a manager. I keep a very special place in my heart for Pittodrie. I have to say that the chemistry which brought together that particular talent and character might turn out to be a once-in-a-lifetime happening.' Govan made the man and Aberdeen made the manager. It was while he was ruling Pittodrie that Ferguson lost his father, saw his mentor Jock Stein die in Cardiff and learned that his mother had the lung cancer which would claim her life within a few weeks of his move to Old Trafford. It was a period during which he saw his sons Mark, Darren and Jason go through their formative years at school, where Cathy felt so at home that it was a wrench for her to move the family south, and where he made deep and lasting friendships which endure to this day. Some of those relationships were with the players who helped him make Aberdeen great. Miller, McLeish and Kennedy have stayed in regular contact with their old boss. The likes of Strachan, Bobby Clark, Neil Simpson, John McMaster and Peter Weir see him now and again. Plenty of others have his number stored in their phones. Throughout his 26-year tenure at Manchester United there was an open-door policy for his Aberdeen favourites. Very few of them will hear a bad word said about him.

Aberdeen was the prototype for United. A club where he had to prove himself before establishing a dictatorship. A club with boardroom stability and absolute trust between manager and directors. A club committed to finding and shaping its own young players to Ferguson's specifications. A team built around a back four, a formidable central defence and an outstanding captain who was the embodiment of Ferguson's own intolerant hunger out on the pitch. A style based on strength, intensity, width and relentless attacking. An attitude built on character, spirit, aggression, fearlessness and ambition. A club where Ferguson became the greatest, most successful manager they had ever known. He knocked Rangers and Celtic off their perch in Scotland long before Liverpool and all the others were knocked off theirs in England.

Aberdeen's peak seasons were 1982-83 and 83-84 but narrowly failing in two strong title races meant they did not qualify for the European Cup in either of them. How would the side who triumphed at Gothenburg have fared in the 1983 or 1984 European Cups? Certainly they were stronger than the Dundee United team which beat them only once in six attempts in 1983-84 but reached that season's European Cup semi-final and went out to a Roma side which lost the final on penalties. 'I'm not saying we would have won it, but it would have been nice to have had a crack at it,' said Leighton. 'When we got into the European Cup the following season the team wasn't the same. We'd lost Gordon, we'd lost Rougvie, we'd lost McGhee. We had brought in good players but it wasn't *that* team.' It is an intriguing 'what if'. Ferguson's teams at Pittodrie were every bit as reflective of his football ethos as all those who landed thirteen league titles and two European Cups at Old Trafford. If things had been different he might have lain his hands on the European Cup fifteen years earlier.

When Ferguson called it a day and retired as United manager in 2013 the BBC presented him with a special award at the Sports Personality of the Year ceremony. 'After a successful eight years at Aberdeen . . .' said host Gary Lineker, before lingering on all the subsequent successes in Manchester. Seven words? To span the battles and the glories of Pittodrie, Hampden, Parkhead and Ibrox? To do justice to the clashes with Liverpool, Ipswich, Hamburg and Bayern Munich? Seven words for Gothenburg? For 'a disgrace of a performance'? There was a time when Lineker would have received a phone call about that, from a furious young Glaswegian giving him both barrels about anti-Aberdeen bias.

TWENTY-THREE

THE DAYS OF OUR LIVES

In the early summer of 2023, exactly forty years on from their peak, the boys were back in town. For four days they were a force to be reckoned with again. By now the players had their own WhatsApp group – title: 'Gothenburg Greats' – and for weeks there had been mounting interest and chatter among its elite membership about gathering for a major celebration. They teased each other, fired out one-liners, figured out who was coming and asked for details on what was planned. Gradually, with a bit of work and cajoling, everyone said yes, okay, they were in.

The fortieth anniversary of beating Real Madrid in Gothenburg was a big production. As a city and a football club Aberdeen pulled out all the stops. First there was a cinema premiere of *Aberdeen '83: Once in a Lifetime*, a classy documentary for the BBC which featured interviews with Ferguson and many other key characters. The following night, a gala dinner. Then the centrepiece of it all, a prestigious event in which the Freedom of the City of Aberdeen was presented to the Gothenburg squad and to the club itself in front of 2,500 fans at Pittodrie. Cue Willie Miller being photographed looking more dandy than ever in a specially made red-and-white fedora with the ceremonial scroll tied to it with a ribbon. Finally, the next day, the unveiling of a plaque commemorating Gothenburg at Pittodrie's main entrance and a parade of the greatest Aberdeen team before the current one played out a drab goalless draw against Hibs.

Laughs, stories, getting mobbed for selfies and autographs: they were like kids again, these guys who had subsequently managed Scotland, Celtic, Rangers, Aston Villa, Nottingham Forest, Leicester City, Wolves and – two of them – Aberdeen. Since the Fergie years they had loved and lost, become dads and grandads, been married, divorced and even widowed. Guys like McGhee, Leighton and Strachan who had shied away from some of the previous events were all back together for the fortieth and it felt like the biggest blow-out of the lot. Maybe it would be the final one which almost all of them could attend.

There was no Ferguson – the explanation given was that he felt it was the players' moment and his presence would have overshadowed that – but he sent a message by video: 'I think back to forty years ago and who can forget that wonderful night? The players were fantastic, the support was fantastic. Do you remember thousands of them went on that boat, the *St. Clair* going across the North Sea? What a time they had. These are memories that always flash back in my mind and it was such a wonderful event. Just recently, it came to my notice that Aberdeen were the last team to beat Real Madrid in a final, forty years ago. So well done to the players and well done to the club.'

The four days of celebration, of making Gothenburg feel like it was yesterday, also finally addressed an injustice. After four decades Dougie Bell finally got his medal. The club and AFC Heritage Trust lobbied Uefa and Europe's governing body agreed to provide additional medals for Bell and also for Ferguson, Archie Knox, Teddy Scott and the Donald and Anderson families in recognition of towering 1980s boardroom figures Dick and Ian Donald and Chris Anderson. 'I was really chuffed getting it,' said Bell. 'It made me feel more a part of things. It was great playing the games in the run but having missed the final and not got a medal, that just completed it for me. There had been talk about it for years so for it to finally happen was a really powerful moment.'

So over the four days there was a sense of completion in some ways, but nothing could help them get over a staggering loss. There were laughs and fun with the boys again, but not quite enough of them. For all the joy they had, a shadow hung over everything because the whole Gothenburg team wasn't there. It will never be fully together again. At the Freedom of the City event there were ten of the starters, all five substitutes, and one front row chair left empty for the boy with a personality big enough to fill every seat in Pittodrie.

In May 2018, Neale Cooper, the Dons' precious 'Tattie', died in hospital after suffering a heart attack near his home. At fifty-four he was the youngest of the Gothenburg team and the first to pass away. A Dons A-lister, too. If anyone represented the youth, fun and effervescence of Aberdeen in the 1980s it was the kid with that mop of blonde curls and irresistible, infectious personality. Cooper, who Fergie wound up to smash Charlie Nicholas. Cooper, who had the cheek to pull off that forward roll in front of the Rangers end after lashing a fourth goal into their empty net in the cup final. Cooper, the towering midfield presence with athleticism, aggression and class. Cooper, with his escapades in the city's pubs and clubs, playing his cat-and-mouse game to escape the manager's clutches. Cooper, with all his stories and the best Fergie impersonations in the house. He was the club's lovable wee brother. He could have anyone in fits of giggles within seconds and he would be in stitches along with them. He would grab a team-mate by the arm, or a fan, or anyone, and say, 'Wait 'til I tell you this one,' to launch into another anecdote.

A life and a hero poignantly remembered by a red number four shirt draped over an empty seat.

Losing Cooper devastated the whole club and remains raw to this day. Miller, always so hard and impassive, choked and had to walk away from his interview when asked about Cooper on *Once in a Lifetime*, unintentionally giving the documentary its most powerful moment. The great captain was just as moved at the premiere, at one point doubting whether he could go through with a planned question-and-answer session after the screening. He did, on the condition that he wasn't asked about Tattie because he couldn't trust himself to keep it all together. 'When you lose someone like that it really does hurt,' he said. 'Everybody loved him.'

Cooper had suffered a serious heart attack in the previous summer of 2017 and spent time in a hospital bed contemplating that he had almost become 'the first Gothenburg boy to go'. That episode and his tragic passing served as the first upsetting reminders that time was marching on for the great Aberdeen boys.

Just before he turned sixty, another of the younger Gothenburg players, John Hewitt, began suffering chest pains and had a heart attack while on a lunchtime walk. Thankfully he was treated and recovered. Twelve days after his long wait ended and he had his 1983 medal, Dougie Bell had a heart attack and was told he would require bypass surgery.

And then there was Ferguson. All of football had held its breath when news broke in May 2018 – just three weeks before Cooper's death – that Ferguson had needed emergency surgery after collapsing at home with a brain haemorrhage.

He was seventy-six and had retired from management five years earlier. GET WELL SOON SIR ALEX said the front page of Aberdeen's *Press & Journal* newspaper, reporting how 'messages of support have been flooding in from across the north-east'. Ferguson was in intensive care for four days and in hospital for a further fortnight before being allowed home. He was back at Old Trafford for a match four months later, made a speech when he returned to Pittodrie for his statue unveiling and, at eighty-one, made valuable interview contributions to the fortieth anniversary documentary and celebrations.

When the Gothenburg Greats walked out at Pittodrie in 2023 the fans who remembered them at their formidable best had Cooper in their hearts and affectionately applauded the famous group of old friends teasing each other or grumbling about bad ankles or knees or being thicker around the waistline and thinner on top. Each of them was still easily recognisable forty years on, still the individual components of a truly exceptional football team.

'I always remembered us being fit and organised and having drive, but there was more to it than that,' said Strachan. 'That team could play any game, anytime, anywhere. They were like a four-wheel-drive Range Rover. They could handle anything.'

Ferguson and many of his men will make fewer returns to the north-east now. Perhaps in some cases they will never be back at all. The statue and the fortieth celebrations felt like the last grand thank yous to a manager and players who made the whole of Europe sit up and pay attention to Aberdeen.

What they did is immortalised in that gleaming new plaque at Pittodrie. 'These are the giants of our game,' it says. 'Those were the days of our lives.'

ACKNOWLEDGEMENTS

Around one hundred people played a part in *Fergie Rises.* Without the initial cheerful nagging of agent Mark 'Stan' Stanton it would not have happened in the first place. It was worth it. Thank you to Pete Burns at Polaris for his endless enthusiasm and support for this paperback edition. A raised glass to Dave Innes, who helped at the very beginning and at the end, and whose 'Doug Rougvie Is Innocent' T-shirt inspired a chapter title. Mark McGhee's help and advice were highly valued. To John McMaster, thank you for putting a Gothenburg medal in my hand.

For one reason or another, a debt is owed to all of the following: George Adams, Douglas Alexander, Charlie Allan, Keith Anderson, Ian Angus, Eamonn Bannon, David Begg, Dougie Bell, Raman Bhardwaj, Eric Black, Alan Brazil, Darryl Broadfoot, Jock Brown, Terry Butcher, Brian Campbell, Bobby Clark, Charlie Connelly, Robert Connor, Kersten Constanze, Steve Cowan, Jim Duffy, Tom English, Alan Ferguson, Ian Fleming, Willie Garner, Chris Gavin, Frank Gilfeather, Richard Gordon, Richard Gough, Alan

Grant, John Grant, Peter Grant, Bryan Gunn, Billy Hamilton, John Hewitt, Tony Higgins, Graham Hunter, Brian Irvine, Thomas Jordan, Stuart Kennedy, Archie Knox, Jim Leighton, Craig Levein, David Lindholm, Dave Macdermid, Kenny MacDonald, Archie Macpherson, Walker McCall, Ally McCoist, John McGarry, Brian McGinlay, Derek McGregor, Tommy McIntyre, Dave McKinnon, Stewart McKimmie, Alex McLeish, Jackie McNamara Senior, Dave McPherson, Tommy McQueen, Maurice Malpas, Joe Miller, Willie Miller, Johnny Metgod, Steve Morgan, Pat Nevin, Charlie Nicholas, Jonathan Northcroft, Malcolm Panton, Ian Paul, Ian Porteous, Davie Provan, Derek Rae, Harry Reid, David Robertson, John Robertson, Doug Rougvie, Karl-Heinz Rummenigge, Neil Sargent, Neil Simpson, Gordon Smith, Kenny Smith, Billy Stark, Danny Stewart, Kevin Stirling, Gordon Strachan, Dom Sullivan, Ian Taggart, Peter Weir, Chick Young, and the staff at Central Library, Aberdeen, and The Mitchell Library, Glasgow. I'd also like to thank those who helped and have sadly passed away since the original edition of this book was published in 2014: Ian Redford, Ron Scott, Walter Smith and the incomparable, unforgettable Neale Cooper. Aberdeen will always miss you. Sincere apologies to anyone omitted from the list due to forgetfulness: trying to keep the 80s alive uses up a lot of headspace.

To Sharon, Tom and Charlie. And to Donald from Glenlivet and Ruby from Torry, thank you for the Dons and for everything. What a time we had when our team were kings.

BIBLIOGRAPHY

Atkinson, Ron – *Big Ron: A Different Ball Game*, André Deutsch, 1998
Barclay, Patrick – *Football, Bloody Hell! The Biography of Alex Ferguson*, Yellow Jersey Press, 2010
Burns, Jimmy – *Barça: A People's Passion*, Bloomsbury, 1999
Campbell, Tom & Potter, David – *Jock Stein: The Celtic Years*, Mainstream, 1998
Crick, Michael – *The Boss: The Many Sides of Alex Ferguson*, Simon and Schuster, 2002
Docherty, David – *The Celtic Football Companion*, John Donald, 1986
—— *The Rangers Football Companion*, John Donald, 1986
Ferguson, Alex – *A Light in the North*, Mainstream, 1985
—— *Managing My Life: My Autobiography*, Hodder & Stoughton, 1999
Ferrier, Bob, & McElroy, Robert – *Rangers Player by Player*, The Crowood Press, 1990
Galbraith, Russell – *The Hampden Story*, Mainstream, 1993
Gordon, Richard – *Glory in Gothenburg*, Black & White, 2012

Halliday, Stephen – *The Essential History of Rangers*, Headline, 2002
Harper, Joe with Allan, Charlie – *King Joey: Upfront and Personal*, Birlinn, 2008
Harris, Harry – *The Ferguson Effect*, Orion, 1999
Johnston, Willie with Bullimore, Tom – *Sent Off at Gunpoint: The Willie Johnston Story*, Know the Score Books, 2009
Keir, Richard – *Scotland: The Complete International Football Record*, Breedon Books, 2001
Kelly, Stephen F. – *Fergie: The Biography of Alex Ferguson*, Headline, 1997
Leatherdale, Clive – *Aberdeen: The European Era, A Complete Record*, Desert Island Books, 1997
Leighton, Jim – *In The Firing Line: The Jim Leighton Story*, Mainstream, 2002
MacBride, Eugene, O'Connor, Martin & Sheridan, George – *An Alphabet of the Celts: A Complete Who's Who of Celtic FC*, ACL & Polar, 1994
Macpherson, Archie – *Jock Stein: The Definitive Biography*, Highdown, 2007
McColl, Graham & Sheridan, George – *The Essential History of Celtic*, Headline, 2002
McDougall, Frank with Holmes, Jeff – *McDougoal: The Frank McDougall Story*, Macdonald Media, 2010
McNeill, Billy – *Hail Cesar: The Autobiography*, Headline, 2004
Miller, Willie with Robertson, Rob – *The Don: The Willie Miller Story*, Birlinn, 2008
Rickaby, Jim – *Aberdeen: A Complete Record, 1903–1987*, Breedon Books, 1987
Ross, David – *The Roar of the Crowd*, Argyll, 2005
Smith, Paul – *Gothenburg Glory*, Aberdeen Journals, 2008
—— *Aberdeen FC Who's Who: Every Red Ever*, Pitch, 2012

Strachan, Gordon with Webster, Jack – *Gordon Strachan: An Autobiography*, Stanley Paul, 1984
Webster, Jack – *The First 100 Years of the Dons*, Hodder & Stoughton, 2002

The Daily Record, *The Evening Express*, *The Evening Times*, *The Glasgow Herald*, *The Press & Journal*, *The Scotsman*, *The Sunday Mail*, and Aberdeen Football Club match programmes 1978–1986

INDEX

H

I

J

K

L

M

N

O

P

R

S

T